# STRIKE

*To Karl Arakelian with appreciation for your ongoing car*

# STRIKE

A NOVEL

SET IN THE BREAD AND ROSES STRIKE

1912

JOSEPH J BAKEWELL

*Joseph J Bakewell 7/30/13*

ISBN 978-0-971-87018-5

Unabooks

P.O. Box 322

Boxford, MA 01921


Printed and bound in the United States of America

FOR MY READERS
YOUR PATIENCE AND SUPPORT

# STRIKE

## Prologue

During the early and mid nineteenth century, the textile mills of New England grew in number and efficiency. Early workers, including thousands of young women, left farms for jobs and a better life in mills located in fast-growing cities on the Merrimack and other rivers. Later, these cities were a magnet for waves of immigrants who came to escape conditions in their native lands.

Many came from Ireland as a result of the great famine during the late 1840's. Others came from Germany, England and Canada. Their children became managers and supervisors in the mills, police, firemen, merchants and professionals. New waves of immigrants from eastern Europe, the Balkans and even Syria took their places at the looms and machines.

In the late 1800's, increasing capacity resulted in competition and its concomitant pressure on prices. The mill owners resorted to cost cutting by improving efficiency and continuously reducing wages. By the turn of the century, life for low-level mill workers became intolerable.

The mill owners were comparatively unaffected as an increasing number of immigrants arrived to take jobs at almost any price. In Lawrence, Massachusetts, William Wood rose to become the head of the American Woolen Company and the wealthiest man in the state by mastering cost accounting and related innovations directed at minimizing wage costs.

State governments were just beginning to recognize and deal with the plight of workers. After the Triangle Shirtwaist fire in New York City, in which over one hundred young women leaped from windows to lie crushed on the ground in front of horrified spectators, Al Smith and others helped to pass laws dealing with the safety and health of workers. Starting in 1892, Massachusetts passed a series of laws reducing the hours of a workweek. In 1911, the Commonwealth passed a law requiring the workweek for women, and children under eighteen, to be reduced from fifty-six to fifty-four hours as of January 1, 1912.

Workers assumed that, as in earlier workweek reductions, their pay would remain constant. On January 11th, the first payday of the New Year, they discovered otherwise, and a spontaneous walkout ensued.

The strike of 1912, later known as The Bread and Roses Strike, became a major turning point for workers and industry throughout the United States. It was the first time unskilled workers, represented by a union, won a strike.

This work of fiction uses authentic strike history and some details from it as a backdrop. It is the story of an Irish-American family, an Italian family, and how they coped with life-changing consequences of the strike.

For those with an ongoing interest in the strike and related issues, I recommend: The Visitors Center and The Immigrant City Archives, both in downtown Lawrence; the Lowell National Historical Park; and the book, *Bread and Roses,* by Bruce Watson.

# CHAPTER ONE

At the start of 1912, Lawrence, Massachusetts was going to hell with itself, and Amos Flanagan felt himself being pulled in its wake. Almost every aspect of the city's life had deteriorated, and now, to top things off, the Italians were out on strike.

Descending the front steps of the police station, he turned west, hunching his shoulders against the gray mixture of snow and mist. He barely noticed his surroundings; shops prepared to close, removing sandwich-board signs from the sidewalk and merchandise from the windows; horse-drawn wagons, hacks, and the occasional motor-car or truck contended with each other and the snow as they strived to complete their day's work. His face stung with the cold and, where it wasn't shielded by the brim of his black bowler, it dripped with melting snow. Cold water began to leak in around the edges of his collar, he cursed, "Shit, and winter's just starting."

Turning left on Hampshire, he headed for Canal Street where the strikers were trying to shut down the Atlantic and Pacific mills. An argument raged in his head: strictly speaking, the strike wasn't his concern; he was a police inspector. Ah, but also a father; his nineteen year old son, Paddy, worked as a supervisor in the mill on Canal Street. And who knew where this thing was going? It had started with violence and could only get worse. If anything happened to Paddy, it would be on his head, he knew it. Molly would blame him; she never wanted Paddy working in the mills in the first place.

Oh, and the job—his job. On January 1st, the entire city government had been reorganized under a new mayor and aldermen. They were putting in their own people; "Who knows? Maybe I'll be back in uniform, bashing heads and either getting stabbed or shot by some crazy wop."

Approaching Canal Street, he was comforted by the sight of a familiar figure. Patrolman Michael Casey stood under an overhang next to a delivery platform on the corner. Amos would recognize that belly anywhere. Casey's frontal profile resembled that of a melting snowman, consisting of a near continuous slope from the top of his rounded helmet, over his walrus mustache, to the low-slung belt that tucked his great coat under his stomach. He had difficulty getting on and off street cars these days but, billy club in hand, he could bull his way through a crowd well enough.

Casey spotted him and touched his club to his helmet. "They sure know how to pick the weather," he said, pointing to a group of pickets gathered around the main entrance to the Pacific Mill, a long, five-story, red brick building, located across a canal bridge about a block away.

"They could hold out longer in summer," Amos said.

"Shorter's better."

The two had a long history, starting when Amos joined the force, and Casey was assigned to mentor him for a few weeks. Several years later, when Amos had developed contacts in the Italian community, he learned of an extortion scheme—Irish cops shaking down Italian merchants--Casey was implicated. The Italians wanted action; Amos vacillated, the 'code of silence' weighed heavily.

Finally, he went to Casey. "It's just a question of time, Michael. They're going to their priest."

"Yeah, he's already in contact with Father Riley. It's over anyway, Amos, but thanks for keeping it under your hat."

Five years later, Casey had a chance to reciprocate. The two went to arrest a Polish man, accused of molesting young girls. Earlier, Amos heard an hysterical account from a young mother. "He's destroyed my little girl. You should see the bruises and the blood." He had vengeance on his mind when he and Casey pulled the man out of his apartment. The man struggled and cursed them, Amos shot him dead.

Casey placed a hand on his shoulder. "Amos, you've got to control yourself, this is a terrible thing."

Amos looked at him, wide-eyed, he was stunned, unable to believe what he'd just done, wanting to pull it back. In a hoarse whisper, he said, "I know."

Casey nodded. "But it was in self-defense. I saw the whole thing; he had a gun, I'll just go and find it."

He did, he 'found' the gun and perjured himself. They never spoke of these things, each man understanding that loyalty was part of the fabric of their profession.

Amos studied the crowd gathered around the mill gate and spilling back onto the small, arched, iron bridge. There were a few women, and all were dressed in whatever winter clothing they possessed, about a third held umbrellas over their heads. The dark clothes and black umbrellas stood out against a thin layer of snow, in fading light and drizzle, giving the scene a funereal feeling. Amos experienced a sudden urge to pray for them.

"Some got inside," Casey said.

"Are they wrecking the machines?"

"I don't think so. The militia is in there too. I think they got 'em."

"How can they win if they wreck the machines? There won't be any work."

"Don't ask me; I'm not Italian. What do your friends on the east side think of all this?"

3

"My Italian friends? They don't work in the mills, and I haven't been over there since Christmas but I'm sure they don't like it--bad for business--bad for everybody. They like things nice and quiet."

"I must be part Italian," Casey said. "I like things nice and quiet." He shuffled his feet and flapped his arms in and out. "I'll be glad to get inside for a pint after this."

"Molly will be worried about Paddy. Do you think he'll be able to get out all right?"

"I'll keep an eye out for him, Amos."

"No sense me waiting around then."

Just as he turned to go, screams bellowed out from the bridge.

Casey said, "Will you look at that."

"Good God."

They watched as streams of water came from fire hoses behind the high, black, iron gate and brick wall, cascading onto the pickets, making a mockery of umbrellas. The hoses soaked those in front, and they jammed together, scrambling back across the bridge where they met resistance from those at the back; several stumbled and slipped down in the slush underfoot; others stopped or turned back to lift them, and they all held to each other until they reached Canal Street where they regrouped and went off to seek someplace dry and warm.

"And the week's just started," Amos said.

The two men stood, watching the scene until Amos turned to leave. "When you spot Paddy, look after him, will you Case?"

"I will Amos. I will."

*******************

Paddy Flanagan climbed the cast-iron staircase set against the red brick wall at one end of the long mill building, his footfalls a clanging, bell-like, sound reflected from the wall on his right, a sound strange to his ears only because everything else was so eerily quiet. On the third floor, he walked the narrow aisle next to the windows overlooking the canal. To his left, row upon row of looms, each tethered with a wide leather belt to an overhead drive shaft. Normally, they raised a deafening roar; now silent, they watched him pass in the gloom. It was dark outside, and he would be getting home almost two hours later than usual; his mother would be worried, but there had been no chance to get word to her.

He'd just come from a meeting where he listened to older men talk about earlier strikes and how they mostly tended to peter out. The meeting had puzzled and disturbed him--from the sound of it, they were entering a contest, a combat, in which no quarter was to be given, or expected. He got along very well with the operatives, as the workers in his charge were called. They were all girls, some as young as sixteen, or, with forged papers, younger. "I'm like a brother," he thought, "an older brother." It was not possible to imagine them as opponents—the enemy.

He felt a chill and rubbed his arms as he stopped to look at the canal below where a thin layer of snow covered the arches of the bridge, tool-shed roofs, and everywhere but the alleys and streets where pickets, police and militia swarmed earlier. It was quiet now, cold and getting colder.

Why should the Italians give in? What did they have to lose? He knew the numbers. Six dollars a week—just enough to cover the rent and food. No wonder they dressed like gypsies and sent their kids into the mills.

Two days earlier, out of curiosity, he watched a big meeting of strikers held on the common. A small group of

5

women left the meeting early and passed within earshot, one of them saying, "It's only right. We want bread."

Another agreed, "Yes, and roses too."

They all laughed. "Bread and Roses."


He moved away from the window and continued to the tiny office where glass walls gave a view of the looms. He took his woolen cap and long coat off the rack and proceeded down the other stairwell. Outside, the cold nipped at the passages of his nose, and he made a note to add a sweater under his coat next time. Several soldiers stood in a group, close to the shed near the gate. One stepped away to unlock and open the gate for him to slip through. "Watch the ice," the soldier said.

Crossing the bridge, he held onto the rail; the water from fire hoses had mixed with the slush to form a thick slippery skin underfoot. Not much danger of flopping over into the canal, but the very thought gave him the chills. He smiled. Roses? What a crazy idea. But why not? Spotting Casey off to his right, he waved and Casey raised his club as he turned to go.

Turning left on Canal Street Paddy headed for Broadway and the bridge over the Merrimack. The Flanagans lived on the other side of the river. He heard something, a sound from near the three-story building to his right. He turned ready to face whoever it was, but no one stepped from the shadows.

He heard it again, a low moan. Most likely a cat. Turning to walk away, he just noticed a dark bundle near the wall. He paused, staring at it. It didn't move. Probably some drunk, slipped on the ice. It was late, he was cold and he had to cross over the damn bridge to get home. Would he mention this? Could he? What would his da say?

"There are a lot of miserable people out there. You're forever coming across some poor bastard in trouble. Don't walk away. See if you can help—at least a little. It's a short cut to heaven, lad."

"I'll worry about heaven next summer," he murmured as he stalked off. He'd gone about twenty feet when he stopped again. "Shit." Then he began to run but only for a few more yards. "God, it's cold." He heaved a deep breath and turned around. Returning to the bundle, he bent close. "Do you need help?"

# CHAPTER TWO

After leaving Casey, Amos walked two blocks to Broadway where he stepped onto a streetcar, nodded to the conductor, and rode across the bridge. The steamy smell of wet clothing assaulted his nostrils, making it harder to breath, still, with the sloppy weather, it was better than walking. He got off in front of the fire house on South Broadway where a fireman paused as he was about to close the large door, he waved, and Amos returned his greeting. A horse snorted just before the closing; the bolt clunked, not to be lifted until the next day—or an alarm sounded. The comfort of a pint beckoned him from Jack's pub, a block away, but remembering that he had to go out again after supper, he turned the corner.

In the dark, the nearest electric street light providing barely enough light to avoid tripping over the barrels of garbage waiting for pick-up along the sidewalk, he thought about how the short days that made winter seem so much longer and colder. At 55 Crosby Street, he opened the gate and looked up at the pride of his life, a gray, two-story, wooden house, sitting on a lot not much bigger than the foundation. They bought it and made improvements using Molly's inheritance from her mother--and they still had a decent nest egg. There were not many on the force who would do as well. The stairs, barely visible in front of him, were so familiar it mattered little. Inside, he removed his hat and coat placing them on the rack while the aroma of cooking and the warmth of steam heat began to leach tension from his body.

Molly, who stood by the stove wearing a long, dusty-rose, dress and a gray apron, gave him a look when he stepped into the kitchen—as if he'd done something wrong. "You're early?" she said.

"I've got to go out again."

She turned, looking, waiting, saying nothing, but her blue eyes told him she wanted to know more.

He pulled out a chair and sat, facing her from across the table. "Some woman complaining that her husband is trying to kill their kid. He gets home later. I want to talk to him."

"Some kids could use a little killing. The kid's probably bigger than the father."

Amos laughed. From a bowl of newly washed micks, sitting on the table, he picked a wet potato, rolled it in his fingers and then replaced it. "This is serious; the kid's only thirteen."

"Well, he'll have you looking out for him now."

"That's why they pay me."

She wiped her hands on her apron and stood close to him, reaching out to brush back an errant lock of his, still mostly red, hair. "That's it then? Just the money?"

He slipped his arm around her waist, pulling her close. "I don't suppose Kathy could finish fixing the dinner?"

She picked up the bowl of potatoes and moved away. The back of her, with her brown hair rolled up in a bun, never failed to hold his eye, he could look without having to provide an explanation.

She glanced back. "Aren't you the rascal? What would the children be thinking?"

"You think they haven't figured it out yet?"

She waved a hand at him and began to cut up the potatoes. "Paddy should be home."

"I stopped by the mill. Casey's there. He'll look after Paddy. Besides, I think the pickets have gone home." He told her about the fire hoses.

She nodded. "Would you like a sandwich now, then some of this when you get back?"

He pulled his watch from his vest pocket and popped it open. "Good idea; my man should be home soon from his shoe store."

Twenty minutes later, on his way out the door, Amos said, "If Paddy's not home when I get back, I'll go find him."

\*\*\*\*\*\*\*\*\*\*\*\*

Paddy repeated the question. "Do you need help?"

No answer. He reached down, anticipating the discovery of a bloodshot-eyed drunk with half his teeth missing; the bundle felt cold and soaking wet. Bending closer, looking for the head; he pulled back a wet scarf. Two eyes rolled to the side and stared back at him, looking like those of a frightened dog. He leaned to get a straight-on view of the face. This was no drunk, but an olive-skinned, dark-eyed girl. For a moment, they just stared at each other; her eyes clearly indicating fear.

Why would she be afraid of him? "I want to help you."

Her mouth moved, but nothing came out.

"Can you stand up?"

She looked as if she was trying to speak.

He leaned close but heard nothing—not even her breathing. How to help, without scaring her more? "Let's see if we can get you up," he said, reaching for her shoulders, but she pulled back. He waited a few seconds to see if she would get up and run off before he asked, "Do you speak English?"

No answer. He had an idea. He unbuttoned his coat and the neck of his shirt, reaching inside he pulled out the crucifix he

11

wore on a chain. He dangled it in front of her and then made the sign of the cross. "I want to help you." He moved his hands in a lifting motion. She tried to stand, and he helped her get to her feet. But then her knees buckled and she stumbled into his arms. He scooped her up, held her for a moment and then carried her toward Broadway. "I'll take you to my mother. My momma mia." He repeated this several times but, looking down, he saw her eyes turning dull and her head rolling back. "Oh, God. Don't die on me—not that."

She was Italian—but maybe not. Lebanese? Possibly French-Canadian? There were over twenty different nationalities in Lawrence, many recent arrivals. At times he felt like an alien in his own city. Last summer, he, and his friend, Frank Dunn, explored the city on bicycles, visiting a dozen countries in four hours.

There were no streetcars in sight on Broadway. Without stopping, he turned to cross the bridge as fast as he could, talking to her constantly. "I'm strong. I'll get you there. My mother will know what to do. You're pretty light."

Near the other side, he was sweating profusely, stopping he set her feet down close to the guard rail. Propping her against the rail, he tried to catch his breath, all the while, holding her to keep her from slumping down. Her eyes now clear, she appeared to study his face. He thought her to be a little older than most of the girls in his charge at the mill.

Breathing became easier, and his heart stopped racing. "I need to get you home," he said. "But I have to carry you a different way." He  bent to put his right arm behind her knees. With his left at the small of her back, he lifted her and draped her over his left shoulder. She had to be really scared. He was going to pat her and say something reassuring, but that might have frightened her even more. They were on South Broadway, and he could almost run with her now. "Good Christ. If anybody sees me, I'll never hear the end of this." He flew past the fire house and up the street. By the time he reached the front steps, his lungs were burning and perspiration dripped from his nose. Pausing to catch his breath, in gasps, he murmured to her. "We're home—You're going to be okay—My mother will know what to do—You'll see." He pushed on, up the stairs.

Staggering down the dimly lit hallway, he burst into the kitchen where Molly, Kathy, his younger sister, and his little brother Neal were at the table, just finishing supper. He was so winded he could not speak. They all jumped up and stepped back from the table. Molly, with her hand up to her throat came toward him. "Mother of God. What have you done?"

Paddy slipped the girl down and held her out. Molly's jaw dropped and she caught her breath. She stepped forward, reached out to touch the girl and then turned. "Neal, clean off the table and then get out of here. Kathy, run in and get some towels and blankets. Paddy, set her down here." She pulled out a chair. "Help me get her coat off."

Paddy propped the girl in the chair and gingerly helped his mother with the girl's lumpy, swollen, wet coat. He wasn't sure about where to put his hands. "She must have been hit by the fire hoses," he said.

Molly was not interested. "Get on with it, Paddy. She'll catch her death."

He worked more aggressively, and they had her coat off.

"Hang that by the stove," she said.

When he hung the coat and turned back, Molly had the girl's hat off, and she looked more alert. He gazed at her--even dazed, wet and disheveled, she was beautiful. Molly took note. "You go in the front with Neal and don't come back till you're called."

Kathy returned to pile towels and blankets on the table. Without a pause, she stepped to the stove and picked up the large, copper, laundry kettle, bringing it to the sink for more water. For a fourteen year old, gangly, leggy kid, she was strong.

Paddy smiled and paused on his way out the door. "Maybe Kathy could bring me a crust of bread?"

Molly raised one arm. "Out."

She draped a towel over the girl's head, rubbed it a few times and then started aggressively to unbutton her blouse. Kathy dropped to her knees and struggled to get her shoes off. "These are good shoes," she commented. The girl remained limp against the back of the chair.

They kept working on her, pulling and peeling blouse, shoes, stockings. When her chemise came off, Kathy's eyes fixed on her breasts. "My, my," she said.

Molly scolded. "We'll have none of that. Get the laundry tub."

Finally, with Molly Lifting her like a rag doll, and Kathy stripping layer after layer, they had her clothes in a pile, the girl covered in towels and blankets, and her feet in warm water. They continued to work on her. They rubbed her legs, her arms and her head, Molly, strong and full-figured, and Kathy, still growing and skinny, their Irish-white hands contrasting with the soft tint of Italian skin.

Molly held her head, looking for any sign of progress.

The girl blinked and spoke. "My name is Maria Petrella."

"Thanks be to God," Molly said. "Kathy, make some tea."

"I went out before supper to find my brother."

After some tea and a bit of the stew, earlier set aside for Amos, Maria announced that she was feeling much better. As Molly continued to fuss over her, Kathy hung on every word as Maria told them about herself—all the while, thanking them profusely. She seemed miraculously recovered.

14

"My father is a business man. He has a tailor shop on Union Street. My older brother works at the Pacific Mills—at least he did until the strike. And I want to be a teacher." She ended by saying, "I can go home now. My parents must be frantic."

Molly allowed herself a short laugh. "Your clothes won't be dry until tomorrow, and it would not be good to be going out again tonight."

Maria protested, but Molly was adamant. "I'll send my son to your house. He'll talk to your parents and bring back some clothes. And then we'll see."

"My family is going to be very upset."

Molly put her hand on Maria's forehead and then her neck. "You've had a shock, dear. You still have a chill. It won't do to send you out again to catch your death." She called Paddy into the kitchen where he moved to observe Maria. They made eye contact, and then she stared down at her hands, resting on her lap. Her black hair had been combed out and spread down over her shoulders to dry. He saw Italian girls every day at the mill, but never one like this.

Molly said, "I want you to go to her house, tell her parents what happened and bring back some dry clothes for her." Paddy looked puzzled. Molly continued. "She speaks English and she's quite intelligent."

Paddy turned to Maria, who smiled, revealing, near-perfect, white teeth as she looked directly at him. He felt himself redden as she took her time, giving him her name and address. He nodded, in no hurry to leave. Finally, he said, "Okay," and then turned to Molly. "I'm starving."

Without a word, she went to the breadbox, took out a loaf and sliced off a piece. "Here's your crust. I'll feed you when you get back."

# CHAPTER THREE

Amos crossed South Broadway and spotted a horse-drawn wagon, followed by a streetcar, both making their way toward him. The horse's head bobbed up and down, leaving puffs of vapor in its wake. He waited under the awning of Donovan's butcher shop. "Damn, how long is this going to take?" He thought about stepping out--ordering the wagon to one side. No need, the wagon pulled to one side and stopped to let the streetcar pass. Immediately, a layer of steam covered the horse—a fuzzy aura. It snorted and raised its head as he passed in front of its nose to board the streetcar. The car felt steamy, electric heat from under the seats combining with that of a dozen bodies, all wearing wet coats. Amos wiped the foggy window with the side of his hand and checked to be sure he'd be able to see when to get off. He unbuttoned his water-proof, waxed coat—a Christmas gift from Molly, but he was still too warm.

Two streetcars later, he crossed the Spicket River and stepped off onto Park Street; the Wilcoxes lived two blocks down. He didn't get to this part of town very often, the homeowners were mostly lower middle-class merchants and tradesmen—not much crime, aside from the occasional housebreak.

He found the house, a single-family dwelling, well maintained with white paint and blue trim. A porch spanned the front of the house, and there appeared to be a good sized back yard. He turned the thumb key to ring the rotary bell; the door opened a crack to reveal a thin woman with large sunken eyes. He held up his badge. "I'm here to talk to you about your son and husband, Mrs. Wilcox."

She didn't move or speak. He wondered if he had the right house, or perhaps she wasn't Mrs. Wilcox. "Is there a problem?"

"He'll be home soon."

"Your husband?"

"Yes."

"Good. I want to talk to him too. There won't be a problem—I promise."

She stepped back and, with her eyes down and head bowed, held the door open.

They sat in the living room after the woman removed the sheets covering the chairs and the couch, revealing furniture that appeared to have never been used. Amos declined an offer of tea and took out his notebook. She spoke softly. "I don't want William, my son to hear." She perched on the front edge of a padded, armless chair, folding her hands and resting them on her lap, a thin woman, hair pulled back, she wore an ordinary house-dress of non-descript color and she seemed at pains to keep from fidgeting.

"I understand, Mrs. Wilcox. What is it that makes you fear for your son?"

"I hardly know where to begin. My husband started beating him when he was nine months old." She refolded her hands.

Amos, the street-hardened cop, who had seen and heard it all, sat with his pencil frozen over his pad. Finally, he wrote, "beat — 9 mos." He looked at her, wondering how she fit in. Was she part of the problem? "And he's how old now?"

"Thirteen, and it's still going on."

"Yes," he said. "Go on." He began to scribble, racing to keep up.

"Whenever he did the slightest thing, Bill beat him and beat him, the boy has nervous twitches and hardly sleeps. He would take him out to the woodshed, put his head on the chopping block and threaten to cut it off if he wasn't good. One time, he tied him to a tree and said that the wolves would come and eat him. A week ago was the last straw. William came home

18

late from his paper route; Bill punched him and pushed him out the door. He pulled out his pistol and fired shots after the boy. It's a wonder someone wasn't killed." Her dark brown eyes fixed on him, as if wondering if she had said too much.

"We heard about the shots." Amos put down his pencil and studied her face, now contorted and wet with tears. "Why didn't you come to us earlier?"

She stared at him as if she hadn't heard and then, reaching up to the neck of her dress, she pulled it down, and he saw the burn marks. She pulled up a sleeve—more of the same. The marks looked like he'd done it with a poker. He put up his hand to stop her.

She continued. "He said I'd find my boy in the river if I ever told."

Amos searched for something to say. He had a vision of putting Bill Wilcox in the river, himself. Suddenly, the woman stiffened; she had the look of a frightened animal. "He's home."

They sat waiting, she with her hands in her lap, and Amos sitting back as he put his notebook away. Sounds in the hallway were followed by footsteps, and Amos looked up to take in Bill Wilcox, the husband and father, as he strutted into the room and stood with an exaggerated erect posture.

He'd been expecting a big man, a bulky man. This one was small, thin—the image of a shoe store owner, used to smiling and ingratiating himself to customers.

He smiled at Amos. "Oh, hello. I'm Bill Wilcox." His thin, pointed, mustache moved up and down emphasizing the movement of his mouth.

Amos nodded and did not get up to accept the hand offered. "I'm Inspector Flanagan." He got up slowly, towering over Wilcox. "I want you to put your hat and coat back on." He reached inside Wilcox's jacket, deftly removing a pistol from its holster. "You won't be needing this." He slipped it into his own pocket.

19

\*\*\*\*\*\*\*\*\*\*\*\*\*\*\*\*\*\*\*\*\*\*\*\*

When Paddy got to South Broadway, the streetcars were running less frequently. It was well after seven and getting colder. He waited, continuing to peer down the street. "Shit, I could freeze to death here." Turning, he headed north. Approaching the Merrimack, he felt the wind penetrate his clothes, blowing downstream, it seemed to push the river along. At the bridge, he held his collar, putting his head down, he trotted across and kept trotting all the way to Common Street. "Maybe I can build up a little heat." There were no streetcars there either, but the wind wasn't as bad so he turned right and kept going, taking a short-cut across a corner of the common.

He was not familiar with Maria's address on Garden Street but he knew that it was unlikely to be a tenement house. He found a well maintained, three-family, house spaced far enough from its neighbors to allow access to a small barn in the rear. He wasn't sure which floor Maria said her family lived on so he went up the steps and bent to read the mailbox. Someone heard him and the door opened. "What do you want?" The question came from a strong-looking, clean shaven, olive-skinned man, younger than himself.

"Are you Lorenzo, Maria's brother?"

No answer. Whatever his name was, he looked ready for a fight.

"I've come about Maria Petrella. I'm looking for her family."

"I'm her family. Where is she?"

"At my house."

Lorenzo's jaw dropped, just a bit.

"She's with my mother and sister."

20

A woman's voice came from behind Lorenzo, yelling something in Italian. He turned and yelled something back. The woman appeared, wearing an apron over a dark dress, her black hair, streaked with gray lay smooth over her ears. She gestured at Paddy while continuing to yell at Lorenzo.

Lorenzo said, "You better come in."

They moved inside, and the three of them stood crowded together in the narrow hallway while Lorenzo kept talking to the woman—apparently Maria's mother, while she continued to gesture and voice loud questions in Italian, apparently meant for Paddy. Three teenage children peered from the kitchen at the end of the hall, and Paddy's stomach reacted to the aroma of Italian cooking. One of the teens came forward, a girl of about thirteen. She pushed her way to stand in front of Paddy and point at her mother. "She speaks English, you know. It's just that she's so excited."

Paddy, pleased at being treated as a person rather than a box found on the doorstep, said, "I appreciate that. If I could just explain; everything is okay."

The girl, who was taller than her mother, put her arm around her shoulder and spoke softly in her ear. The mother nodded and turned to address Paddy. "Oh my God, we've been so worried. I am Maria's mother. Please tell me what is happening." Lorenzo tried to break in, but she shoved him to one side and waited expectantly for Paddy to answer. Her dark eyes glistened and fixed on him like an eagle's.

Paddy spoke slowly while she stood with her hands together, as if in prayer.

"I found her lying on the street." He gestured at the floor. "She was wet and so cold she couldn't speak."

The girl said something to her mother in Italian, and the mother looked frightened.

Paddy continued. "I carried her home to my mother. She's warm now."

21

The mother took his hand and squeezed it as she continued to look hopefully into his face.

He grasped her hand. "And she can laugh, she's going to be fine. I came to tell you and for some dry clothes."

She moved his hand up and down, smiling with tears running down her face. A stream of words came from her, some of them English, but he understood nothing, except that she was happy.

The other two came from the kitchen, and all six people crowded together in the narrow hall, talking excitedly in a disorienting mixture of Italian and English. Paddy felt that he was their hero. But not Lorenzo's, he looked angry. The mother issued instructions, and the two teenaged girls and a younger boy, disappeared into the back. She motioned Paddy to step into a small room and take a seat. Paddy held his hand out to Lorenzo. "I'm Paddy Flanagan."

Lorenzo just looked at him. "I know who you are."

\*\*\*\*\*\*\*\*\*\*\*\*\*\*\*\*\*\*\*\*\*\*\*\*\*\*\*\*

Amos sat Wilcox on a bench against the wall just inside the police station and walked over to explain the situation to Morioraty, the night-duty desk sergeant. "This guy belongs in a nut house. He's been beating the shit out of his kid and burning his wife with a poker. Put him up for the night, will you? I'll figure out what to do with him in the morning."

Morioraty gazed past Amos at the figure on the bench. "You can never tell by looking at them, can you?"

"No."

"I'll see he's taken care of."

Recalling his own past and knowing that some members of the force were inclined to mete out a bit of their own 'justice' to those accused of despicable crimes, he said, "No rough stuff, Mory," and turned to go. Morioraty motioned a patrolman to bring Wilcox forward.

He was sorely tempted to stop in at Jack's for a pint—it would help him get his head straight. But if Paddy wasn't home yet, Molly would not take kindly to his coming in with the smell of beer on his breath. By the time he reached the house, he had himself talked into a cup of tea, some dinner, and a nice chat with Molly.

Neal was the first to greet him. "Da, you'll never guess what happened." Amos reacted as a father. "Is Paddy home?"

"That's part of it, Da."

"Oh Christ." He charged into the kitchen.

"Ah, you're home," Molly said with a big smile.

He looked to Kathy, who stepped back, gesturing at a figure sitting in a chair and covered with blankets. It was too small to be Paddy—And the hair... He stepped over for a closer look.

"This is Maria," Molly said. "Paddy brought her home, soaked to the skin and near froze to death."

"Ah." Amos continued looking at her, trying to get himself oriented to the situation.

Maria spoke. "Your son saved my life. He's gone to get me some dry clothes."

"Oh." He hadn't expected her to speak English. Why was that, he wondered? "Did you fall in the river?"

She laughed, and he was struck by her beauty. "I went to the Pacific Mill, looking for my brother. And..."

"The fire hoses. I saw them." He smiled and bent to touch her hand. "It looks like you're being well cared for."

He sat where he could observe her. What a marvelous counterpoint to the Wilcox affair—his family saving someone's life. And here she was in his very own kitchen.

He looked to Molly. "It's not right, you know, treating people like that—peaceful pickets, women. The mill owners are going to regret this."

\*\*\*\*\*\*\*\*\*\*\*\*\*\*\*\*\*\*\*\*\*\*\*\*\*\*\*\*\*\*

Paddy sat, trying to make conversation with Maria's mother. He gestured. "You have a nice home."

A smile, a nod, but no response.

"The children are nice--well behaved."

More of the same.

Finally, the older girl came from the back of the house with a bundle of clothes, he stood up to accept it, but Lorenzo stepped in front and grabbed the bundle. "I'm going to get her," he said to his mother. She said nothing but seemed to accept this. Paddy shrugged. "Let's go."

When they gained the sidewalk, Paddy said, "It's a bit of a walk—maybe we can catch a streetcar."

"We can walk."

Paddy was six feet tall, strong and athletic. He could move and, at that point, he had no warm feelings for Lorenzo, who was at least six inches shorter. "You said that you know me. From where?"

"I work at the Pacific Mills."

"So you're one of the strikers?"

"That's right. But don't worry; I'm glad you helped my sister."

24

"I wasn't worried."

"You should be. There are big changes coming. People like you won't have any work."

"No? Who's going to run the mills?"

"The workers."

"Yeah. The same ones who are busting up the looms and beating up other workers?"

"It has to be done. The owners will not give up. We have to take what is ours—what was built by labor."

"You've been listening to too many crack-pots. We have laws in this country."

"The workers will win."

"We'll see." Paddy picked up speed.

They walked the rest of the way in silence. Paddy set an aggressive pace and enjoyed glancing at Lorenzo to find him struggling to keep up. There was a streetcar headed south on Broadway, but Paddy ignored it.

At the house, he bounded up the front stairs and, before opening the door, waited on the porch for Lorenzo. He led him to the kitchen where the table, with its green and white, checkered oilcloth, was positioned against the wall opposite the cast-iron gas stove. Amos sat alone, eating his dinner at the far end of the table.

"Da, this is…"

Lorenzo interrupted. "Where's my sister?"

Amos put down his fork and glanced at the bundle in Lorenzo's hands. "Are those her clothes?"

"Yes."

Amos stood up and came forward. He was as tall as Paddy and carried another fifty pounds. He thrust out his hand. "So you're Maria's brother?"

Lorenzo grasped the proffered hand and nodded. Amos took the bundle from his other hand and gave it to Paddy. He motioned toward the back rooms, and Paddy disappeared. Amos went back to his chair, sat down and pointed to another. "What's your name?"

"Lorenzo. I want to see my sister." He sat in the chair.

Amos nodded and started eating. Paddy returned and sat down, uncomfortable with the silence. Lorenzo sat with his arms folded, seemingly uncomfortable under the steady gaze of Amos.

Amos said, "He wants to see his sister."

Looking at Lorenzo, Paddy felt a twinge of sympathy. "They'll be right out."

They fell back into silence, the only sound being that of Amos continuing to eat.

A few minutes later, the women emerged from the back—Maria in dry clothes. Paddy remembered his manners and stood up. She went to her brother, held his head and kissed his forehead. "They have been treating me like a princess."

Lorenzo looked glum. "I'm here to take you home."

Molly broke in. "That would be most unwise. She's had a shock to her body and must not go out into the cold again tonight."

Amos stopped eating, pushed his plate away and sat back to enjoy the show. Paddy averted his eyes from Lorenzo, and Kathy placed an arm around Maria's shoulder. Lorenzo stood up as if to argue.

Molly continued. "I'm sure that I can speak for your mother. She would not want to endanger Maria's health."

Lorenzo glared at Maria, who stepped forward to grasp his arm. "I will stay with Mrs. Flanagan." Lorenzo appeared about to say something, but she squeezed his arm and putting her face close to his she whispered something in Italian. His expression changed as he glanced at the others and stepped back.

Snatching his cap from the table, he said, "I'll be back in the morning."

Molly picked up Amos's plate and took it to the sink. To Paddy, she said, "Too bad you didn't get here earlier; your father's just after eating your dinner."

Paddy, recognizing her purposeful use of an Irish expression, turned to Amos, who waved a hand, indicating that she was having him on.

Molly said, "Sit down, Maria. You too, Paddy." She went to the cabinet for a clean plate. "Kathy, find Neal and get yourselves to bed. Maria, would you like a bit more stew?"

Maria sat at the end of the table closest to the door, and Paddy sat at the long side with his back to the stove.

Maria answered, "Just a little, if there's enough." She leaned toward Paddy. "Thank you so much for going to my house to get my clothes. Did you meet my mother?"

"Yes, and your other brother and sisters."

Amos noticed a slight reddening at Paddy's neck.

"I hope that Lorenzo wasn't difficult."

"He's very serious."

She rewarded him with a big smile. The reddening grew. Molly put out two plates of stew and two mugs. "There's tea in the pot."

She set out two more mugs and filled them, pushing one toward Amos. "We'll have our tea inside," she said.

He added milk and sugar, picked up his cup and followed her into the living room. Out of earshot, he said, "She's Italian, for God's sake."

Molly grinned. "Where's the harm?"

"Wait till they get wind of this at the station house. I'll never hear the end of it."

At the table, Maria did most of the talking. "My father was probably working late. He's so worried that the strike will be bad for his business. He was a professor in Italy. But the pay was very low, and he was a Socialist. They were not so popular then. He learned English so he could come to America and teach. There were no jobs for him here, but his father was a tailor, and he knew how to do that. Then he sent for my mother, and the next thing that happened was me."

Paddy laughed. "They got married first, right?"

She did not answer. Paddy felt himself going pale. "I was just teasing."

She reached over to touch his hand. "I know that."

He watched her hand withdraw and for an instant thought of reaching out to take it back. "My father is a police inspector. His parents both worked in the mills but they made sure that he finished high school. That was very unusual back then."

"Did your grandparents come from Ireland?"

"No, but their parents did, during the famine in Ireland. They landed in Canada and were so poor they had to walk most of the way down here for jobs. My grandfather became a carpenter. He helped build Lawrence." Brief glances told him that her eyes were fixed on him as if pulling out his words. "My mother's family goes back to before the Civil War. Her father owns a trucking business in Boston."

She said, "You can certainly be proud of your family. And they've been so good to me."

"I liked your family. Lorenzo has a few ideas that I don't agree with, but…"

"I went looking for him at the mill today. My mother worries that he'll get in some kind of trouble during this strike."

"Well, so far…" He wanted to say that he was grateful to Lorenzo for making it possible for him to find her and to bring her home—if only for this one night. He wanted to tell her that she was beautiful. "It may not last very long. And the soldiers will probably keep things under control."

"Possibly, you could keep a watch out for Lorenzo?"

He nodded while wondering what 'watching out for Lorenzo' meant. He'd figure it out later; what mattered then was the glow of her presence and its effect on him

Molly returned to the kitchen. "I want you looking well rested for your mother tomorrow, Maria."

# CHAPTER FOUR

Paddy went upstairs to his room at the front of the house, and climbed into his bed. It had been a long and arduous day, but he did not sleep; Maria's dark eyes and tantalizing smile refused to leave his imagination. "I'm going to be dead on my feet tomorrow," he grumbled as he sat up and squinted into the faint light provided by the few streetlights in the neighborhood. It was still snowing just enough to surround each one with a glowing, translucent orb. Might she be awake and looking out a window?

Molly would be in early to get him up and out on time, early enough to beat the strikers to the mill. How does she do it, get by on so little sleep? He needed more but he would not get it this night. He'd seen lots of attractive Italian women, some of the girls at his mill were very pretty; he was attracted to them—even fantasized over a few. But fall in love? It never occurred to him—until now. She was like something out of Arabian Nights, all eyes, with a figure and grace of movement calculated to destroy his brain, leaving him without the ability to think clearly just when he needed it most.

He felt as if he'd barely dozed off when Molly rousted him for breakfast. He sat at the table and finished buttoning his shirt as she set a plate of eggs in front of him. They spoke in whispers.

She said, "She seems to be sleeping soundly."

"That's good."

She looked into his face. He raised his eyes, offering her the briefest of smiles.

She heaved a sigh, nodded her understanding, and went back to the stove.

The cold air did its job; he was fully awake when he reached Canal Street. It was still dark with a faint glow in the southeastern sky, but some strikers were already at the gate. They gave him dirty looks but said nothing as he strode past. Inside, he joined Ernst Meyer, a German loom fixer, and his crew, in running the looms on his floor. The familiar hum and clacking gave him a sense of comfort when he sat in the tiny office, gazing absent mindedly at a rotating overhead drive shaft and wondering what he would be doing with his time until the strike was settled. With his eyes still fixed on the shaft, his mind drifted back to Maria. It would have been so nice to see her before I left the house. She'll be gone before I get home, and I'll go crazy with figuring out a way to see her again. Damn.

\*\*\*\*\*\*\*\*\*\*\*\*\*\*\*\*\*\*\*\*\*\*

Amos got to the station before Morioraty was due to go off duty. He told Amos that Wilcox passed a quiet night and was eating his breakfast. Amos ordered him brought into one of the tiny interrogation rooms where he sat and said nothing when Amos entered.

"Did you have a good night?" Amos asked.

Wilcox shook his head.

"Ah, then you won't be wanting to stay here?"

Wilcox stared at him. "A man has a right to be safe in his own home, to raise his family without the police sticking their noses in."

"You'll have to be safe somewhere else. You can't go home."

"What? I better talk to my lawyer."

"That's your right. You can do that. But before you get your lawyer, I'm going to arrest you for attempted murder."

32

Wilcox stared at him, his mouth agape.

"We can go another way. You'll still have your lawyer, but later. Meanwhile, you'll be able to attend to your store."

Wilcox nodded. "I'm listening."

"You get a furnished room. You stay away from your house, your wife and your kid. Your wife gets ten bucks a week. And we get your lawyer and a judge to work something out."

"This is outrageous. I'm a law-abiding citizen. I pay my taxes. I've got friends in this town, some in high places. I could have your job. And what did I do? Just trying to be a good father. What's wrong with that?"

Amos sat, arms folded, his head leaning to one side, with a very unsympathetic expression on his face. "Assuming you're finished, I'd like your decision."

Wilcox hesitated, pursed his lips and lowered his eyes. "I'll do it."

"You're god damned right, you will."

Twenty minutes later, Wilcox was out the front door, and Sergeant Jimmy Kerrigan, Amos's old friend and schoolmate, was at the desk. He motioned Amos over. "Our new City Marshal wants to see you."

"Ah, yes, the mayor's son-in-law. I wonder what took 'em so long. Who have they got, taking my job, Jimmy?"

Kerrigan shrugged. "You're about to find out."

He waited in the open doorway until City Marshal John Sullivan motioned him in. He sat in a straight-backed, wooden chair and took in his surroundings while Sullivan got up to close the office door. There were not many changes in the room: on the wall behind the desk hung a picture of Sullivan's father-in-law, Mayor Scanlon, and one of Sullivan shaking hands with Alderman Cornelius "Con" Lynch, the new Director of Public Safety. Amos noticed some personal items sitting on a side table, apparently waiting to be setup on display. A baseball, a bat and mitt reminded him of earlier times when he and Sullivan played together as kids and later at department picnics.

Sullivan sat down behind his desk, putting two fingers under his collar to pull it away from his neck. Amos thought he looked a bit uncomfortable. But that would be only natural, given the nature of the meeting.

He gestured toward the baseball equipment. "Old times, Amos, heh?"

Amos allowed his eyes to go to the table. "Yeah, I still get out now and then to hit a few."

"Well, maybe this spring then?"

"Right." It was just talk. Sullivan had grown fat and ruddy faced. There would be no more running around the bases for him.

"Amos, so much has been happening, we've not had a chance to talk. Of course, you know the system—how it goes. The new man always wants his own people—it's their reward for helping him get elected."

"Yes, I've been wondering when you'd call me in. The other shoe, and all that."

"We made some changes right away, but your situation is a bit different."

"You want me on your baseball team?"

Sullivan laughed. "Not exactly. It seems Mister Wood has put in a word for you."

Amos sat up straight. "What, William Wood, the richest man in Massachusetts? He doesn't know me from Adam."

"It seems he does, or, at least, he knows of you and he wants you to stay in plain-clothes so you can help us with certain kinds of information."

34

"And what kind would that be?"

"We want to know what the Italians are thinking and what they're planning to do."

Amos's mind flashed back to the previous night. They couldn't possibly know about the girl. "You need somebody who speaks Italian."

"We need somebody with connections. Somebody they trust."

How did the girl and her crazy brother fit into this? "I won't spy on my friends."

Sullivan smacked his desk with the flat of his hand. "Amos, it's important. The Wobblies are in town. There's going to be violence, maybe some killing."

"I understand. I'll do my job, public safety will come first, but I won't give over my friends and I won't lie to them."

Sullivan pulled on his collar, folded his arms and sat back. "I don't know how Con and Wood will take this. They want to break this strike—and fast. So do I."

Amos stood up. "I've got my helmet and billy club ready to go back on the beat. Let me know."


The last time he'd gone over to see Joe Lamastro was before Christmas and that was strictly a social call. He went late on a Friday afternoon, but Lamastro was still busy with someone, so he waited in the outer office and chatted with Connie, Lamastro's wife and office manager. Joe always said that she knew the business better than he did. Maybe he was being modest, but Connie sure was smart. No one could spend five minutes with her and not know that. And she was interesting to look at, always wore simple dresses, belted at the waist, but she experimented with her hair, using combs to arrange it so that it never looked the same.

"It will be twenty years, Amos."

It took him a second; she was talking about the first Lawrence Columbus Day Parade in 1892, when he met Joe and Connie. Father O'Reilly organized it. He twisted Amos's arm—hard—to pitch in and make it happen. Amos had just joined the police department, and the older cops slagged him over his involvement. "You don't *look* Italian." "Here, let me smell you—Yeah, he's Italian."

The Lamastro's had arrived in Lawrence only months earlier. They came from New York City with enough money to start a small importing business in the fast-growing textile city, known for its immigrants. They dealt in Italian wines, cheeses and olive oil.

A new world opened to Amos; he ate Italian food and learned to drink a little wine. The music was wonderful, and he was excited by the exposure to another culture. Joe and Connie were his teachers, but they often told him that he was their window on Lawrence. Molly went along with it, even enjoyed his involvement with the Italians, but she was more socially conservative. And then there was the baby, Paddy; he kept her busy.

Over the years, the Lamastros became leaders in the Italian community, helping others with letters, money sent home, and passage for relatives being brought over. People came to them for advice, even on family and personal matters. They knew how to keep secrets, and there were many secrets to keep.

When Joe came out of his office with a woman, Amos averted his eyes; she had obviously been crying. Lamastro saw her out and returned to a tall, dark, wood cabinet, set against the wall, nodding to Amos, he opened it to pull out a bottle of grappa. "She wants to go back to Italy," he said with a nod toward the door. "It's a long story. Maybe someday I can tell it."

That was before Christmas, before the strike. He couldn't just stop in now—too many eyes—too many people waiting to connect anything the police did to Lamastro. They would meet in secret, a certain little room in the basement at City Hall would do. He'd call Joe and make arrangements.

\*\*\*\*\*\*\*\*\*\*\*\*\*\*\*\*\*\*\*\*\*\*\*\*\*\*\*\*

To avoid the strikers, Paddy came to work earlier the next day and every day that week. There had been violence on Monday; a young Syrian man had been bayoneted by one of the militia. The crowds of strikers and their parades continued, and almost every hour a new rumor spread inside the mill, many having to do with the arrival of Wobblies in Lawrence. The older men talked about their reputation for violence, anarchy and the destruction of property. It sounded ominous, as though some kind of natural disaster, a huge storm, was moving toward the city.

It was all new to Paddy. He kept busy running looms to fool the strikers into thinking that they were not needed. They made no cloth, just ran, clanking away, combining in a roar that hurt Paddy's ears. He stuffed them with raw cotton. It helped, but not as much as when Ernst Meyer showed him how to rub cotton against a candle until it felt waxy and then roll it into small balls to fit in his ears. Since the start of the strike, he was getting to know Meyer, who always wore a black, narrow brimmed hat with a silver medallion stuck in the hatband.

When he had a spare minute, he went to the windows. Feeling foolish, he checked on the strikers, hoping for a glimpse of Maria. He spotted Lorenzo once. He'd have to find some way to contact her. At supper that night, he mentioned seeing Lorenzo. Kathy caught on to what he really wanted to say— she'd been teasing him about Maria all week. "They still deliver the mail, you know."

He looked at her, feeling stupid.

On Friday the first scabs arrived, and he was busy training them all day. Ernst Meyer came by when he was getting ready to go home. He pushed his black hat back from his forehead. "They found a cache of dynamite."

"Dynamite! Where?"

"The cops got a tip. It was in a Syrian tailor's shop."

"A Syrian? That doesn't make any sense. They don't even want to be on strike."

"Syrian, Lebanese, Italian. They're all crazy. But I'll tell you this. The militia never should have stabbed that Syrian kid. Revenge is big with these people."

# CHAPTER FIVE

Kevin McNulty, a quiet, white-haired, unassuming soul had been a janitor at City Hall for as long as Amos could remember, although, he knew him better as an usher at Saint Patrick's. He owned one, dark-blue, suit and he wore it every Sunday, summer or winter. Amos imagined that it came off as soon as he walked in the door at home to be brushed and hung carefully lest it show signs of wear before the undertaker put it on him for the last time.

After a visit to the toilet in the basement at City Hall, Amos occasionally stopped in at Kevin's tiny office down the hall. The visits were short, Amos rarely sat down; just a few words about the parish and some personal small talk. He was careful to stay in one spot--in addition to wiring strung on the walls and ceiling, there were pipes overhead and some along the floor near the walls. In between, were crates of supplies, a little table, and two simple wooden chairs. It was all clean, none of the layers of dust to be found in the basement at the police station.

When Amos told him what he needed, McNulty's only questions were: "When do you need it?" and "Would you like anything with your tea?"

"Friday afternoon, and just tea will be grand. How's Margaret these days?" He knew that Kevin's wife suffered from an old injury to one of her legs.

"She's not getting about much. It's the ice; she's terrified that she'll slip. I bring a few things in."

"I'll send Kathleen over to see what she needs."

"No need, Amos. We manage."

"It's good for kids to do these things."

McNulty smiled softly, just enough for Amos to know that he'd said the right thing.


At the appointed time on Friday, Amos returned. Leaving the door ajar, he sat behind the tiny table wondering if it ever occurred to Kevin to put in a larger light bulb. The door opened and Lamastro stuck his head in to look around the room. "You Irish have a flare for the dramatic," he said as he moved gingerly around the obstructions to take the other chair. "Some news, heh?"

"Yeah. I wonder what they planned to do with all that dynamite, blow up one of the mills?"

"I know the family. They don't seem the type."

"The tip came from Breen, the funeral director. His father was a great mayor and a fine man, but I never cared for this guy."

"I don't know him. And anyway, you wanted to see me about something before this dynamite business came up."

"That's right, but it's all tied in." Amos related the details of his meeting with Sullivan. "It's not about the job, Joe, but I am a cop, and there are things going on here that are different from any of the earlier strikes. And, of course, you know that Paddy works at the Pacific Mill. These Wobblies scare the crap out of me."

"I share your concern, Amos. And it's not just the Wobblies; some of my countrymen are doing things that could wind up hurting a lot of people—most of them Italian."

"What can you tell me?"

"A few things, but first I have something to say. The Italian strikers are not your big problem. There are some bad, violent men in there, but they're easy to spot. You probably already know who most of them are. It's the ones from New York you've got to look out for."

"New York?"

"They're Sicilians and they're not union people. They're here to intimidate and maybe even kill somebody."

"Do you know where they are?"

"Try the rooming houses on Valley Street. And I understand a couple have taken rooms in the tenements."

"Armed to the teeth, I imagine."

"No doubt."

******************

Paddy spent most of the weekend stewing over the idea of writing a letter to Maria, He had trouble just talking to girls; a letter felt risky, you can't correct yourself, a misunderstanding could be deadly. But there seemed to be no other way. He struggled through several attempts before writing,

*Dear Maria*

*I hope that by now, you have fully recovered from your ordeal. I'm writing to tell you that I did see Lorenzo. He seemed to be doing all right, but I'm cooped up all day, and he's outside, at least getting some exercise.*

*My last exercise consisted of carrying you home that night. I still smile to think of what might have happened if I met a cop or a priest while I had you draped over my shoulder.*

*My mother tells me that the jacket I wear to church is too short and getting shabby. When the strike is over and we can all move about, I'll stop into your father's shop and see if he can fit me up with something I can afford.*

*Sincerely,*

*Paddy*

41

He mailed the letter on Tuesday. When he got home the following Saturday, Kathy pointed to a package on the kitchen table. He lifted the cover.

"They're delicious," she said.

He picked up one of the small pastries and bit into it.

Kathy said, "They're Italian. I bet the mother made them."

Paddy was now more interested in the note, sticking out of an envelope, which sat on top of the pastries.

There were two notes. The first:

*Dear Mrs. Flanagan,*

*Thank you for rescue of my daughter. Our family rejoices from your kindness. You know another mother's heart.*

*You and your family will be in my prayers every day of my life.*

*Blessings on you,*

*Sophia Petrella*

The second note was in a broader, more confident hand.

*To the Flanagan family,*

*My heartfelt thank you for your kindnesses. You are true good Samaritans, and I owe you my life. Please accept these pastries (I made them myself) as a small token of my gratitude.*

*To Paddy,*

*My father is looking forward to making you a fine jacket for free. Also, it would have been nice if you carried me from your home back to mine. I might have enjoyed the ride.*

*Sincerely,*

*Maria*

Molly entered the kitchen just as he finished the note and was picking up another pastry. "Leave a few of those for your father, but not that note from Maria."

Kathy giggled.

Paddy said, "But Da likes Italians."

"He loves them, but he's concerned about you. There are traditions, you know." She turned to Kathy. "And not a word out of you. Go get your clothes ready for Mass tomorrow."

Kathy left them.

"What do *you* think, Mom?"

Molly put a hand on her son's arm. "She's beautiful, an angel, but you have to be realistic. You don't want to be hurt. And look at how you met her; it was an accident."

"It was a miracle."

Molly laughed and squeezed his arm. "I have the feeling that you'll be needing another miracle before this is over."


\*\*\*\*\*\*\*\*\*\*\*\*\*\*\*\*\*\*\*\*\*\*\*\*\*\*\*\*\*\*\*\*


Amos entered the police station. It was his intention to tell Sullivan about the Sicilians, but Charlie Vose spotted him from down the hall and motioned with his head. He wanted to talk about something.

Until recently, Vose had been Amos's boss. He'd just been demoted by Con Lynch, the new Director of Public Safety, from Lieutenant and Chief Inspector to Inspector. As Amos strode up, Vose said, "Congratulations on your escape. You must know the Pope, or something."

"I don't. But it helps to drink a little red wine with Italians now and then."

Vose led Amos to a small empty office. "Do you actually like that stuff?"

"Some of it's pretty good."

There was a small table and several chairs in the office. Vose closed the door and they sat down to one side of the table; neither man wanting the separation implicit in sitting across from each other.

Vose reached into a vest pocket for a small snuff box. After sniffing a pinch into each nostril, he began. "Amos, I don't know how long Lynch will have the whip hand, but better times are coming back sooner or later. I'm hoping that we can help each other in the meantime."

Amos paused while Vose snuffled into his handkerchief, and then asked, "Did you have something in mind?"

"I do. I got assigned to the dynamite find this afternoon. There's something about it that doesn't feel right. And there are some people who think that the Italians are behind it. If a connection can be made, some higher-ups in this town would be grateful."

Amos gazed off. "You mean some higher-ups who'd like to break the strike?"

Vose said nothing but the way he squeezed his lips together said yes.

Amos continued. "Well, from what little I know, these particular Syrians don't sound like the type to cook something like this up by themselves. And there are some new characters in town—some Sicilians from New York—heavily armed. We can probably book a few on gun charges. Maybe they had something to do with the dynamite." Without mentioning Lamastro, he told Vose what he knew about where to find the Sicilians.

"This is good, Amos. This is good. I'll square it with Sullivan, tell him I got it from you, and we can keep working on it together."

44

"That would be grand, as long as you won't be upset if we find that the Italians had nothing to do with it."

Vose gave him a sharp look. "Of course."

Amos went to the inspectors' room to catch up on some paper-work. He'd been at it for almost an hour when he glanced up to see Michael Casey's bulky frame standing just outside the door. They looked at each other, and Amos understood that Casey had something on his mind but did not want to come into the room. Amos went to the door, and Casey said, "I was just headed to the toilet." Amos grinned and followed him down the hall.

A brief survey of the stalls established that they were alone. Casey took a large Police Department manila envelope out from under his coat. "This can't leave the station," he said, handing it to Amos.

"What's in here?"

"It's evidence. I got it—that is I borrowed it—from Maguire. It's what the dynamite was wrapped in. You'll want to be looking it over."

Amos hefted the envelope.

Casey said, "You only need to look it over."

"Okay. I'll look at it here." He motioned toward one of the stalls.

Casey whispered, "I'll be in the hall, just outside. Leave it in the stall."

Casey left. Amos went into the stall and opened the envelope, finding some wrinkled papers taken from some kind of magazine. He unfolded and spread them out as best he could while standing with his back against the door. They were all from *Shadyside,* an undertakers' trade magazine. He put the papers back in the envelope and propped it up behind the toilet. Outside, as he passed, Casey said, "Isn't it interesting that an undertaker would tip us on where to find the dynamite?"

45

"Indeed, it is."

# CHAPTER SIX

It was never defined in so many words, but the Flanagan family made it a custom to eat together on Saturday evenings. They discussed the events of the previous week and plans for the next. All of them knew what the main topic would be that night. Throughout the day, everyone in town had talked of little else but the dynamite. Even Neal was anxious to hear if his da had any new information or details.

Amos arrived home late in the afternoon. He was left to himself while he washed up and went into the living room to read the paper for a short time before dinner. Little was said as they sat down. A family member might comment on the weather or make some other innocuous observation, but otherwise, until prayers were said, the meal served and partly eaten, no serious discussion started. On that evening the ritual was followed while the older members, with mild amusement, observed Neal's enthusiasm for getting past the formalities. His prayers were loud and clear and he helped in every way: he passed the potatoes and turnips quickly, and held out his plate for Molly to serve his slice of lamb. In between, he kept watch on his father.

When the appropriate moment arrived, Amos cleared his mouth, straightened up and said, "I'll tell you as much as I can."

For the benefit of Neal and Kathleen, he went over the important details. And then, without telling them how he knew, he mentioned the undertakers' magazine, in which the dynamite had been wrapped. "It's printed in English," he added.

Neal piped up. "Some Syrians read English." He looked around. "Don't they?"

Paddy laughed. "Not if they can help it. You know, Da, the Syrians don't want this strike. They want to continue working."

Molly asked, "Do you think the dynamite was planted?"

"It's a bit of a mystery for now."

Molly read her husband's eyes; the subject was closed. "I'm sure that you'll get to the bottom of it." She turned to Kathleen. "Would you start the kettle, Luv?"

After dinner, Paddy helped to clear the table; he went to the basement, stoked the fire in the furnace, shoveled in some coal, cleaned out the ashes and carried the barrel out to the back of the house. Then, with Molly's permission, he went out to join his friend, Frank Dunn, in his darkroom. Frank was a part-time photographer who loved to experiment, and Paddy enjoyed working with him. The fascination of standing together in the dim light provided by a candle behind a red filter and watching images emerge in the tray of developer, seemingly from nowhere, never grew old.

The darkroom was in the basement of the Dunn family home on Newton Street where heat radiated from a small pot-bellied stove, which Frank had fired up well before Paddy's arrival. With the electric lights on, they worked to mix the chemicals, using water warmed on the stove. They filled the trays, and Frank checked the temperature in each, explaining, "The developer is the only one that's really critical." They closed the door, lit the candle, and turned out the overhead light. "We're going to make some prints tonight," Frank said.

While they waited for their eyes to adjust to the darkness, Frank squinted at the thermometer and asked, "Is your da involved with the dynamite?"

"Yes. He found out something interesting yesterday." Paddy told him about the *Shadyside* wrapping.

"Did he say what issue it was?"

"I don't think so. What does it matter?"

"You know Turley's funeral home on South Broadway, right? Well he wanted some pictures of one of his parlors when it was empty. I was over there two weeks ago. Photographers learn to notice things, you don't want to waste plates so you check

48

details. You don't want something in the picture that will distract, like a calendar or another picture—unless they're important. Anyway, I'm in his office and I happened to notice these magazines you're talking about; all laid out  by date, so's you could tell if one was missing."

"Was one missing?"

Frank laughed. "I'm not *that* good." He slipped a sheet of photo-paper out of a box and closed it. "I forgot to put the cover back on once. That was expensive." He took a glass plate from a rack and laid it on the photo-paper. Both were in a little frame which he closed, clamping them together. "Close your eyes; I'm going to do the exposure."

Paddy closed his eyes, and Frank counted. "One, two, three…twenty-five. Okay."

"I didn't see the plate," Paddy said. "What's it a picture of?"

"It should be interesting. I was trying to capture the feeling of winter, by taking a picture of bare trees against the sky and snow." He opened the frame and slipped the photo-paper into the developer.

Paddy bent forward to stare into the liquid. "The developing is going to be really critical, isn't it? You want to get that high-contrast, stark look, without overdoing it."

"Right. It may take a few tries. Try to remember exactly what it looks like as I take it out, so we can go a little more, or less, on the next one."

They watched intently until Frank removed the photo-paper and placed it in the tray of fixer.

Paddy asked, "Do you think all the funeral homes keep their back issues of that magazine?"

"How do I know? Wouldn't it be funny if Turley was the only one and *that* issue is missing?"

"Yeah. He sure looks like a trouble maker."

They laughed.

"Let's see what we got," Frank said, turning on the overhead light.


\*\*\*\*\*\*\*\*\*\*\*\*\*\*\*\*\*\*\*\*\*\*\*\*\*\*\*\*\*\*


Molly assigned Kathleen to do the dishes and Neal to dry them. "I'll be checking them very carefully," she said, before adjourning to the living room with Amos.

He settled into his customary easy-chair but did not reach for the newspaper alongside; this was a time for talk. He waited, studying the raised floral pattern on the iron plate that sealed the rarely used fireplace and recalled, not for the first time, how it was before central heating.

Molly settled into her rocker, a few feet away. "I'm worried, Amos."

He nodded. She was worried about Paddy, as she often did as he took ever more confident steps on the road to manhood. This time, he shared her concern. "There are more of these Wobblies coming to town. And we've got some gunmen from New York here as enforcers."

"Was the dynamite found in the tailor's shop intended for blowing up mills, do you think?"

"I don't know. I doubt they had any such intention. The Syrians seem to be a peaceable lot. Maybe that dynamite was planted."

"By Wobblies?"

Amos shook his head. "By the mill owners."

"My God!"

"Keep it to yourself. I am worried about Paddy though. Who knows where this thing is going."

"What can we do? Should we get him out of there?"

A thought flicked across his mind: 'Does she ever worry about me?' "There's not much we can do; he's a man now. He has to make his own decisions."

"Amos, he's just making a start."

"I know. I can give him some advice, but I can't tell him what to do."

"You'll never forgive yourself if anything happens to him."

"And he'll never forgive me if I order him about."

Molly sat back, put her knuckles up near her mouth and sighed. A moment later, she spoke. "He picked a fine time to fall in love with an Italian girl."

"Is that still going on?"

"I'm afraid so. I don't suppose you'll be telling him not to do that?"

Amos clasped his hands together and shook his head. "Oh God. What to do? What to do?"

"You can ask God about it tomorrow at church," she said, getting up to go into the kitchen.

************************

On Sunday afternoon, Paddy left the house and went to the Common. He thought that there would be some kind of strike meeting going on, and his heart soared with the hope that he might see Maria in the crowd. He walked past the new YMCA building on Lawrence Street and noticed a crowd gathered near

51

Haverhill Street, about half-way across the Common. He turned in that direction and stopped in front of Trinity Church to study the crowd across the street. The day was clear and cold, but at least a thousand people were listening to a man with bushy black hair and a black, fluffy, bow-tie ranting in Italian. Paddy was too far away to understand what he was saying, even if it had been in English. It didn't matter, he wasn't there to listen to a speech.

Crossing the street, he walked onto the grass and circled behind the crowd, using his height to try to spot Maria. He walked to a spot near Jackson Street, where Maria might pass on her way home and, with his arms folded, he leaned against a tree. What little warmth the January sun offered comforted him.

The speech ended and groups of people drifted away from the crowd. He pushed off from the tree and studied the women coming his way—no Maria.

From his left, a man spoke. "Too bad you don't understand Italian; you might have learned something." It was Lorenzo.

Paddy grinned, pushed off the tree and faced him. "I wish I did. It might come in handy."

Lorenzo stood there, dressed in a thick brown jacket, his neck wrapped in a plush maroon scarf, but he wore no hat. He was alone and seemingly in no hurry to move on. "You're wasting your time here. My father has forbidden my sister to come to these kinds of meetings."

"Smart man."

"He is a smart man. He'll probably forbid her to see you anywhere."

"I understand that he was a professor in Italy."

Lorenzo moved closer. "Yes, and he's thinking of going back. Things have changed there."

Through some, unspoken communication, they began walking together toward Jackson Street.

"Your father has been here a long time."

"He'd rather be a professor than a tailor."

"I would too. You have a nice family."

"You do also. But it doesn't change anything; the Union will win this strike. Things will never go back to the way they were."

"Do they have unions in Italy?"

"I don't know much about Italy. I was born here and I'm going to stick with the IWW."

"The Wobblies?"

Lorenzo nodded, and they parted company at the corner. Paddy made his way home, still trying to come up with some way to see Maria. He found himself in front of Frank Dunn's house and still had no idea of how to go about it. Frank was home, and his mother offered Paddy a cup of tea. Then, with cups in hand, the two of them went to the basement to look at the prints made during the previous evening. The pictures were still hanging from a clothes line, just as they had left them. They took them down and spread them out on a table, using small, smooth stones from a white crock on the work-bench to weight the corners.

Frank went into the darkroom and came back out with a large diameter magnifying glass. "Here, try this," he said, handing it to Paddy.

Paddy remembered the day the two of them had gone to the graveyard in North Andover to take pictures. He examined the image. "It looks cold."

"Doesn't it? But it was hot as hell that day. Remember? He gestured at the table. "Take some for your scrapbook." He handed Paddy an envelope.

"I will." He picked up a print of a gravestone. "I wanted to ask you about something. Remember Maria?"

53

"Yes. I haven't seen her yet, but you've sure got me looking forward to it."

Paddy put the situation to Frank, including his recent encounter with Lorenzo.

"So," Frank said, "with the possible exception of Maria, herself, these Italians are not looking at you as any kind of prize catch."

"I guess not."

"That didn't stop Romeo."

Paddy drained his tea cup. "I'm hoping for a happier ending."

"Well," Frank said, as he perched on a stool. "It doesn't sound like singing love songs under her window would be a good idea. How about a go-between?"

"A go-between?"

"Yeah. You must know some Italians."

"They're all friends of my father. But there is one who might help."

********************************

Amos listened carefully when Paddy told him about Frank's observation of the *Shadyside* magazines in Turley's funeral parlor. He thought it over. It was unlikely that all the undertakers kept their back issues. And if one of them had used the November issue to wrap dynamite, he had probably discarded earlier ones. But it had to be checked out, and the obvious place to start was Turley's.

As far as Amos was concerned, there could not be a less likely suspect than Liam Turley. He was getting on in years, a bit frail, and somewhat forgetful. His charity was well known in the community; many a poor widow buried her husband and never received a bill. Amos knew him well. He could ask questions and trust Turley to keep it under his hat. He found him in his office on Monday morning. On seeing Amos, he struggled to his feet. "Oh, Amos, I do hope that this is just a friendly visit?"

"It's not about a funeral, Liam. It's information I need."

Turley lowered his small frame back into his chair. "I'll try not to disappoint you, Amos, but I'm not known for having much information these days."

Amos had already noticed the *Shadyside* copies, laid out on a side table just as he had expected. "I think you can help, and I know you can keep things to yourself."

"Oh, absolutely. Without question."

Amos moved to the table. The stack was laid out so that the issue date of each copy was visible. "It's about these magazines." He picked up the November edition.

"You're welcome to whatever's there, Amos."

"I'll just borrow this one." He said, as he walked over to take a chair in front of Turley's desk. "Why do you keep so many?"

"Guilt. I haven't read one in years but I know I should. All I do is leaf through some of the oldest ones before I throw them out."

"Isn't that the way of it though? None of us do all the things we're supposed to do. There aren't enough hours in a day. The trick is to forgive yourself. I'm getting good at that. Is there anything useful in these?" He held up the magazine.

"Oh yes. I read it when I was younger. I learned some useful things."

\*\*\*\*\*\*\*\*\*\*\*\*\*\*\*\*\*\*\*\*\*\*\*\*\*

Paddy explained, before he left the house on Tuesday that he would not be coming straight home after work. He didn't say that he planned to go to the Lamastro home in Jackson Court on the other side of the Common.

Paddy knew Connie and Joe well. As a boy, he had been to their previous home, a flat on Elm Street, many times, and he recalled their return visits to his family. He stood in front of their new home, a two-story, brick, row-house and wondered why, without children, they needed a house of this size. He had been inside twice, but the last time was over two years earlier.

Connie answered the door and recognized him immediately. She welcomed him into the parlor where a fire glowed from inside a glass-jeweled, pot-bellied stove. The flickering flame caused the red, green and yellow bits of glass to twinkle and cast soft, moving, colors onto the dark walls and drapes. She turned on the light, and he observed draperies and satin-covered furniture of a quality that he did not recall from previous visits. "This is all very nice," he said. "Is it new?"

She smiled. "We've been making improvements." She gestured to a chair. "Would you like a glass of wine?"

He declined, and she left him to find her husband.

Lamastro entered wearing a thick dressing robe. He removed his glasses as he came forward with his hand outstretched. Paddy stood up, and Lamastro commented. "You certainly have grown. Not a boy anymore?"

Connie, who was just behind him, said, "Isn't he handsome?"

Paddy grinned, and they all sat down. Lamastro asked, "Would you like a glass of wine? I have some of your father's favorite."

"Thank you. No. This is just a short visit."

"Your family is well?"

56

"Yes."

"Did your father send you?"

"No."

"Does he know you're here?"

"No."

"Hmm. You want some information?"

"No."

Lamastro laughed. "I give up."

Paddy hesitated. "It's about a girl."

"Ah."

The Lamastros looked at each other. Connie asked, "Is there a problem?"

"It's a…Yes, there's a kind of problem."

Lamastro asked, "Can you tell us the nature of the problem, Paddy?"

Paddy nodded as he looked to one and then the other. "She's Italian."

Again, they exchanged glances. Then, Lamastro said, "I think I'm beginning to understand. Would this be the girl you brought home, half frozen to death? Maria Petrella?"

"It would."

Connie clasped her hands. "This is interesting."

"It is. I know her," Lamastro said. "I know her father very well, and the family. Are you in love with her?"

Paddy whispered, "Yes."

Connie sighed. Lamastro sat back, plopping his hands onto his lap. "Is she in love with you?"

"I think… I hope so. I don't know."

Connie gave Paddy her most sympathetic look and gently shook her head. Lamastro rubbed his forehead and smoothed his mustache before continuing. "I can guess the rest. Of course, Paddy I want to help you, but there are difficulties. You need to know what they are. First off, your father is a trusted friend. I can't do something behind his back that I know he would not want." He paused and then continued. "I won't lecture you on the traditions and cultural issues. Italians are very proud, especially the immigrants; they know they are not accepted. They cling to the traditions of the old country. In some ways they become exaggerations of what they'd be like in Italy. A man like Alessandro Petrella would have total say over whom might be allowed to court his daughter. I'm sure he would never accept an Irishman."

"I'm an American."

Lamastro smiled and nodded. "As is Maria. There is an additional problem. I'm working with your father—in secret. You can't come here again until after this strike business is over. You understand?"

Paddy slumped in his chair and stared at his shoes. "I wouldn't do anything to hurt you or my father."

"I know that, Paddy. And I want to help you—but this…It's not possible."

Paddy stood up. Connie spoke to her husband. "We can't leave it like this."

"What can I do?"

"I'll do it," she said and turned to Paddy. "You can meet in a church or the library. If she is willing, I'll get word to you."

Lamastro stood up. "I didn't hear any of this." He took Paddy's hand. "God bless you. We'll see more of you after the strike. Yes?" He paused, shook his head. "Don't do this. Don't torture yourself." He turned and left them.

Connie saw Paddy to the door. She looked outside for passersby and then hugged him and kissed his cheek. "Whatever happens, it will be God's will."

# CHAPTER SEVEN

The strike that brought Maria into Paddy's life now seemed to be pulling her away; he felt as though he were standing alongside the Merrimack, longing for Maria, while she sat in a small boat, drifting away with wind and current.

Life in the mills grew more threatening every day, and Amos cautioned him repeatedly on the possibility of violence. The warnings seemed prophetic when Big Bill Haywood, a Wobbly leader from New York, arrived on Wednesday.

That afternoon, Ernst Meyer, who seemed to have a lot of time on his hands, came by to relate the latest rumor. He took off his little black hat and flicked off some imaginary lint. "That lunatic from New York, that Haywood fellow, he's dangerous. He gives a speech; he wants to overthrow the government. And he's telling the workers to destroy the mills." With that he put his hat back on, picked up his tool box and moved on, leaving Paddy to wonder how this might affect his pursuit of Maria.

Everyone inside the mills wondered if there were enough soldiers to protect them. On Friday, they were more optimistic after learning that Joseph Ettor, the Wobbly organizer whom Paddy had seen speaking on the common, had gone to Boston to meet with William Wood, President of the American Woolen Company and king-pin of the mill owners, regarding a settlement.

Paddy worried about the strike, but it all seemed strange, and he had difficulty imagining that something terrible would actually happen to him. Besides, life in the mill was all secondary; he spent more time thinking about Maria and wondering if Connie would be successful and if Maria would want to see him.

\*\*\*\*\*\*\*\*\*\*\*\*\*\*\*\*\*\*\*\*\*\*

"Now what?" Amos asked himself as he left Turley's Funeral Parlor and looked for a northbound streetcar. Breen had tipped the police to the dynamite in the Syrian tailor shop. His funeral parlor was the one to search for copies of *Shadyside*. Would November be missing from his collection? Did he have a collection like Turley or did he get rid of the others?

Amos did not like Breen—never had. He was a social climber; loved to butter up the mill owners. His only claim to any kind of status was that his old man had been mayor all those years—a good one. Breen would be against the strikers and he'd help the owners if he could; a lot of cops would do the same. Amos would have to keep his suspicions very close and he needed to get to those magazines before somebody tipped Breen.

There was very little activity at the station house when he arrived. His long-time friend, Sergeant Jimmy Kerrigan, sat behind the tall desk. Amos greeted him. "It's nice to see friends in such high places."

"I'm just sitting here, waiting for someone like yourself to bring in another lunatic." Kerrigan was a big man, not fat but bulky, his arms filled the sleeves of his jacket. He favored an occasional cigar, but Amos was grateful that he never left the stinking butts on the desk

"You won't have long to wait, Jimmy; there are more Wobblies coming this week. And, in the meantime, there's this dynamite thing."

"Will you be bringing me some Italians?"

Amos scanned the room; there was no one within earshot. He motioned Kerrigan to the side of the desk where they could put their heads close. "Jimmy, I need some help. Not a soul can know."

"Amos, you know you have my bond."

Amos proceeded to tell him about the magazines and what he needed from Breen's funeral parlor.

"I have the very thing you need downstairs. Do you remember Eddie Foyle?"

"Yeah. Fast Eddie, skinny kid, always getting into some kind of fracas. What did he do now?"

"Something that you may be able to take care of. We got him in here on a charge of bastardy."

Amos laughed. "Oh, I'm good at that kind of shit."

"Amos, he works at Breen's"

"Ah. And who's the lucky girl?"

"Mary McGreevy."

"That one. I assume her father made the charge. What the hell does Willy McGreevy want with a son-in-law like Eddie?"

"What choice does he have? Besides, Eddie's not a bad sort; he's settled down, and he swears he's not the father."

"And you believe him, of course. But that Mary's no prize; she could be pulling a fast one. You let him out, and I'll see what I can do for him with McGreevy. Just get me the information on those magazines, and not a peep out of Eddie."

"Timmy Coyne brought him in; he'll be asking questions."

"Tell Coyne there's a priest involved, but that it's all on the quiet for now. Negotiations are in progress; Foyle's going to do the right thing, and that's why you let him out."

"I won't tell Coyne who the priest is. You can stand me a pint when this is over."

Willy and Nora McGreevy kept a little candy store on Market street just off South Broadway. They were both in the store when Amos popped in and motioned Willy before proceeding into the storeroom at the back. Willy gave his wife a questioning look before following. The room was nearly dark, separated from the store by a curtain; most of the available light filtered in through dirty, frosted, windows—one of them in the back door, and the other in the wall alongside. Among the, mostly empty, boxes there was a small table, but only one chair.

Amos gestured to it. "Rest your feet, Willy. I'll only be a few minutes."

McGreevy sat down and placed his hands on the table, waiting for Amos to start.

Amos propped one hip over a stacked box. "What I'm here about is not entirely police business. I'm feeling more like a father right now."

McGreevy offered no sign of encouragement. His expression was almost cold.

"Eddie Foyle claims to not be the father."

McGreevy remained motionless.

Amos knew Mary McGreevy to have a bit of a reputation but he had no idea of how far the truth went. He gambled. "There's some saying that he could find ways to convince a judge."

Willy's hands moved to the center of the table and he lowered his eyes.

"No doubt the girl's in the right, but I've been involved in these cases before. It works best when it's kept private. The girl goes away, and…"

Willy folded his hands, placed them between his knees and lowered his head. "I've got six kids, Amos. I've not got a cent to my name." He looked at Amos now with a different expression—a pleading in his eyes.

"There's help, Willy." Amos paused, waiting to see how McGreevy reacted. Then he asked, "With your permission?"

Willy nodded, and Amos went to him, placing a hand on his arm. "I'll be back." He started to leave but turned back with an afterthought. "You know, sometimes they wind up getting married after it's over."

Amos couldn't get out the front door without indulging in a bit of chocolate. He picked a piece out of the case and left two pennies on the counter for Nora, who was busy with a customer. On the sidewalk, it occurred to him that he had not heard from Wilcox or his lawyer. He'd have to stop in at the shoe store.

*****************************

Paddy went to the office to get his jacket and hat before leaving the mill on Saturday. He found an envelope, with his name on it, pinned to his jacket. His boss, white-haired, Kevin O'Shay, sat at the desk, wearing his bowler, glasses, and scribbling away. Paddy unpinned the envelope and showed it to him. "Did you see who left this?" O'Shay, not known for his sociability, shrugged and shook his head.

Paddy opened the envelope. Inside, he found a note and a ticket to a matinee at the Broadway Theater on Sunday. The note was from Connie:

P.

Be sure to attend. Destroy this note

C.

He slipped the ticket into his pocket, tore up the note and envelope and put them in the trash outside. At home, he casually mentioned that someone had given him a ticket to the show.

Molly said, "How nice."

Amos said, "Must be a lousy show."

Paddy laughed.


The theater was half full when he arrived twenty minutes early to find his aisle seat in the next-to-last row on the right side. He got up twice to let people pass, but the row behind him remained empty. Clearly, the house would not be full; the strike was taking a toll on all the businesses in town, and that was too bad because, contrary to Amos's joke, he had heard that it would be a good show.

The house lights dimmed, and Paddy felt his heart sinking in unison. Just then, an usher and two young ladies appeared at his shoulder. He rose, and they slipped into the seats next to him. Maria's smile, and her brushing against him, raised goose bumps and a giddy feeling, causing him to forget to breathe until he sat down.

Maria sat next to him and gestured to her companion. "This is my friend, Carla,"

Paddy reached across Maria to briefly take Carla's hand. Before letting go, he looked straight into Maria's face. He had never been this close.

A spotlight illuminated the center of the stage, and a man stepped out from behind the curtain. He started to juggle steel rings; an attractive, dark haired woman dressed in white tights and a leotard covered with rhinestones stepped out with more rings. They were soon tossing twelve rings to each other. The act concluded when the spotlight went off as they tossed flaming torches back and forth in the darkness.

Next, the curtain opened and a family with six kids sang and danced. The smaller children played it for laughs, but all were talented in singing and dancing.

As the performers went off, Maria reached for Paddy's hand. He was almost startled by her touch but he clasped her hand with both of his.

She whispered, "Carla is very discrete—a very good friend. Sometimes, I go with her on Sunday to visit her grandmother in Haverhill."

Paddy was still tingling with the effects of her being so close; it took him a few seconds to catch on. "Haverhill. Grand; I hardly know a soul in Haverhill."

Another smile, as she pulled his hand closer.

"Next Sunday?" he asked.

She let go of his hand and reached into her purse. "The address," she said, handing him a slip of paper. Then she said, loud enough for Carla to hear, "Carla is going to need a lot of help with her poor, sick grandmother."

Carla grinned at both of them, revealing a large gap between her two front teeth.

\*\*\*\*\*\*\*\*\*\*\*\*\*\*\*\*\*\*\*\*\*

On Monday, Amos intended to follow up on Wilcox. Was he staying away from his wife and kid? And why hadn't his lawyer been in touch? Also, he hoped to get some results regarding the *Shadyside* issues at Breen's funeral home from Fast Eddie. But even before he got to the station house, he knew that his plans for Wilcox and Breen would have to wait.

Early that morning, a group of strikers had attacked streetcars on Broadway. The cars were filled with replacement workers. Strikers had smashed windows and thrown pieces of ice at the occupants. There were injuries and several cars were out of commission. Later in the day there was to be a large strike rally on the common. When Amos entered the station, he immediately sensed an air of agitation. Officers were scurrying about, and no one had time for more than a nod in his direction.

Kerrigan motioned him to the desk. "The Son-in-Law," as he referred to the City Marshal, "wants to see you."

"Any idea what he wants?"

"I'm certain he knows nothing about you looking to nail Breen on this dynamite thing, but he's not going to like it when he does find out. Right now, it's the streetcars. He's getting all kinds of grief from higher ups, and you can imagine what *they* get from William Wood and his cronies."

"Yeah. It's something, isn't it? We never had this before—all this violence."

"Those guineas are crazy."

"It's the hard men from New York that scare me."

Amos turned toward Sullivan's office. He peeked in to see Sullivan sitting at his desk with his glasses on, writing furiously. Amos tapped on the doorpost and walked in. Sullivan slapped down his pen, tore off his glasses and smacked his desk with the flat of his hand.

He stood up, red faced. "Amos, we left you in your job so we could keep track of those god damned Italians. Do you know what they did this morning?"

"I do." Amos helped himself to a chair. "And it's no secret who the agitators are. You know the names as well as I do."

Sullivan strutted around behind his desk and leaned forward to smack it again. "We need arrests. We need to start putting people in jail."

"I've already given information on some gunmen from New York. They're in jail now. Were any arrests made this morning?"

"Of course. What I need to know is what they're going to do next."

"You need someone on the inside for that. Someone who speaks Italian."

"Or," Sullivan put both hands on his desk and leaned toward Amos, "we need some good—at least plausible—reasons to arrest the leaders."

Amos put his hand up to his chin and nodded as if he were seriously considering what Sullivan had just said. At that point, any doubts that he had about whether the dynamite had been planted were rapidly disappearing. "Yeah, that's an interesting way to look at it. I'll work on it and keep you informed."

"All right, Amos. Just remember, we need to look like we're doing something here."

"Right." Amos got up to leave. "John, have you ever been in the tenements on Common Street?"

Sullivan looked at him as if he had not heard the question and then answered. "I couldn't stand the stink."

"The Italians don't like it either. You can imagine how desperate they are for something better." He continued out the door and passed in front of Kerrigan.

"Amos," Kerrigan called, softly, setting a cigar to one side.

He went over to the desk and leaned close.

"Amos, Eddie Foyle was here; he just left. He says the journals are all there—except for last November. You're one smart cop."

Amos grinned. "Ah yes. Now we can pay Breen an official visit. I'll see Judge Waters and get a warrant. I'll need somebody to go in with me."

"Bring Casey."

"I will, Jimmy, and tell Eddie I've got something started for his situation."

Amos left Kerrigan, went out into the hallway and ascended the stairs to the judges' chambers on the third floor. He did not need to see Judge Waters himself; Billy Conboy, Waters's clerk, would do. They had been close while in grammar school together at Saint Mary's until Billy got left back in the fifth grade. Later, they played baseball for the Lawrence Stars; a friendship started, but it died out when Billy got a job at the courthouse and took up heavy drinking. No doubt, he'd been helped down that path by some of Lawrence's less upstanding lawyers.

He found Conboy in a small entry-room, just outside of Waters's office. Billy greeted him with a grin, which revealed the need for some serious dental care. Amos knew that he never drank on the job and that he was always clean, shaved, and decked out in a fresh white shirt. Helen, his wife, was a saint; getting Billy up and out everyday must leave her exhausted. She did the same for their three kids. The kids' manners were exemplary—no spark though, never said a word.

"Amos, a sight for sore eyes. How's Molly and the kids?"

"Grand, Billy. They're all grand. Just a bit worried about Paddy, working in the mills and all. And your family?"

"All grand. Little Tommy's graduating. He'll likely get a prize for spelling. But this strike is a terrible thing, isn't it? Those Wobblies are a bunch of lunatics. You should arrest the lot of them."

Amos laughed. "We may do just that, but Judge Waters doesn't like it when we break the rules."

"True. True. Is there something you wanted from the judge?"

70

"Yes, there is. But first, I want to emphasize the need for confidentiality. If this leaks out, I'll be asking the judge for a full investigation."

Billy adjusted his glasses and cleared his throat. "Absolutely, Amos, and I'll be sure to pass that on to the judge."

Amos paused for a few seconds, thinking to add that it wasn't the judge he was worried about but he moved on, explaining the situation to Billy, who sat completely still until the end when he said, "Whew. I'll prepare the warrant and get word to you as soon as it's signed."

"Thanks, Billy. My best to Helen—and good luck to Tommy."

Leaving the building, Amos noticed some people gathering on the common. They drifted toward the far end, out of sight. Another damn meeting, he thought before turning toward Essex Street where he planned to stop in at Wilcox's shoe store. The streetcar violence that morning renewed his concerns for Paddy. If things kept escalating, he'd have to listen to Molly and pull Paddy out of the mill.

A streetcar came up Essex Street marked for South Broadway--he changed his mind; Wilcox could wait until later. He'd take care of Fast Eddie first and at least get one thing off his agenda. He rode across the river and got off in front of Saint Patrick's.

The housekeeper, Agnes Scully, opened the rectory door, gave him one nod and stepped back to admit him. He asked for the pastor, Father Kavanagh, and she showed him into the great man's office. "I'll see if he's in," she said, leaving him to his own devices. He'd been in the office many times on some sort of parish business; it never ceased to fascinate him. Why did priests have so much clutter?--Every inch of wall space was covered--A picture of the Pope and a papal flag hung behind the desk, along with a picture of the archbishop and Kavanagh.

71

There were many pictures of him, posing with dignitaries at all kinds of ceremonies, and enough holy pictures to fill the remaining spaces including the tops of side tables. A grouping of small daguerreotypes in silver frames occupied a corner table, Irish parents and relatives, from the look of them.

Kavanagh strode into the room, making a show of setting his prayer book on the desk before swishing his cassock around to sit in his high-backed chair.

"Sorry to trouble you, Father, but we're working a tight schedule because of the strike." Amos sat himself down.

"Not at all, Amos. God knows, we're praying for these…" He tapped his fingers on the desk. "these aliens to come to their senses. Mister Wood and the other owners are right not to reward criminal behavior."

"Uh, yes Father. I've come on a related matter, but it's police business, and I can't reveal too much. I hope you'll understand."

Kavanagh folded his hands on his desk and nodded.

Amos told him about Mary McGreevy and her problem.

"This hardly sounds like police business."

"But it is."

"She must know who the father is?"

"She thinks she does, but that's the part I can't discuss. What I need is a place for the girl to go away, someplace where the nuns will take care of her and find a decent home for the baby."

Kavanagh sat back and folded his arms, a look of disgust on his face. "This doesn't come free, Amos. These things cost money."

"Indeed, Father. But this is one of those times when some bread needs to be cast on the waters."

"The money is needed for other purposes."

"True, but I'm thinking that it's not that much when compared to the money I help raise from policemen in the parish, and the money Molly raises with her cake sales and special events. And I'm here every Sunday helping with the collections and counting the money."

"All right, Amos. All right, but I want you to see that McGreevy comes up with fifty dollars."

"It may take him a while."

Kavanagh threw up his hands.

"Thank you, Father."


As he reached the bottom of the stairs and stepped onto the sidewalk, Amos glanced upward at a few clouds, and the sun--still low in the southern sky, it cast a bright but tepid yellow light on the building behind him. It seemed to be getting colder, and the wind had picked up. He pulled out his watch and popped open the cover. Eleven-twenty; Neal and Kathleen would be walking home soon for their lunch, but it was too cold to stand around and wait for them. He tipped the watch to gaze at Molly's picture on the inside cover before snapping it closed. She probably wouldn't be up for a quick roll-in-the-hay, but a little time without the kids would be nice. He crossed South Broadway and headed home.

What to tell her? She'd already know about the streetcars that morning, be even more worried about Paddy. He felt an inner pressure building as he got closer to the house although she had said very little since the strike began; they had that quiet kind of understanding--once an issue was raised and discussed, it was left to rest until one of them had a reason to speak of it again, or an undefined time had passed and one of them felt it necessary to bring it up.

Molly's father, Patrick, had been after him for over a year; he wanted Amos to quit the force, move to Boston and take over his trucking business. At Christmas time, he had made it clear that Amos would have to make up his mind soon as he, Patrick, was feeling old age coming on and he said that, if he was going to provide anything for his heirs, he had to sell or get Amos to run the business. Molly made no secret of wanting him to be demoted to patrolman; it would make the change more palatable.

He found her at the stove, stirring a pot of soup. She turned her head to him as he entered. "Did someone report a disturbance at this address?"

He slipped behind her and wrapped his arms around her waist. "Smells good," he said, his right hand slipping up over her left breast. "I don't suppose it could just simmer there for a bit?"

"And have the children walk in on us? They may be young but they're not stupid."

"After lunch then?"

"I can't believe that, in times like this, you'd leave the citizens of Lawrence unprotected for any more time than necessary." She leaned her head back against the side of his, murmuring, "After lunch."

Well after two o'clock, he re-crossed the river and walked up Essex Street. The sun was already lowering in the southern sky, but the wind had died, and his spirit was renewed. He stopped under the awning at MacCartney's One Price Clothing Store where he studied the latest fashions for women. The new skirts were much slimmer and used far less cloth. He wondered if the strikers knew about this and at least considered that the owners might be up against a tough market. The strikers certainly needed more money, their living conditions were deplorable, but their timing stunk.

He continued down the street. There were no customers in Wilcox's shoe store, only a clerk, who informed him that,

"Mondays are always slow. Mister Wilcox has taken the afternoon off."

"Where might he go on a cold day like today?"

"Mister Wilcox does not say."

"I'll be back."

Amos toyed with the idea of going to Wilcox's home to make sure he was sticking to their deal. The slimy bastard was getting under his skin. But first he wanted to see if Conboy had gotten his warrant signed.

At the station house, the scene resembled the one early that morning: near chaos.

Kerrigan jerked a thumb at him. "The "Son-in-Law" wants to see you right away."

"Sullivan? What does he want now?"

Kerrigan leaned forward. "There was a riot on the common. A woman shot dead, and one of our men stabbed."

"Jesus. Who?"

"Oscar Benoit, he's going to be okay. Do you know him?"

"Not well."

"Let's hope things don't escalate from here. By the way, here's your warrant for Breen."

Amos accepted the warrant, barely glancing at it. He looked into Kerrigan's eyes. "A man can't relax, even for a minute, can he, Jimmy?"

# CHAPTER EIGHT

Paddy scurried across the bridge that morning, squinting against the flurry of snow that blew into his face. As he slipped through the gate, one of the soldiers called to him from the small guard house. "You won't get much done today, Paddy."

He waved to the soldier, wondering what he meant, but it was cold—he didn't stop, clanking up the metal stairs, he entered the office, took off his coat and was rubbing his hands together when Kevin O'Shay motioned him over. He took off his glasses and cleaned them. "We're in for a hard day, Paddy. There's been an attack on our replacement operatives."

"My God, what happened?"

"They hit the streetcars on Broadway. I just came from there myself. Rocks, ice, they smashed windows. People were hurt. I was near the back door in the second car. I slipped out and got away. They were screaming, Scabs! Scabs! We won't have many workers here today." He heaved a sigh of resignation. "We'll do what we can."

Paddy went to the window and watched a thin line of workers coming through the gate.

The day passed in a strange, surrealistic way. Occasional clouds cast a gray, suffused light over what was normally a hectic, noisy field of shuttling looms. Fewer than half the machines were running, and most of these, bare of thread spools, simply clacked away, making nothing but noise.

Late in the day, Ernst Meyer showed up to work on several of the unused looms. Paddy went over to talk to him. Meyer, a stocky man of about forty, had the broad hands and fingers that went with his trade. He openly discussed his

Socialist beliefs and was active in some kind of German Socialist organization. Paddy assumed that the little silver medallion in his hatband had something to do with that.

As usual, his opening remark had to do with the replacement workers. "All they know how to do is break looms and make rags."

"And, you heard what happened this morning?"

"Ya, but that's nothing. I just heard downstairs, there's been a killing."

"What?"

"An Italian girl; she got shot near the common. And a cop got stabbed."

"Was there a riot?" Paddy wondered about his father's whereabouts.

Meyer shrugged. "I don't think so, but now it gets interesting. Who knows where this goes?"

"My mother is going to be upset."

"She wants you to stay home?"

"She wants to move to Boston."

"I should move to Boston. How can you do that? Your father's a cop."

"Her father has a business there."

"Lucky."

"But I'm in love with a girl who lives here."

Meyer put down his tools and stepped close to Paddy. "There are not many secrets in this mill. I heard about your girl. You should understand that when there is violence and strife, people cling to their own kind. You Irish stick together like glue. The Italians will do the same."

Paddy, who had been thinking of little other than the next time he would see Maria, felt a chill across his shoulder blades. He didn't like to think of Maria having some kind of ethnic loyalty that might get in the way.

Meyer said, "And, unless I miss my guess, the cops will try to please the mill owners by trying to pin the shooting on the Italian strike leaders."

Paddy blinked and walked away. The strike was getting more complicated, more dangerous; it was too much to think about. All he wanted was to see Maria--he was going to Haverhill that Sunday no matter what. She would do the same. She had to.

\*\*\*\*\*\*\*\*\*\*\*\*\*\*\*\*\*\*\*\*\*\*

Amos slipped the Breen warrant into his pocket and turned toward the City Marshal's office. Sullivan was on the phone when he arrived at the doorway, he waved Amos to a chair and wound down his conversation. "Yes sir, I intend to do that. Yes sir, I'll report back." He flipped the phone cord over the edge of his desk, set the speaker stand down and placed the earpiece back on its hook. He paused, looking at it for a few seconds as if it were some strange object before swinging around to face Amos. "You heard what happened?" He smacked his desk.

"I did."

Sullivan placed his hands, palms down, on the green blotter pad and wet his lips. "This could be the beginning of a disaster for us, Amos--or maybe an opportunity."

"A young woman has been killed."

"Yeah, Anna Lopizzo. A nice girl, apparently, on her way to visit a friend. Had nothing to do with the mess near the common."

"Do we have a shooter?"

Sullivan paused. "Some are saying that this guy, Ettor, did it."

"Joseph Ettor, the Wobbly strike organizer?"

Sullivan nodded as he pulled at his collar and stretched his neck..

"Are there witnesses?"

"That's where you come in."

Amos couldn't suppress a short laugh.

"Listen, Amos, even if he didn't pull the trigger, he certainly has set things up so that people aren't safe to walk the streets. We can knock down this strike and solve the murder, all at once. But it will only work if we get some Italians to testify. And if he didn't do it, he can probably find out who did."

Amos said nothing as he watched Sullivan's hands fidgeting on the desk, and his eyes blinking as he waited for a response. He felt sorry for his old friend; the situation was chaotic, over his head, and the pressure from the Mayor, his father-in-law, siding with the mill owners, had to enormous. "John, I'll get right at it and be back tomorrow with something."

"Don't fail me, Amos; I've got to have something."

Amos got up to leave, thinking that Breen's head on a silver platter was not what Sullivan had in mind. He found Casey waiting at the door to the inspectors' room.

Amos asked, "Did Kerrigan send you?"

"Yes, he told me about the warrant. You're pretty sure Breen's our man?"

"It's a good bet. We're going in first thing, before anyone knows what's going on. By the way, has anything being tipped on this killing?"

"I'm hearing that a cop did it. There was a dust-up when Oscar Benoit got stabbed."

"An accident?"

"Sounds like it to me."

"Any idea of whose gun went off?"

"Would anyone around here tell you if he knew?"

Amos wasn't sure if that meant Casey knew the answer and was not going to tell, or something else. All he said to Casey was, "Okay, meet me outside Breen's at eight tomorrow morning."


\*\*\*\*\*\*\*\*\*\*\*\*\*\*\*\*\*\*\*\*\*\*\*\*\*\*\*


As soon as the few operatives on the floor quit for the day, Paddy shut down the looms, retrieved his hat and coat, nodded to O'Shay, and was on his way home.

He strolled into the kitchen and said to Molly, "It was pretty quiet at the mill today."

She said nothing but looked at him as if she were checking to see if his appearance matched his statement. "I'm happy to hear that."

"I'll wash up," he said, as he disappeared into the back.

When he returned, there was a cup of tea sitting on the table. She motioned to the chair in front of it, and he sat down, already certain that he knew the subject.

She sat across from him. "The money you're making at the mill won't count for much if the violence keeps up."

"I know, Ma, but…"

"It's not as if we have no choices."

"If you're talking about Boston, I don't think Da wants to go. Do you?"

She took time to come up with an answer, while he took a few sips of tea.

"Your father is not a quitter. I know he likes his work, and it's important. He tries to do right by the little people. But it's not like before; it's more politics now. That's not his game."

Neal sauntered into the kitchen, plainly thinking about joining the conversation, but Molly shooed him on his way.

Paddy asked, "Has Da been talking about it?"

"He has a lot on his plate right now, but my father can't wait much longer."

Paddy leaned back, thinking of Maria, wondering how much time he had before moving to Boston was unavoidable.

She sensed his mood. "It's not that far to Boston, you know."

"You don't think Da would leave just to get me out of Lawrence, do you?"

She smiled. "I might, but you know your father; he would want you to make your own decisions. He might even stay on your account, and that's why I wanted to talk with you, Paddy. The world is changing, an education is important."

"That's what I've been saving my money for."

"You can make some money and also get an education in Boston."

He slumped forward, his elbows on the table.

"I don't object to the girl," she said. "It's not that. Besides, she wants to be a teacher, you know. An education might help you in more ways than one. And it would make more sense to live in Boston if the two of you ever actually got married."

She rested her left elbow on the table and placed fingers at her chin. He felt her eyes, waiting for a reaction, his stomach, all knotted up. How did she know so goddamned much without his having said anything? He needed to think things out on his own—away from the pressure of having to answer her.

\*\*\*\*\*\*\*\*\*\*\*\*\*\*\*\*\*\*\*\*\*\*\*\*\*\*\*

The next morning, as Amos stepped from the streetcar at the intersection of Hampshire and Oak Streets, he spotted Casey waiting on the far corner. He was fifteen minutes late, and it was bitter cold; he hoped that Casey had not been early. As he crossed over, Casey hunched his shoulders and shuffled his feet.

Amos said, "Sorry, they seem to be missing a few streetcars after yesterday's fracas."

Casey took his hands out of his coat pockets and rubbed them together. "I just passed Marad's tailor shop, where they found the dynamite. It's only down the street a bit. Do you think Breen was a customer?"

"I think he said that's how he knew about the dynamite."

"Will we be going in now?" Casey stomped his feet.

"Yeah, let's go."

They crossed Oak Street and, as it was too early for the funeral parlor to be open, they went around to the back where a young man answered the door. He said his name was Albert and that Breen was still upstairs, probably having his breakfast.

Amos waved the warrant. "Show us to the office and tell him to come down."

They followed Albert into a narrow, dark hall and then into a large workroom. Amos never liked being in funeral homes. He especially did not like being in the backrooms or basements where he might encounter a naked body lying on a

83

table, and where strange smells assaulted his nostrils. They passed close to a body, but only the gnarled feet stuck out from under a sheet.

Breen's office was ice-cold and dark. Albert turned on an overhead light, another on the desk and turned the valve on a steam radiator before leaving them. Casey stood next to it, rubbing his hands together.

Amos grinned at him. "That's going to help a lot."

"It's better than being outside." The radiator began to hiss, a small jet of steam coming from the valve. "There we go. That's more like it."

Amos nodded at a table in the corner where Eddie Foyle said they would find the magazines. Casey went over and started to collect them in a stack, his head bobbing up and down as he hummed to himself and checked the dates. Amos took a seat in front of the desk and folded his arms for warmth. He checked the walls where he found the usual crucifix and holy pictures along with pictures of Breen posing with various members of the clergy. Several pictures included Father O'Reilly, the pastor of Saint Mary's, just a block away. Another wall was covered with pictures of Breen's father as mayor of Lawrence. Some copies of the same pictures hung at city hall. Amos liked the one of Mayor Breen leading a parade with the police department just behind him.

He turned to see the current John Breen coming through the door without a collar on his shirt and wearing a heavy cardigan sweater. His hair looked as if he'd barely run a comb through it, and his eyes kept blinking as if not ready for the day—Just the way Amos wanted him.

"Ah, it's you, Amos. A bit early isn't it?" He nodded to Casey as he circled his desk, took his seat and rubbed his hands together. "Did Albert turn on the heat?"

"He did," Amos said. "As you can imagine, after yesterday's goings on, we're very busy down at the station and we need a bit of clarification regarding the dynamite."

"You should be asking the Syrians."

"We will. We will. Now, John, I understand that Marad's is not your regular tailor shop?"

"Right. I use Doyle's, but I had a few repairs. I thought that, with the strike, Marad would need the business. That's how I came to be in there."

"But you wouldn't think that the dynamite would be out where a customer would see it?"

"No. I gave him a coat over a week ago and I had more with me. He had to look for the coat, and I helped him. That's when I spotted it under some papers."

"I understand it was wrapped?"

"Yes, and I said that I wasn't sure, but from the shape, it looked like dynamite."

"Did you notice what it was wrapped in?" Amos glanced over to Casey, who tapped on the stack of magazines he had taken from the table and nodded. Amos understood this to mean that the November issue was missing.

"No, Amos. I didn't want him to see me looking at it." Breen appeared more alert now, his fingers drummed on the back of his left hand.

"That's a pity. You might have noticed that it was wrapped in a copy of *Shadyside.* The November issue."

Breen turned. Casey held up the stack and nodded.

Amos said, "It's cold out, John, you'll be wanting a coat and hat." He reached into his coat pocket for the warrant and held it up to Breen. "This is the warrant."

With Breen booked and in a cell, Amos invited Casey to breakfast at Weigel's on Essex Street. After some hot coffee and while waiting for his eggs, Casey asked, "Where do you suppose Breen got his hands on twenty-eight sticks of dynamite?"

"It's certain he's not going to tell us. I've been wondering how to find out. You got any ideas?"

"Maybe our friend, Albert?"

"Or Eddie Foyle. Which reminds me; I've got to get that bastardy charge dropped."

They returned to the station just after ten, and Amos, anxious to avoid Sullivan, went upstairs to report to Judge Waters. The judge wasn't in so he explained why he had arrested Breen to Bill Conboy and then stayed awhile, swapping reminiscences before heading downstairs.

He went to the inspectors' room to retrieve his coat and found Charlie Vose busy filling out forms. Vose looked up. "Looks like we got Anna Lopizzo's killer, thanks, in part, to you, Amos."

"Really?" Amos sat down.

"Yeah, some witnesses identified a guy named Caruso. This one doesn't sing. Picked him up at that same rooming house on Valley Street where the Sicilians stayed, the one you told me about. This Caruso guy's a walking arsenal. But I want to hear about Breen."

Amos struggled with how much to say. He knew that Vose wanted to curry favor with Sullivan, Con Lynch, and the mill owners, but he and Vose had been friends over the years, and they'd likely be working together for some time.

"It wasn't difficult, Charlie. The dynamite was wrapped in an undertakers' magazine, and it was Breen who told us where to look in Marad's shop."

"He can't be that stupid."

"You wouldn't think so."

"He had no reason to do it on his own account."

"Right."

Vose paused and folded his arms before speaking. "Amos, I know what you're thinking, that I'll do anything to get my old job back—or at least, keep this one." He looked away. "And maybe you're right. Don't tell me anything."

"It's just easier if fewer people are involved."

"I understand. By the way, your Italian friends are going to be angry. Sullivan's got a warrant out to arrest those Wobblies, Ettor and his sidekick, Giovannitti."

Amos left, thinking it was time to see Joe Lamastro.


\*\*\*\*\*\*\*\*\*\*\*\*\*\*\*\*\*\*\*\*\*\*\*\*\*\*


Paddy went to work on Wednesday wondering if recent events were making a strike settlement impossible. He was early and didn't need to get out on the floor right away. Kevin O'Shay still had his overcoat on. He was arranging things on his desk. Paddy pulled a chair over and sat down.

"Mister O'Shay, what do you think of these arrests?"

O'Shay turned to him and removed his glasses, setting them on the desk. He looked surprised, perhaps annoyed at Paddy's temerity—just sitting down and starting a conversation. "The dynamite business has got to be dealt with. But I'm not at all sure that arresting the strike leaders is a good idea. Unless, of course, it can be shown that they are clearly guilty—which I'm inclined to doubt."

"But do you think we're getting any closer to a settlement?"

"That I wouldn't know, Paddy." He picked up his glasses, put them on, nodding toward the looms.

By mid-morning, Paddy had things running as they were before the streetcar violence—replacement operatives were making rags while over half the looms remained idle. His thoughts were elsewhere and, for once, not entirely about Maria, he was concerned about a reaction to the arrests of the Wobbly strike leaders. He wasn't afraid for himself but he knew that many Italian men owned revolvers. Every week there were several arrests of men caught carrying loaded weapons and he knew from his da that some of these were violent men brought in from out of town. Would they shoot cops in retaliation for the arrests?

Any kind of shootings would add to the pressure from his mother; she might even insist that he quit his job immediately and move into Boston to live with his grandfather. How would he get to see Maria then? If only she would fall madly in love with him; they could work out something.

Ernst Meyer showed up after lunch, ostensibly to fix looms but he seemed more intent on having a chat. Paddy wondered why he bothered to do anything; both their pay amounts were determined largely by how much good cloth was produced on the looms in their charge. There were no bonuses now; they were both going through the motions for half-pay.

"Your father has been busy, Paddy. Doesn't he know that the mill owners will be very unhappy with him locking up Breen for planting that dynamite?"

"How do you know about that?"

"Ask your father how long the Lawrence Police Department can keep a secret."

"My father tries to do the right thing. He doesn't care who's not going to like it."

"I believe you're right about that, Paddy. But did you notice how fast they locked up those two Wobblies, Ettor and Giovannitti for being involved with shooting that girl?"

"Maybe they were involved."

Meyer shook his head and gave Paddy a knowing look.

"Are you going to tell me who did?"

"This is just for your father. The cop did it. There's a girl, Greta Zurwell, lives next door to me on Prospect Street, number 371. She saw Benoit, the cop, shoot Anna Lopizzo."

"Oscar Benoit is the cop who was stabbed."

"Greta didn't stab him; she's only sixteen. Maybe somebody else saw him shoot and tried to get him." Meyer picked up his tool box and moved down the aisle.

89

# CHAPTER NINE

On Wednesday, Amos arranged to meet Lamastro in the same little room at City Hall on Friday. He then headed for Breen's funeral parlor, hoping to find Eddie Foyle.

Entering the front door, he met Albert, now dressed in a grey suit with black tie. On seeing Amos, he stiffened and waited for Amos to say something.

"Albert, I'm here on a personal matter. I need a word with Eddie Foyle—in private."

"I'll get him." Albert looked around. "This parlor is empty," he said, gesturing to the room on his right.

Amos waited in the hallway. Foyle appeared, his eyes flitting about.

"I'm the only one here, Eddie. We can talk in there."

They entered the room, dimly illuminated by a single overhead bulb, and sat on two of the chairs set against one wall for mourners. The center of the room was clear of the usual small chairs, revealing a large dark maroon rug. The long wall, opposite the entrance, was draped with velvet of the same color. Several small kneeling benches occupied the space usually reserved for a casket.

Amos said, "You don't need to worry; Albert thinks I'm here about the other matter—the McGreevy business."

"Are you?"

"No but I can tell you that I've made arrangements, and the charges will be dropped. I need to get over to McGreevy with the papers."

"Thanks. Why *are* you here?"

"I need to know where the dynamite came from."

Foyle shook his head. "I don't know anything about that."

"Would Albert know?"

"I don't think Breen tells Albert much about anything."

"The dynamite was wrapped here. Somebody carried it here or had it delivered. Will Albert talk to you?"

"He's not what I'd call social."

"I need to find out how Breen got that dynamite. Maybe there was some unusual activity or visitors around here just before the discovery. See what you can do."

"All right, I'll try. I'm in the clear, am I?"

"Don't celebrate just yet."


\*\*\*\*\*\*\*\*\*\*\*\*\*\*\*\*\*\*\*\*\*\*\*


That evening, Paddy relayed Meyer's story regarding the girl who had seen the shooting. Amos shook his head and wrote down the girl's name, 'Greta Zurwell'. There was no discussion.

After supper, Paddy went to his room, ostensibly to read. Instead, he brooded over how events were overwhelming his pursuit of Maria. He decided to drop in at Petrella's Tailor Shop on Union Street. Maybe he was nothing like Lorenzo described. He had an excuse: he could pretend to be checking on Maria's health after her ordeal, and he could also see if Petrella remembered the offer of a free jacket. Mostly, he wanted to meet Maria's father and assess how resistant he might be to an ongoing courtship.

He was of two minds when it came to the possibility that Maria might be there helping her father. He'd have to play-act, making believe he hadn't seen her since the rescue. If it happened, he hoped she'd be convincing in her reactions. The possibility of seeing her thrilled him, and helped him gloss over the risk involved.

The following day at quitting time, he went to Common Street and took a streetcar to Union. Most of the shops on Essex and Common Streets were closing for the day, with awnings rolled up and whatever merchandise had been on the sidewalks already inside. A few late shoppers scurried along in the cold with baskets clasped close and shawls pulled tightly around their heads and shoulders.

He had gambled on finding the tailor shop open, and it was. A nattily-dressed manikin torso shared the small front window with some cloth samples spread around its base. He stepped into a small room, a counter on one side and two walls hung with clothing on hangers; a single bulb hung from a wire provided the only illumination, leaving dark shadows to fill the corners and spaces between the hangers.

A bell over the door announced his arrival, and a familiar figure emerged from a back room. On seeing Paddy, Lorenzo stopped. A murmur came from the back, and he turned his head to answer. "It's that Irish capitalist." Paddy surmised that he would normally have answered in Italian, but it would not have had the same effect.

Alessandro Petrella appeared, he stepped forward and spoke softly to Lorenzo, who nodded and returned to the rear. Petrella smiled at Paddy, revealing fine even teeth. He removed his glasses and came forward to extend his hand. "I am most delighted to meet you."

Paddy noticed his eyes, dark with strong brows—a handsome man. "You know who I am?"

Petrella laughed. "It is not so difficult. Please come inside; Lorenzo is just leaving."

They passed through heavy drapes to a well lit workroom where Lorenzo was putting on his coat. He stepped directly in front of Paddy. "Your father is a hero to us for catching Breen, that Irish bastard."

"I'll tell him that you approve."

Lorenzo grinned and passed through the drapes. Paddy turned his attention to Petrella who opened both hands in a gesture to what was obviously the most comfortable chair in the room.

"I'll only stay a minute," he said as he removed his coat and sunk into the overstuffed dark-brown chair.

Petrella reached into a cabinet to produce a bottle of red wine and two small glasses. "Just a small blessing on such a cold night."

Paddy was barely aware of his surroundings, his eyes fixed on Petrella, a lean, athletic man with a receding hair line, a trim mustache and goatee. To Paddy he looked like pictures of old world royalty--intelligent and exuding self-confidence. He wondered what such a man might make of him, a struggling, third generation, Irish immigrant.

The small glasses full, Petrella handed one to Paddy. "To your very good health."

They touched glasses, and Paddy took a sip, thinking that there could not be a worse time to get a little tipsy. "I guess you're wondering why I'm here?"

Petrella sitting just a few feet in front of Paddy, next to a large work table, answered, "For your jacket perhaps?"

Paddy wondered if he should just agree and keep his visit short and simple, but Petrella seemed so warm and open, it felt like a good time to get to know him—at least a little. "I was wondering if Maria is okay, fully recovered from getting so cold and wet?"

Petrella took a second sip of his wine, set the glass aside, put one hand up to his chin, then rested it on his lap and, looking at Paddy in a kindly way, he said, "You are strong, and that is good. You saved our daughter's life. Someday, when you have children of your own, you will know how grateful we are to you, and to your family."

"She's in good health then?"

"Yes." Petrella sat back. "You know, Paddy, in some countries it's understood that when you save someone's life, you are responsible for that person for the rest of your life."

Suddenly, Paddy felt uncomfortable. Was there no secret? Had Joe Lamastro tipped him, or Maria confessed everything? "I don't know much about other countries. This one is complicated enough."

"Indeed it is. And no one expects you to be responsible for Maria."

Paddy judged it best to say nothing. He just smiled and nodded. A pause followed and he felt awkward. "I'm keeping you from your family." He began to get up.

"Not at all. Please stay a few minutes. Tell me, how is the strike affecting you?"

Paddy sat back, relieved at the change of subject. "I'm afraid that the violence may get worse. Not afraid for myself really, but my father is a police inspector."

"I know. Your father seems a good man. We have a mutual friend, you know?"

"Joseph Lamastro?"

"Yes. We both would love to see the real killer of Anna Lopizzo arrested. She was a friend to my wife."

"I don't think my father is assigned to that case."

"The two they arrested had nothing to do with it."

"My father already knows that."

Petrella grinned. "Tell him that there are people over here who are trying to help." He got up, removing a tape

95

measure from around his neck. "Since you are here, let me take your measurements."

When Paddy left shortly after, he had the feeling that if Petrella knew about him and Maria, he at least was not taking any action right away.

\*\*\*\*\*\*\*\*\*\*\*\*\*\*\*\*\*\*\*\*\*\*\*\*\*\*\*\*\*\*\*

Amos wasn't quite sure how to go about dealing with the tip regarding Greta Zurwell having seen Oscar Benoit shoot Anna Lopizzo. Accusing a fellow police officer of even a minor offense was always touchy, and if the charge didn't stick, the aftermath could get ugly. And Benoit was entitled to some sympathy and consideration; he had, after all, been stabbed during the disturbance.

He consulted with Kerrigan, who knew Benoit better than he did.

Kerrigan said, "I think it would be best to just test the water a bit by making some discrete inquiries before jumping in, Paul Martin works that beat. He speaks German, you know. I'll have him talk to the girl. We'll see what he thinks."

"I leave it to you, Jimmy. And I wouldn't mind if someone else makes the arrest, if it looks like Benoit did do it."

"If I can help it, Amos, you won't be pulled into it. But. speaking of arrests, where are you with that guy, Wilcox?"

"Oh, Jimmy, I've been so busy, and that son-of-a-bitch is dodging me. I know it."

"You shouldn't be doing this, Amos. Your neck's out. Bring him in and let the court handle it. You've got enough on your plate."

"You're right, Jimmy. I know you're right. The trouble is, if he's in jail, there's no money for his wife and kid. I'll give him one last chance."

Kerrigan shook his head but said nothing.

Feeling relieved at having the Benoit-Lopizzo matter off his plate, Amos set off to confront Wilcox before meeting Joe Lamastro at city hall. When he stepped into the shoe store, Wilcox was busy with a customer. Amos took a seat near the window and waved off the sales clerk. He watched the interaction of Wilcox and his plump, middle-aged female customer, wondering how a man could behave in such an obsequious manner, and if the woman found it as repulsive as he did. Perhaps, after a day of behaving this way, Wilcox went home with a secret desire to beat-up somebody—his wife or kid, whomever he came across first?

The woman left without buying anything, but judging from Wilcox's manner, he was every bit as pleased as if she had bought several pair of his most expensive offerings.

Wilcox turned to Amos wearing the same unctuous smile. "Inspector, I'm sorry I was not here to greet you on your last visit."

"I came by to find out why we have not heard from your attorney, as agreed."

"Of course, Inspector. My attorney, Mister Curtis, practices in Boston and, unfortunately, he has been very ill. I've been remiss in not advising you. But he's much better now and has promised me to give the matter his immediate attention."

"That's nice. Let me have his address, please."

"Certainly. Unfortunately, I don't have it here. You can appreciate, with my new arrangements, things are a bit disorganized. I keep those sorts of papers at my lodgings. I'll put the information in the mail."

Amos was not at all sure that Wilcox was telling the truth, but he was almost out of time. "You'll do it today, or I'm taking you in. Understand?"

"Yes. Consider it done."

"Meanwhile, I assume that you're keeping our bargain?"

"Of course, Inspector. And if Mrs. Flanagan has need of a pair of shoes, send her round. I'll treat her to the best."

Amos nodded and headed out the door, wondering if Wilcox had just offered him a bribe.

He got to the basement at City Hall early enough to talk briefly with the janitor, his friend, Kevin McNulty. But knowing that Lamastro would prefer complete privacy, he asked Kevin to leave. He sat in the tiny room, very aware of being alone. He was often by himself but seldom as aware of the sensation, as he was just then; it seemed to bring a special perspective to his thinking. Had he been a cop too long? Had it changed the mechanics of his brain so that it worked differently from those of normal men? He knew that, as a cop, he constantly judged people, attempting to read their intentions. He'd just done it with Wilcox. It could be dangerous, even life threatening, to a policeman not to do this. But did it wind up warping his view of life?

There were not many men with whom he felt completely comfortable, trusted implicitly; most were cops, but Joe Lamastro ranked with the best. Where the hell was he? He needed the company of his friend to pull him back into a more pleasant frame of mind.

Lamastro slipped in. "Well, Amos, I sometimes come to City Hall on business so this makes sense. But, I must say, this room gives a certain conspiratorial feeling to these meetings."

"Yeah, it's great, isn't it? Like two kids in a secret club house."

Lamastro grinned and briefly shook Amos's hand before sitting down. "I have some interesting information for you—the name of Anna Lopizzo's killer."

Amos had a sudden sensation—he was in some kind vortex. It didn't matter what he did; Anna Lopizzo was manipulating him from beyond the grave. He couldn't help but utter, "Another one?"

"What's that?"

"Nothing, Joe. Tell me what you know."

"Yes, well first, I should tell you that this information comes to you because of Paddy's good deed in rescuing Maria Petrella. The family feels a great debt of gratitude to Paddy and to all the Flanagans."

"Paddy outdid himself that night."

"Did he tell you that he stopped in on Alessandro Petrella, Maria's father, at his tailor shop the other night?"

"No, but I'm not surprised."

"Something to do with a new jacket, I understand."

"Of course, what better place to get one? Especially, in the middle of a strike, and him being on half pay."

Lamastro laughed. "Well anyway, it seems that her brother, Lorenzo, whom I believe you've met, is very active in the strike committee and he told his father what actually happened."

"You know these people, Joe. How credible is this version? We've already got eye witnesses for two different suspects."

"I know about Joseph Caruso. And arresting Ettor and Giovannitti? That smacks of strike busting. I don't know about any other suspects but I do know Alessandro Petrella. He is a man of great intelligence and common sense. I know that he was very thorough in questioning Lorenzo and that his heart is pure."

99

"Okay, I was hoping to get out from under all this, but apparently, God has other plans."

"The man's name is Pasquale Carapatsi. He was brought in from New Jersey as a strong arm. One of the radical people from New York thought it would be a good idea to shoot a cop. It would let everyone know that they mean business, keep them in line, maybe even send a message to the mill owners—they could be next. Anyway, Carapatsi hides in the crowd, tries to do his job but botches the whole thing and kills Lopizzo. Petrella says that several people have agreed to testify. Right now, Carapatsi is on the run. You need to catch him before he leaves the country."

Amos sighed. "What have we got to go on?"

Lamastro handed him a piece of paper. "He stayed at a rooming house on Union Street. The landlady will give you a description."

Amos took the paper, folded it and slipped it into his breast pocket. "So Paddy went to see her father?" He looked into his friend's face. "He never mentioned the visit. Why would he go there, I wonder? Do you think he's trying to win the father over?"

"Ostensibly, he was just inquiring about Maria's health."

Amos laughed. "And did Petrella believe him?"

"He didn't say. You should meet him yourself."

"I suppose you're right, I should meet the man. Who knows what kind of trouble Paddy is getting himself into?"

Amos lost no time following up on Carapatsi. As soon as he and Lamastro parted, he walked over to the rooming house on Union Street, a white, three-story, wood frame building. Seven steps ascended to a small porch and the front door. He held up his badge when the door opened. Mrs. Goldberg seemed to expect him, without asking his name, she stepped back and led

100

him into the parlor. She motioned to the couch and she sat down on a straight-back, wood chair; its seat padded with a thick brown pillow. She was about sixty and plump, but her movements were quick and purposeful. She smoothed her gray apron and primped her hair. Amos sat and took out his notebook.

"He was only here a month," she said. "He paid each week in advance and was very quiet. He was out every evening, but I never smelled any liquor. I do know that he was seeing some woman but he never brought her here. I clean the rooms, so I know these things. And I found this under the radiator after he left, down in the hole around the pipe—there's a little cover there that you can lift up." She reached into her pocket and held out a cartridge casing. "Boarders sometimes hide things down there."

Amos bent across to take it from her—a .32 caliber. "Did he say anything when he was leaving?"

"Very little, just that his work was over and he had to catch a train."

# CHAPTER TEN

The interminable wait was over; Sunday arrived, Paddy had butterflies. He had a story ready—a lie, just in case his parents were curious about where he was going after Mass and breakfast. He planned to tell them that he and Frank Dunn were going on an outing to take some pictures. Unfortunately, the day did not look that promising for pictures; it was overcast and cold--a snowstorm was possible. His story would be hard to put over.

Another strike incident added to his anxiety. On Saturday, a stick of dynamite had been thrown over a passing railroad car in front of the dye factory at the intersection of Broadway and Water Street where the tracks ran alongside the street. A soldier was standing guard near to where the dynamite landed. Fortunately, the stick turned out to be in poor condition, but as Amos explained to Paddy, in that part of town, anyone could throw dynamite over a passing train and escape before the train had passed out of the way. If it happened, and someone was killed, a wave of retaliation and violence might follow, ending all hope of a peaceful settlement.

To Paddy, it all seemed like some kind of conspiracy designed to thwart his pursuit of Maria. Strike violence was escalating; the weather threatened. All he could do was pray that neither Maria's nor Carla's parents would forbid a trip to Haverhill. He did just that at the nine o'clock Mass, which he attended with Neal and Kathleen.

Molly had their breakfast ready when they got home. She had gone to church earlier, and Amos was going to serve as an usher at a later Mass. Paddy tried not to hurry, he wanted to appear relaxed and unconcerned. Inwardly, he was anything but; surely someone would ask him about his plans for the day, and Kathy could almost be counted on to give him the needle about something. His parents made light conversation about trivial subjects, and when Kathy started sniping, Amos told her to be

103

quiet and mind her own business. It occurred to Paddy that his parents might know exactly what he was up to and had chosen not to embarrass him.

In addition to being cold, it was windy, a typical early-February day, but Paddy hardly noticed; he was so relieved to be on his way and to see the clouds starting to clear. So far, his prayers seemed to be working. At Haverhill Street, he boarded a streetcar which brought him to Merrimack and Main Streets in Haverhill. Carla's grandmother lived across the river in Bradford.

He crossed the bridge and walked up South Main Street. What if she wasn't there? What if Carla wasn't there either? Would her grandmother even know who he was? How long could he stand outside, waiting in the cold?

He paused at the black, cast-iron gate, hung between two granite posts about four feet high. A three foot wood-slat fence extended from each post to the lot boundaries on either side. In all, the lot appeared to be at least one hundred feet wide and two hundred feet deep, extending toward the river in the rear. A white, colonial style, two story house sat twenty-five feet behind the fence. It had a full width porch, which wrapped around one corner. He was sure he had the right house, although he saw no signs of life as he went up the stairs and twisted the ringer on the bell.

A figure appeared behind the lace curtain covering the small window, and the door opened to reveal a slender woman dressed in a full-length gray-blue dress with a small fringe of lace at the top of a high collar. "Mister Flanagan?"

Paddy snatched off his cap, making a mess of his hair. "Yes, ma'am."

She smiled and stepped back to admit him. He glanced over her shoulder to see Carla's toothy grin, and Maria smiling, from a doorway a few feet down the hall. After he removed his coat and hung it near the door, Mrs. Schultz escorted him to the living room where they all made polite conversation until Mrs.

104

Schultz nodded to Carla, who disappeared to make tea and some sandwiches.

Paddy was fascinated by Mrs. Schultz. He had pictured a frail, little old lady who spent most of her time knitting and needed a cane to get around. In between long glances at Maria, he endeavored to learn about Mrs. Schultz.

"This is a beautiful house, Mrs. Schultz—in fine condition."

"Thank you. Mister Schultz, my deceased husband, built it over fifty years ago. Carla's father was raised here."

"That's impressive. What did Mister Schultz do?"

"He owned a carriage and wagon manufacturing business across the river. But surely, you didn't come all this way to learn about me?"

"No, but I am interested."

"You expected a little old lady in a wheel chair?"

Paddy laughed.

"I will see if Carla needs any assistance. You may turn your attention to Maria."

She left, and Paddy turned to Maria. He felt uncomfortable with the distance between them so he moved to another chair, just in front of the sofa on which she sat. An awkward silence followed, during which, he struggled to remember all the things he wanted to say. The words that came to mind seemed too forward, too abrupt. Finally, his desperation forced his mouth to open. And then it closed.

She said, "Surely, you can think of something to say?"

"I love you," is what came out.

She put her hand up to cover her mouth. Was she laughing at him? She took her hand down. "That certainly clears the air."

He started to say something, but she leaned forward as if to speak, and he stopped to listen. She moved her lips, silently mouthing the words, "I love you too."

He held his breath and, as Carla came into the room, realized that his eyes must appear to be popping out of his head.

Carla said, "I trust you two have been using your time productively?"

"You would be amazed," Maria said, while continuing to look at Paddy.

He glanced briefly at Carla and tried, unsuccessfully, not to blush. Amazed? She couldn't possibly be more amazed than he was. Whatever it was that just happened, it felt wonderful.

Mrs. Schultz returned, and all enjoyed tea, some sandwiches and feather-light pastries, which Maria had brought from home. Conversation centered on the recent murder of four people in Lawrence, apparently a robbery. Paddy had difficulty concentrating; he tried not to stare at Maria. The strike also came up, but, conscious of his position and that of Maria's family, and possibly Carla's, he made only a few neutral comments.

They finished their tea. Carla and Maria took the trays back into the kitchen. Mrs. Schultz told Paddy that when they returned, she would be going upstairs to lie down.

Paddy said, "Yes. I guess it's time for me to be on my way."

"Not at all. Please stay on a bit. It has been a pleasure to have you."

"You can't imagine how grateful I am."

"Oh, but I can." She smiled, as Carla and Maria returned. "Carla, I'm going upstairs. Would you read to me for a few minutes?"

"But of course, Grandmother." She gave a little wave to Paddy and Maria as she turned to follow Mrs. Schultz. "I won't be long," she said, obviously teasing.

The lovers turned to each other. Paddy, feeling euphoric and surprisingly self-confident, said, "What do we do next?"

"You could come and sit next to me," she said, patting the cushion to her right.

Yes, he could do that. He got up and came forward, hesitating only to decide how close to her he should sit, too close and she might take offense; too far and it would be awkward to take her hand. He picked a compromise and eased himself down. To his surprise, she adjusted her position, moving closer—inches away. He wondered how long Carla would remain upstairs. He turned to Maria, and she took *his* hand.

"How does your family feel about me?" she asked.

"I'm not sure. I don't think they fully understand the situation."

"Perhaps you should explain it to me."

He grinned, realizing that he was completely unprepared to speak of his hopes, his dreams and fantasies. All he could do was gaze into her eyes while frantically searching his brain for something to say.

"Why don't you kiss me while you're thinking about it?"

His body and his brain seemed to lose contact with reality. He felt himself drifting, dreamlike in a timeless, dimensionless space. He had only a blurred vision of her as he twisted and bent to her lips. The slight warm glow of her face on his was overwhelmed by the sensation of the kiss. Their contact was so gentle that he could distinguish her upper and lower lips from each other. Her left arm reached to pull him tight, and he turned on his hips to push against her, shocked at the lightening flash of his arousal. She continued to clasp him, and he became aware of her deep breathing.

When he moved his right hand behind her neck and began to explore her face with his lips, she pulled back, gently pushing on his chest. "We don't want to be too obvious when Carla comes back."

He swallowed hard and took of coupled of fast, deep breaths. "No, of course not." One last stolen kiss and he leaned back against the sofa, wondering if she was aware of his bone-hard erection.

She moved more than a foot away, straightening her dress and producing a small mirror to examine her face and primp her hair.

"Should I move back to the chair?" he asked.

She shook her head. "Now, you can explain our *situation*."

"Well, it seems that we should be thinking about marriage."

She laughed. "Isn't it a little early for such talk?"

"Yes. But we just…"

"And there are difficulties."

"I know, but we need to plan a way around them."

She looked at him with a serious expression. "Do you have a plan?"

"The strike is making it almost impossible to plan. I might even have to move to Boston because of it. But I can get a job there and go to school. And I could still see you."

"The strike is disrupting everything. My father wants to go back to Italy, and I don't know where I'll be able to get a teacher's job."

"It can't last forever."

"And we'll still be in love."

"Yes."

They sat quietly and then began to talk casually about the strike. Carla returned, and Paddy felt that it was time for him to leave.

Carla said, "My grandmother said that you can come again next Sunday, if you like."

\*\*\*\*\*\*\*\*\*\*\*\*\*\*\*\*\*\*\*\*\*\*\*\*

Amos went to work on Monday wondering if it would be possible to stay out of Sullivan's way and keep warm at the same time. Sullivan would be ripping; not only was Amos not cooperating with the effort to lock up Italians as a way to help break the strike but he seemed to be going in the opposite direction. Breen had been arraigned on Friday. Even Sullivan could figure out that Breen may have been in cahoots with the mill owners. And if he did not yet know about Amos uncovering Greta Zurwell, who was fingering a cop, Oscar Benoit, as the shooter of Anna Lopizzo, he soon would.

When he walked into the station, Kerrigan waved a hand to get his attention and jerked his head toward Sullivan's office. Amos waved back and went down the hall to stash his hat and coat. Minutes later, he strolled into the City Marshall's office; Sullivan looked him over, all the while making facial expressions signifying his pain and displeasure. Amos sat down and raised his hands as if to say, 'What can I do? It's out of my hands.'

Sullivan started. "Amos, at the end of this thing the mill owners have got to be in business, or there won't be any jobs— not for the strikers—and not for us. Which means that the mill owners have got to win, whether you see it that way, or not."

"John, there's no gain in you and I arguing about the strike and its lack of merit. By the time it's over, I think the

109

strikers will be better off, and the mill owners will still be in business."

"No thanks to you. Your latest bit of detective work is playing into the wrong hands. Benoit is innocent. Anna Lopizzo was killed by a .32 Caliber bullet, and we all carry 38's. Don't we?"

"Well, that's nice. I was almost sure he didn't do it. My Italian friends just told me who did—an Italian, you'll be happy to know. There will be witnesses—Italians, but we've got to catch the guy before he leaves the country."

"Could be another way to throw us off."

"The sources are very reliable, and his landlady found a .32 caliber cartridge shell in his room."

Sullivan leaned back, apparently mollified. "All right, get on it. And, for Christ's sake, concentrate on the Italians. Leave the powers-that-be alone."

"The guy's name is Carapatsi. I've got his description, and the State Police are after him." He got up to leave.

Sullivan nodded. "I'm trying to protect you, Amos."

"I know that, John."

He went to the desk and waited for Kerrigan to get off the phone.

Kerrigan asked, "How did it go?"

"Grand, he didn't ask me to come up with an Italian to blame for throwing that dynamite over the train. Anything on Carapatsi?"

Kerrigan shook his head. "We've got everyone in Massachusetts on it; the New York State cops and the New York City cops are all looking. He could have beat it out through Canada. Are you sure about him?"

"Yeah, I got this from the landlady." He showed him the .32 caliber shell casing. "And my Italian friends have got some witnesses for me; it's piling up."

"I hope you can find him. It's always easier to catch the ones who didn't do it, isn't it?"

Amos spent most of the day at his small desk in the inspectors' office and after lunch, he paid a visit to Wilcox's shoe store. Wilcox was not there—no surprise. He wondered if he shouldn't just take Kerrigan's advice and pull him in—let somebody else take care of the problem.

He told the clerk, "I'm waiting for Mister Wilcox to give me certain information. Would you tell him to drop it by the station? Today."

The clerk was non-committal. "I'll tell him that you came by. Does he know what information you're expecting?"

"Oh yes."

"And your name, sir?" The clerk pulled a pencil from inside his jacket.

Was the clerk being deliberately aloof or was he really ignorant of anything to do with Wilcox's private life. Deciding not to make an issue out of it, he slowly gave the clerk his name and title. When the clerk finished writing, Amos said, "I'll be back tomorrow, if I don't get the information."


\*\*\*\*\*\*\*\*\*\*\*\*\*\*\*\*\*\*\*\*\*\*\*\*\*\*\*\*


When Paddy got home from work that night, Molly told him that Frank Dunn had come by to see him. "He'll be home tonight. Something to do with pictures you two have been taking, no doubt. Anything happen at the mill today?"

The dynamite toss on Saturday had upset her. He knew she was fishing for anything that hinted of more violence to come.

"Nothing. Everything was fairly calm. We're expecting some politicians from the State House to visit us this week."

"At your mill?"

"That's what they're saying. I've already been told to keep my mouth shut."

"Good advice; even if it comes from those skinflint mill owners. Get washed. I'll put your dinner out."


Frank's mother answered the door. "Ah, Paddy, Frank said you might be by. You know where to find him."

Paddy removed his cap. "Good evening to you, Mrs. Dunn." He stepped past her and walked down the hallway, waving to Frank's father, who sat in the parlor, reading his paper. In the kitchen, he opened the cellar door and descended. Frank's voice came from the darkroom. "I'll be out in a minute." Paddy perched on a stool in front of the worktable and scanned over an array of new prints—all taken at some kind of shindig.

Frank came out, removing an apron and hanging it on a hook next to the darkroom door. "Did I ever tell you that your mother's a damn good-looking woman?"

"Yes, Frank, and my da agrees with you."

"Shit, you didn't tell him I said so?"

"I did, and he didn't look a bit worried."

Frank laughed and sat on another stool. "That's not what I came by to tell you."

"I didn't think so."

"But it does concern your father." Frank leaned over the work table and selected one of the prints, handing it to Paddy, he

112

pointed to one of the men in the picture. "Do you recognize this guy?"

Paddy took the picture and held it in the light from the single bulb, hanging at the end of a wire over the table. "I've seen him somewhere."

"That's Ernest Pitman, the big contractor."

"Oh yeah; he built the Wood Mill."

"Exactly." Frank took the picture and put it back in its place. "Here's what happened. I took that picture yesterday. I got a job to take pictures at a Christening at the Advent Club on Lowell Street. You know, the usual stuff, a bunch of people standing around some little bundle of joy, looking like statues. Anyway, I had my supply case behind the little bar they had set up and I'm on my knees putting cassettes away and trying to fix my Prosch Igniter. The damn thing failed to go off twice, and I ruined the plates. I can't take pictures indoors without it."

"That thing's dangerous; you're going to start a serious fire one of these days."

"Yeah, the problem was the flame kept going out."

"Okay, Okay. Get on with it. What happened?"

"I'm coming to it. Anyway, this guy, Pitman, walks up to the bar with some other guy. They pour themselves a couple of drinks and stand there, talking. They obviously didn't see me since I'm practically under the table, and Pitman starts telling this other guy how tight he is with William Wood. I thought that was interesting so I stayed down. Next thing I hear is Pitman saying that, as a favor to Wood, he supplied the dynamite to Breen."

"Jesus."

"Yup, and Mary and Joseph."

"Did you see the other guy?"

113

"Yeah, don't know him, but he's in one of these other prints." Frank scanned over the table, picked up another picture and handed it to Paddy. "That's him." He pointed to one of the men posing in a row. "Don't know who he is."

"My da would love a copy of this print. He might even forgive you for giving my mom the eye."

Frank laughed. "Take that one; I'll make another."

Paddy, a cop's son all his life, had an additional thought. "Frank, it's important to keep all this absolutely secret."

"All right, I understand. And now tell me about your big day. You did get to see her?"

Paddy slipped off his stool and put the picture under his cap, which he'd left with his coat by the stairs. He used the pause to reorient his mind to what it was he thought he'd be talking about when he came over—his visit with Maria, and the questions it raised. Frank, two years his senior, was his confidant on most issues, but especially when it came to problems with the opposite sex. Clearly, he had much more experience, although he was always a bit cagey with details.

Finally, reacting to Frank's question, he said, "There were a few surprises,"

"Good ones?"

Paddy grinned and nodded as he hopped back onto his stool.

Frank leaned forward and leered into his face. "You didn't...?"

"Come on be serious."

"Okay, I'm really interested. Tell me what happened."

Paddy related the experience in as flat and matter-of-fact a tone as he could muster but, in spite of himself, he found some pleasant sensations returning as he spoke. He ended by saying, "I think she really meant it when she said she loves me."

114

Frank listened with his arms folded and, at first, said nothing. Then, "So she kind of pushed herself on you?"

"I don't think she was pushing."

"Well, maybe not, but I've always said, 'Girls want more than we think they do.' What do you think you'll do next?"

"I don't know. All I'm seeing are problems right now: Her father; her family; I don't make much money; I need more education. And, on top of that, my mother wants us all to move to Boston--and Maria's father wants to move back to Italy."

"Who was that Dickens character, always said, 'Something will turn up.'? And maybe something will for you. Didn't you tell me she wants to get a teachers' job?"

"Yeah, between the two of us, we'll have half as much money as one person needs to live on."

"I don't know what to tell you, Paddy. Until the strike is over, none of us know what's going to happen next. What does she say about convincing her family?"

Paddy thought for a moment. "Nothing."

"For your sake, let's hope she has some ideas."


Amos was getting ready for bed when Paddy got home. He came out to the kitchen, and the two men sat down, sharing a beer while Paddy related what Frank had told him about Pitman, and Molly put the last of the dishes in the cabinet. She came to sit next to Amos as Paddy gave him the picture and pointed to the man Frank singled out.

"Do you recognize him, Da?"

"Yeah, he's a cop. One of Con Lynch's boys."

Molly leaned to take hold of Amos's arm. "This is getting ugly, Amos. And Paddy mustn't be involved."

Amos looked across the table. "Does Frank know to keep his mouth shut?"

"Yes, Da. I told him; he understands."

"Frank has been very helpful, and you have, as well. But I want the two of you to stay out of this thing. Avoid it. Stay as far away from getting involved as you possibly can. Tell Frank. You understand?"

"Yes, Da. I understand and I'll tell Frank."

Amos tossed down the last of his beer and stood up. "It's been quite the day."

Molly got up to follow Amos into the back. She placed a hand on Paddy's shoulder. "You will stay out of this?"

"I will, Mom."

# CHAPTER ELEVEN

Amos wound the alarm clock and placed it on the night table but he did not turn off the light and lie down.

"Do you want to talk about it?" she asked from behind him.

He rolled back and propped himself up on two pillows. "I don't know what to say."

"Are you going to arrest the man?"

"Pitman? Yeah, when I'm ready. And others are involved. Can you imagine me walking in with an arrest warrant for the richest man in Massachusetts, Mister William Wood?"

"Can't you just leave things take their own course? You've already got Breen, and the dynamite's out of harm's way. Why not let the courts take things from here?"

"You know I can't do that--and there's a lot of dynamite in this town."

"And our son."

He turned to flip off the light. "You think I don't know that?"

They lay in silence until she rolled to put an arm around his chest and her head against his neck. "I'm sorry. I don't mean to add to your troubles."

He squirmed an arm around to her back, pulling her closer. "God damn strike."


Amos wasn't sure of the best way to proceed on Pitman, who obviously was not acting on his own behalf. With the trail now pointing toward the mill owners, possibly including

William Wood, the biggest of them all, he needed to be careful who he talked to. Kerrigan would be his best bet.

He went to the inspectors' room at the station house and worked on reports until the start-of-the-day bustle died down before he approached Kerrigan.

"Well, Amos, what will it be this morning? Another Lopizzo suspect? More dynamite? Your friend, Wilcox? You are going to bring him in?"

"It's not exactly any of those, Jimmy. I need some advice on a matter of some political sensitivity."

"You have come to the wrong man. If I knew anything about politics, I wouldn't be sitting here."

"Given the circumstances, I'll have to make do with yourself." He proceeded to relate what he had learned regarding Pitman and the dynamite planted by Breen. "What do you think? Should I try to get a warrant?"

"The strikers will love it. But considering the reaction you're going to get, I'd get more evidence first."

"Yeah, wouldn't surprise me if some slob confessed to selling the dynamite to Breen."

"Yes, and the slob's family suddenly comes into a bit of money. And, speaking of money, I heard that your deal for getting Eddie Foyle off the hook is not going well."

"Surprise, surprise; squeezing money out of the Church is like pulling teeth. Eddie Foyle, yeah...I should go see him."


As he got off the streetcar, Amos noticed several people go in and out of the front entrance of Breen's funeral home. It was not yet noon, too early for viewing hours. There had to be some kind of funeral preparations going on. He went around to the rear entrance and knocked. Eddie Foyle opened the door, wearing a black rubber apron. "We're just taking in a new stiff, Inspector. I'm busy helping Albert."

"Fair enough, Eddie. I won't keep you for long."

Eddie showed him to a small store room where he turned on a tiny overhead light to reveal a small table and two chairs all crowded together in front of three walls lined with shelves of supplies. "We can talk in here." Neither of them sat down.

"Good, I'm looking for more information on the dynamite."

"And I've got something for you. But first, I want to talk about my situation."

"I'm listening."

"Her old man says he can't come up with the money, and she's got him convinced that I'm the only one ever."

"And you think otherwise?"

"She wasn't a virgin."

"Are you an authority in these matters?"

Foyle heaved a deep breath and sat in one of the chairs. "There are some guys who know her."

"I know how these things go, Eddie, but there are probably a lot of credible people who can honestly say that they often saw you with her."

Foyle folded his arms. "Her old man wants *me* to pay. I haven't got more than ten bucks to my name."

"You are implicated, and you've only got one mouth to feed; McGreevy has a family. Borrow the money from Breen; he needs you right now."

Foyle, now slumped in the chair, nodded. "I'll try."

"And I'll see if McGreevy will kick in at least a part of it. Now tell me about the dynamite."

119

Foyle sat back up. "Okay. I got this from Albert. He thinks it might help Breen in some way. I doubt it. Anyway, he says he saw Ernest Pitman. You know who he is?"

"Yeah."

"He saw Pitman, himself, deliver the dynamite here, using one of his motor trucks."

Amos nodded and gazed off, considering the moment. He had the link he needed, and it felt wonderful. "Okay, Eddie. Thanks, this is very helpful. It's grand. But keep working on the money; I'll see what I can do on the other end. We'll arrange something. I promise."


Amos did not feel quite ready to arrest Pitman. He wanted more time to think about the repercussions and to prepare for them. Foyle's information would be of great help, and his cooperation would be critical. Getting things squared with McGreevy would be good insurance.

There were no customers in the candy store when Amos entered. Nora McGreevy appeared from behind a counter, giving him a decidedly unfriendly look. No doubt, she blamed him for not championing her daughter's cause; he should have nailed Eddie's carcass to a wall—made him pay. "He's in the back," she said.

Amos passed by the long glass case filled with sweets in jars and arranged on trays; the unmistakable scent of chocolate wafted past his nostrils. He found Willy opening some boxes in the back room. "I need a word," he said.

Willy wiped his hands on his apron and stepped away from the shelves. "I should have contacted you, Amos. I've been having my troubles." He gestured to a chair.

"Why don't you sit down, Willy. You look like you've been doing a bit of work. I won't keep you long."

McGreevy sat down and, although the room was cold, took out a handkerchief and wiped his brow. "I haven't got the money, Amos."

"The fifty bucks?" He thought he'd have to bring up Foyle's threat to produce some guys who would say that they had done it with Mary. And they probably had, from what Amos knew.

"Little Margaret's been ill. We've had the doctor twice. And the medicines…"

Amos parked his butt on a packing case and folded his arms. "Eddie Foyle doesn't have it either."

McGreevy hung his head and slowly shook it.

It didn't feel right—pushing McGreevy. "We'll do something, Willy. I'll see how much Eddie can come up with and I'll talk with Father Kavanagh again. Can I tell him that you'll come up with something later in the year?" Amos figured he'd probably have to come up with at least part of the "something" himself. But maybe he could talk Kavanagh into footing more of the bill.

Willy's head bobbed.

"We've got some good story books at the house. I'll send some over for Margaret."

McGreevy looked up. "God bless you, Amos. But isn't it hard? It's so hard sometimes."

Amos stood; a vision of Michael, the two-year-old he and Molly had lost to Typhoid years earlier, flashed into his head. "It is, Willy. Yes, sometimes it's hard."

He didn't stop for a piece of chocolate. And he didn't go to arrest Wilcox as he had planned. He felt down; a walk would clear his head.

\*\*\*\*\*\*\*\*\*\*\*\*\*\*\*\*\*\*\*\*\*\*\*\*\*

Paddy's boss, Kevin O'Shay, was uncharacteristically talkative on Thursday morning. He admitted to being nervous about the Massachusetts legislators, who were touring Lawrence that day. He sat behind his desk, swiveling from side to side. "Paddy, I'll leave it to you to show them what the operatives do. We've got to be very careful about answering any questions. Act stupid, like you don't understand. I'll do the talking, unless Mister Clark answers."

"Won't that make them think that the operatives are even worse off, having a dimwit for a supervisor?"

"Maybe. Just give simple answers. I'll jump in."

"Shouldn't we try to help them to understand the situation? Let them see what has to be done in order to make cloth at a cost that competes with other mills?"

"Listen, Paddy, when you're older you'll understand that these politicians don't give a damn about the mills. They don't really care about the workers either. It's all about getting the newspapers to say nice things about them, so they can get reelected."

"So it's all just for show?"

O'Shay nodded, hung head and leaned forward, placing his elbows on his desk.

"It's disgusting; nobody is in this thing for honest reasons. Look at us, running the looms, trying to fool the strikers into thinking we don't need them. And the newspapers; they're the worst, running sob stories to sell papers. They don't understand a goddamn thing. They make the Wobblies sound like some kind of holy missionaries. Do you know what they're up to this Saturday?"

Paddy sat in amazement; O'Shay hadn't said this much to him since he'd been hired. "The newspapers or the Wobblies?"

"The Wobblies." O'Shay's agitation seemed to be growing. Paddy decided not to ask any more questions. "They're rounding up children, strikers' kids. They're going to ship them off to New York so they can be fed. They could feed them here for half the money. But no, they want pictures and stories in the papers. They'll raise money, but I doubt it will go to the kids. They're just pawns being herded around for the cameras"

Paddy had visions of little tots being marched off to live with strangers, who might not even speak their language. "The kids will get homesick."

O'Shay sighed and sat back. "Yeah." He went back to talking about how to manage the expected visit. Paddy listened, but he was elsewhere, thinking about the children. They were going to be scared, but maybe the experience would wind up being good for them.

Early that afternoon, three men, all in overcoats and bowlers, and a woman bundled up in a fur coat, showed up on the floor in the company of Mister Clark. Paddy buzzed around, helping the replacement workers as best he could. They could only handle half the looms that his regular operatives did, and they were in constant trouble with those. He spotted the group coming his way and noticed that Clark was doing most of the talking while Kevin O'Shay stayed to the rear. Paddy went to the aisle to meet them.

Clark told O'Shay to explain things, and O'Shay told Paddy to point out the details as he brought them up. Paddy found himself moving about one of the looms, pointing to the spools, shuttles and so on. It was easy and left him free to observe the visitors. They paid scant attention to O'Shay, who had to shout to be heard over the noise; they preferred talking into each other's ears.

As they were leaving, one of the men, a burly Irishman, stepped over to shake Paddy's hand and to give him a calling card—"Michael O'Connell, Massachusetts House of Representatives…"

O'Shay waited until they were gone. He turned to Paddy. "No doubt your esteem for our elected representatives has gone up." Then, he turned away, and Paddy, went back to work.

During supper that evening, Molly announced to the family that her father, Patrick Kelly, would visit on Saturday and join the family for dinner.

Paddy was relieved that she didn't say that they were all going into Boston on Sunday to visit his grand da. But something told him that the visit would not be without consequences.

\*\*\*\*\*\*\*\*\*\*\*\*\*\*\*\*\*\*\*\*\*

Amos felt he had enough information to justify questioning Ernest Pitman. He wondered if he should get a warrant or just show up and ask questions. Pitman might be surprised enough to reveal some information about his dealings with William Wood.

The offices for Pitman's construction company were located in the Bay State Building on Essex Street. A telephone call revealed that he spent most of his time at the company's yard on Portland Street in South Lawrence. Amos arrived at the facility, which extended about three hundred feet along the street. The entire front consisted of an eight foot high, unpainted, wooden fence. A wide gate provided access to a large yard bounded by sheds, stables, storage buildings, and more fencing. Piles of manure, sand and stacks of bricks were located in front of the back and side fences. Just inside the gate, Amos spotted a small, faded-red, wood building with a weather-beaten sign over the door "Office." Next to it, several men were engaged in hitching up a pair of horses to a construction wagon; they nodded to Amos as he approached. Although he did not know them, they seemed to recognize him.

The door stuck, and Amos needed to give it a shove. Inside, near the door, he found a low, dark wood railing; behind that were several desks and doors leading to offices. The door to one closed just as he came in. A matronly woman sat at one of the desks, hair piled high, Gibson style, typing a letter. After giving him a forced-looking smile, she asked, "What can I do for you?"

Amos held up his badge. "I want to talk with Ernest Pitman."

"Oh, I am sorry. You just missed him. He's gone off to look at a new site and then he's leaving for a few days to attend some meetings. He won't be back until next week."

"I'll call at his home."

"The meetings are out of town."

"Where?"

"Mister Pitman didn't say."

"When will he be back?"

"He didn't say. Business has been slow, what with the strike and all." Another forced smile.

Every instinct told him that Pitman was dodging him, hiding in the closed office. He toyed with the idea of barging in, but that might precipitate a bigger problem. He glared at the woman. "That's too bad." He nodded to the men outside and went back to the station house.

On his way to the inspectors' room to deposit his hat and coat, he passed Jimmy Kerrigan, sitting at the desk. "His secretary tells me, he's left town, Jimmy. What do you make of that?"

Kerrigan shrugged, and Amos kept walking. He passed Kerrigan again, raising a finger, to indicate that he was headed upstairs. He hoped to talk directly with Judge Waters, but found himself having to deal with Billy Conboy. "I need to speak to the Judge on a confidential matter, Billy."

"The Judge won't be in until next week, Amos. Of course if it's a serious emergency?"

Amos demurred; Pitman may have already been tipped and decided to make himself scarce.

Conboy continued. "I imagine there will be a lot of warrants before this strike business is over. So many strange things going on."

"How true."

"I just heard that one of Wood's people is implicated in that dynamite thing you've been working on."

"Really? What did you hear?"

"Oh, Amos, I hear all kinds of things—lawyers and cops, coming and going. I can't keep track of who and what. I try to stay out of it—try not to repeat things. I don't mind telling you, of course. That's different."

"Yes, I'll have to come up more often." Amos decided the less he said about Pitman, the better. "Billy, get word to me when the Judge is in. And have a nice weekend."


\*\*\*\*\*\*\*\*\*\*\*\*\*\*\*\*\*\*\*\*


Neal had an assignment--he was to sit by the window in the front parlor and keep an eye out for his grand da. He took the job seriously; every time a carriage, wagon, or vehicle of any

126

description came down the street, he stood up and put his face so close to the window that his breath fogged the glass, and he had to wipe it clear with the sleeve of his sweater. Finally, just after four o'clock, a carriage stopped, and a large familiar figure alighted into the light drizzle, which threatened to change into snow later that evening. Paddy was summoned to go out and assist his grand da.

"No need," the old man said, as he arrived at the front steps. "As you can see, I'm perfectly capable of getting about."

Paddy was glad to hear this, as his grand da was as tall as he was and of considerable girth. But he stayed close to his side as they started up the stairs. "We've all been looking forward to your visit."

The old man took his time on the stairs. "The old ticker's not what it was. I don't run to catch streetcars anymore."

"I'm glad to hear that, Grand Da, there's always another streetcar, but I've only got one grand da."

They reached the top. The old man stopped and turned. "That's right, and it's time I should be seeing, more of you."

Paddy grinned and reached ahead to open the door. They all gathered around, helping the old man with his hat and coat. Before his coat disappeared into a closet, Patrick Kelly reached into some inside pockets to produce presents for Kathleen and Neal. Kathleen opened hers to find a box of fancy stationery, while Neal found a small model airplane with a propeller that could be spun with the flick of a finger. The old man said, "You'll be riding around in one of those before long."

Amos withdrew while the rest of the family sat in the parlor, and the children gave the usual accounts of their activities: school, the nuns, best subject. When they wound down, Kelly turned to Paddy, his namesake. "I've been hearing some disturbing news about the violence surrounding this strike. Have you been effected by it?"

Paddy shook his head. "No, I stay away from the demonstrations and I get into work early. Everything's quiet by the time I leave."

The old man glanced at Molly, his daughter, and then back to Paddy. "These kinds of troubles have a way of finding us, no matter where we hide."

In the kitchen, Amos reached to a top shelf in one of the cabinets and retrieved a rarely-used bottle of whiskey. His emotions were always mixed when he thought of his father-in-law, part affection, part respect, and part resentment. Patrick Kelly was a self-made man, who had built his company from nothing and he now held sway over a hundred, some-odd, employees. After the death of his wife, Mary, he'd raised two daughters and two sons, giving all a fine education and a handsome dowry to each of his daughters. The Flanagan house and its modern improvements were all paid for with Kelly's help. Amos never wanted for praise from the old man, but he understood that his own accomplishments never really measured up to those of his father-in-law, even when he won his promotion to inspector.

He returned to the parlor with two small glasses of whiskey. He placed one of them on the small table next to the armchair in which his father-in-law sat, holding court. "Your favorite, Patrick, 'Jamesons'." They each raised their glass, and the old man said, "To your very good health."

They took a couple of sips, and then the conversation drifted to the weather, the recent admissions of New Mexico and Arizona as the 47th and 48th States, and the strike. That morning 150 strikers' children had been shipped off to New York City to be temporarily adopted by sympathetic families. Molly said, "I can't imagine the sadness in the parents' homes tonight."

Kathleen added, "Mrs. Collins says they should have saved the train fares and fed the children here."

Then Patrick Kelly said, "Those Wobblies are a bad lot. Anarchists, Communists, they want to overthrow our

128

government. This strike could be long and ugly, which reminds me of why I'm here. You know, Amos, I haven't come for a strictly social visit."

Molly signaled the children to accompany her into the kitchen, leaving Amos and Paddy to deal with her father.

Patrick Kelly waited, letting silence introduce the gravity of what he was about to say. The younger men waited with no sense of impatience. The waiting was part of their cultural heritage, as when, for centuries past, the shanachie waited while everyone in the little dirt-floored cottage settled down and remained without movement or sound for at least a minute before he uttered the first soft words of his story.

He began. "Amos, have you ever driven a motor car?"

Amos was unsure of the purpose of the question. Automobiles were a popular topic in Lawrence. Everyone on the police force wondered when the department would get its first one and what would it be used for. He, himself, was very interested and had taken advantage of an offer from the Essex dealer on Common Street to take a ride and to drive the car for a short distance.

"I have but I'm not sure that I see any advantage to them, given how much they cost."

Paddy broke in. "I've driven one. My friend's father has one. He's been teaching both of us how to do it."

"Well," the old man said, "they've improved and they'll keep on getting better. As you probably know, Amos, the police and fire departments in big cities are starting to use them. Some of my competitors in the trucking business are getting motor trucks, and I'll have to jump in soon. Think of it: no feeding; no harnessing; no horse shite. It will change our lives."

Amos said, "It will be expensive."

"It will be, but there is no choice. And, for those that think ahead, there will be new opportunities." He turned to Paddy. "Where does your friend's father get his fuel?"

"He goes to the railroad yard; they sell it there."

"And where do you think he'll get it a few years from now?"

Paddy thought about it and looked to his da, who asked, "And you're thinking of setting up to distribute gasoline?"

"It will take special trucks." He paused and looked hard at Amos and Paddy. "There's so much to be done, and I'm getting on. I doubt I can do it all myself. It might be better to sell the business for what I can get now."

A heavy silence hung in the room. The old man broke it. "There's no one but yourself, Amos, and maybe Paddy helping and gradually moving up to take over."

Amos nodded but said nothing.

"Will you think on it?"

"I will."

"I'll be needing an answer soon."

"I know you will. I'll try not to disappoint you—on that score at least."

The old man let it drop, and the conversation went back to family matters. Neal slipped back into the room, and Paddy told him that they had been talking about motor cars, an even more exciting subject, as far as Neal was concerned, than airplanes. This line of conversation continued through dinner. Molly, who knew in advance the purpose of her father's visit, chimed in with her own enthusiasm for this new force in modern life and the benefits to businesses.

Her father said, "I'm surprised no one's mentioned Henry Ford. His cars are less than a thousand dollars, and they're quite good."

Paddy said, "That's what Frank Dunn's father has. He's thinking about turning it into a small truck for his plumbing business."

Amos said, "I can see the day when somebody holds up a bank on Essex Street and makes a getaway in a Model T."

Later, when it was time for the old man to leave, a Buick motor car arrived. The family gathered around as Patrick Kelly put on his overcoat, and everyone wished him a fond good bye. It had stopped raining; Amos, Paddy and Neal all went outside to admire the Buick and see Patrick Kelly off. Molly stayed by the window; these moments were bittersweet. Her father looked well, but she knew his time was coming, the time when all she'd have were memories of snuggling up to that huge person who'd protected and comforted her, surprised her with little presents and taken her to the park on Sundays.

After the kitchen was cleaned up, Neal and Kathleen got ready for Sunday Mass and then for bed. Paddy went over to Frank Dunn's, and Amos and Molly sat in the kitchen.

She said, "I've got a fair idea of what he wanted."

"You didn't put him up to it?"

She laughed. "You know very well he has a mind of his own. What did he say?"

Amos related the gist of what her father had said. "That's where all that talk about motor cars and trucks came from."

"I hope he's feeling all right. It sounds as though he wants to make a decision soon."

"Yes, and I understand that—much better than I did before. It was good to have a straight out talk about it. I can see why he's so anxious to get on with it—while he still has his health and can feel the excitement."

"And what about you?"

"Yeah, I feel it. It's exciting." Amos rubbed the back of his neck.

"Would you like another wee one?"

"You read my mind."

She got up, fetched a small glass from the cabinet and poured a small amount of Jamesons from the bottle, still waiting to be put away. She set the glass in front of Amos and sat down across the table. "What do you think you'll do?"

He held the glass close to the table and rolled the whiskey around the bottom, looking at the amber liquid as if he expected a revelation—an answer perhaps to her question. "I can't just walk away in the middle of this thing. I feel there's something important at stake, and that things will go badly for too many people if I just quit."

"And when *this thing,* whatever that is, is over? What then?"

"We go to Boston."

"And if it's too late?"

He slugged down the whiskey. "I don't know."

# CHAPTER TWELVE

Paddy left the house right after lunch on Sunday. No one asked where he was going. His nose felt the bite of frigid air, but there was very little wind and not much snow on the ground. It was already the middle of February, and so far there had not been a great deal of snow. That was good; with only one chance each week to see Maria, a heavy snow on Saturday or Sunday would be devastating.

An hour later, he got off the streetcar in Haverhill, walked up Merrimack Street and crossed the bridge into Bradford. By the time he turned off onto South Pleasant Street, the cold had penetrated his coat and he ran the short distance to the house. When Carla opened the door, he almost pushed her aside to get in. She helped him with his coat. "God, it's cold," he said. Her goofy smile cheered him. "We just got here," she said, as she led him into the parlor where he handed a small gift of chocolates to Mrs. Schultz and rubbed his hands together. "Thank you," she said, "Carla and Maria have only just arrived, and I was asking about the children who were sent off to New York."

Paddy took a chair closest to Maria.

Mrs. Schultz continued, "Maria, you said that you know some of the families?"

"The mothers did not want to do it," she said. "The fathers insisted. They said that the strike leaders told them that it would be a wonderful experience for the children. They would be treated very well, and it would be a great service to the union and for the strike."

Mrs. Schultz said, "It sounds as if the parents were being coerced."

"The leaders said the children will be well fed, and the strike will be shorter because of their service."

Paddy wanted to ask what Lorenzo said about it but he didn't want Maria to feel that he was in any way hostile to her brother.

Mrs. Schultz turned to him. "Surely, you must have an opinion on this subject?"

"I can tell you my mother's reaction. She feels terrible for the mothers of the children."

Maria added, "His mother is a saintly woman—so kind."

Paddy smiled at her and continued. "For myself, I also have sympathy for them. And I don't trust the Wobblies—not one bit. It's all for the newspapers and to raise money for the union."

They talked on about other things, and Carla made some tea. Paddy grew increasingly nervous. He needed to talk to Maria about the situation with his grand da and what might happen. They needed to do some kind of planning. He was also dying to touch her, to kiss her.

Finally, the tea was gone, and Paddy was about to ask Maria to brave the cold for a short walk when Mrs. Schultz suggested that Carla accompany her upstairs for a short time so that he and Maria might have a private conversation. Paddy thanked her, saying that there was something he had to discuss with Maria.

As soon as Carla and her grandmother left, Paddy lost no time in telling Maria of his grandfather's visit, finishing by saying, "I may have to move to Boston."

She listened and then with a wan smile leaned forward to kiss him lightly on the lips. "There are so many difficulties," she said. "This strike seems to be ruining our lives. My father is more determined than ever to go back to Italy. I don't have a chance of getting a teaching job, and the little money I used to

134

get for teaching English has dried up. And that's on top of you being Irish—with a father who's a policeman."

Paddy felt a strange sensation rising in his chest--a feeling of anger. Was this how she felt?

She stopped to gaze at him for a moment and then pulled him to her, kissing him passionately. "But I do love you." He kissed her back, feeling warm and relaxed. Of course, she was only expressing the difficulties.

His brain bordered on panic as he searched for some kind of action that would give them a sense of stability, allowing them to plan how they were going to live happily ever after. He poured it out, "We need to stop hiding. We need to tell everyone that we're in love and set up a regular courtship. My family will be all right with it; they know you already. My father has Italian friends, and my mother mentioned that living in Boston might be better for us if we get married."

She listened, placing a hand on his cheek, before responding.

"My father has been corresponding with friends at the University of Rome. He believes they will offer him a position soon. He wants to take me with him. He says I can earn some money teaching English and I can attend the University. If he found out we're talking like this, he would be very angry. He'd want to leave right away."

Paddy hung his head and tried to think.

There was no time for a second kiss. Carla and Mrs. Schultz returned. Carla said that she had to return to Lawrence early. Paddy got up to retrieve his coat and to thank Mrs. Schultz. She said, "Do plan on coming back next Sunday. I can see that the two of you are going to need all the help you can get."

He took her hand. "I don't know where I'd be without your help."

To Carla, he said, "I owe you some big favors."


When he turned the corner onto South Main, Paddy noticed two men standing across the street under a sign identifying 'Webster's Ladies Shoes and Slippers' factory. A strange place to be standing on a freezing Sunday afternoon, he thought, although it didn't seem as cold as earlier. They shuffled around in the cold, and, when he passed, he noticed them cross the street to follow him over the bridge. That seemed odd, but his mind was elsewhere.

If Alessandro Petrella was offered a position at the University in Rome, he would leave right away and take Maria with him. He would also leave with her if he got wind of how serious he and Maria were about each other. But did Maria have to go with him?

The germ of a solution popped into his head. His grandfather wanted him in Boston—along with his family. Maybe he'd accept Maria as a start. Maybe Maria could live with Patrick Kelly and get a teaching job in Boston. Why not? The old man was always supporting causes, including some that were not popular. He had a flair for the dramatic, for helping the underdog.

He reached the other side of the river, barely noticing the horse-drawn hack that stood at the corner of Merrimack Street. The door opened as he approached, and a man jumped out, blocking his path. He moved to pass, but another man came from behind to grab his arm. "Get in," the first man said. As Paddy resisted, a third man took his other arm, and the first man put a gun to his throat. "Get in."

Paddy was stunned, his mind momentarily blank. He climbed into the cab, followed by the man with the gun. Another man got in on the other side, and Paddy found himself sandwiched between two large, heavy men, whose faces were partly covered by scarves. He saw the third man climb up front, and he felt a lurch as the cab started off, turning left onto

136

Merrimack Street. The men breathed heavily, and the vapor from their lungs filled the small space inside the cab. They rolled down the black, wax coated shades, covering the windows and dimming the light. Paddy's breathing quickened, and his heart pounded.

The first man pushed him forward. "Bend." He held his gun low so Paddy could see it even with his chest on his legs. The second man pulled his arms back and tied his hands tight enough to cause pain. When he finished, he pulled Paddy's collar. "Up." Paddy started to ask why they were doing this. The second man said, "Shut up, or I stuff your mouth." They had accents that he couldn't identify; they did not sound Italian. He nodded, and the man tied a large bandana around his head, blocking his eyes.

The men said nothing more. Paddy tried to concentrate on the sounds outside,

the horse's hoofs clopped on the pavement in a regular rhythm; the cab creaked, and the rubber rimmed wheels thumped over cobblestones. His heart and breathing slowed. Where were they taking him? He heard the clang of a streetcar bell; the sound of the horse's hoofs and the wheels turned hollow as they rumbled across a bridge. Horse-drawn carriages and wagons passed often going in the opposite direction. He heard a train in the distance and twice heard motorcars. His general sense was that they were headed back toward Lawrence. Wherever they were going, it was not a short trip. And why? Why were they doing this? Who were these men?

Had Maria's father sent them? He recalled their conversation; she said her father mustn't know—an Irishman with a cop for a father. Maybe the old man knew about them already—Lorenzo could have followed Maria. And now, he wanted to put the fear of God into Paddy—make him give up Maria. The Italians are crazy. They're all crazy; look what they did in the mills. And all those guns. And sending their kids to New York. But her father? He's a professor.

137

What else? he thought. I could be the wrong guy. Maybe they got the wrong guy. "I'm Paddy Flanagan." He blurted.

He felt a piece of cloth pressing against his lips. "You want this?"

He shook his head.

"We know who you are. Your father's a cop."

The other one said, "Yeah, one who doesn't pay attention to his betters."

His da? This had something to do with his da?

That was it until the cab stopped. He heard trains, not far off—a rail yard perhaps?

They helped him, guiding his foot to the step, and balancing him until he was on the ground. They led him a short distance onto a wooden platform and held him still while someone opened a heavy sliding door. His foot caught on something but he remained upright, standing on a rough floor while the door slid shut behind him. As they steered him around some obstacles, he smelled fresh-cut lumber and kerosene. Another stop and another sliding door. The hand on his arm signaled him to move. "Step up." He raised his foot to feel ahead and then stepped up onto a wooden floor. He heard the door close behind, as a hand pushed him forward and turned him around. "Sit." The hand pushed him down onto some kind of stool.

His heart started pounding again; he felt weak, a little trembly and helpless. What were they going to do to him?

This place was a little warmer; he smelled a cigar and tried to listen to a low, muffled conversation well away from him. He understood nothing. The door slid open and then closed; heavy footsteps came toward him; he felt hands on his head, and the blindfold came off.

He blinked a few times in the dim light of kerosene lanterns and tried to focus on the object in front of him. The first

138

thing he saw was a revolver in a light brown leather holster, worn like a huge belt buckle on the stomach of a mountain-sized man with a full black beard and glinty black eyes. The man stepped back and sat next to a table in the middle of the room where he picked up the stub of a cigar from a dish, lit it and sat staring at Paddy while he puffed away. A lantern on the table illuminated his face from the side, giving his beard and features a stark, Halloween-mask, appearance.

Paddy said nothing, waiting to learn what the rules were.

Finally, the man crushed the cigar out and pushed the dish away. He leaned forward, putting his elbows on his knees. "I treat you okay." His English was rough with a strong accent. Eastern European? "You do one wrong thing; I beat you so you can't move. Understand?"

Paddy nodded. He understood all right. But what the hell was happening? The man leaned back, continuing to observe him.


\*\*\*\*\*\*\*\*\*\*\*\*\*\*\*\*\*\*\*\*\*\*\*\*


Amos folded his Sunday paper and went into the kitchen for supper where Neal and Kathleen were already in their places. He brushed past Molly on his way to the sink. Washing his hands, he glanced back at the table. "Where's Paddy?"

Molly answered, "He's not home."

"Did he say he'd not be home?"

"He said something about maybe going to Frank's after he got back."

Amos put the towel back on rack. "Got back from where?"

She gave him a look.

"I see." He pulled out his chair.

Kathy chimed in. "He should have come home to tell us."

Amos said, "We'll take care of it, Kathleen."

Amos was annoyed; he had enough to worry about, including the aftermath of Patrick Kelly's visit. He didn't need an argument with Paddy, especially if it had something to do with that Italian girl. He wanted to get into the situation with Molly, let off some steam, but not with the kids sitting there—taking it all in. It was a quiet supper; what little conversation took place came to a halt whenever there was a sound from the vicinity of the front door.

Later, with Neal in bed and Kathleen getting ready for school and bed, he and Molly sat close to each other across one corner of the kitchen table.

"It's not like him, Amos. He's never done this before."

"He's never lost his head over a girl before."

"Oh yes he has. You just never knew."

"This is different. They're both of age. He could be planning to marry her, for Christ's sake."

"Getting upset and taking the Lord's name in vain won't help matters."

"This is crazy. Can you imagine—an Italian wedding—an Italian daughter-in-law?"

"Suppose she was Joe LaMastro's daughter?"

"That would be another matter altogether."

"You haven't even met her father."

He leaned back, putting both hands up to hold his head. "My God."

Kathleen came in to announce that she was going to bed. She kissed them and skipped down the hall.

Molly said, "Maybe he's at Frank's and lost track of the time. Catherine probably fed him."

"I'll go over there if he's not home soon."

# CHAPTER THIRTEEN

The man turned his attention to a newspaper while
Paddy rolled his eyes around the room. It was large, about the
size of a classroom at Saint Patrick's, but the ceiling was lower.
The floors, the walls, and the ceiling were all finished with rough
boards, and sheets of coarse canvas covered the three windows.
A small pot-bellied stove sat in the center of the room, its stack
heading straight up through a sheet of metal flashing attached to
the ceiling; buckets of coal and ashes sat on either side.

"You hot?" the man asked.

Paddy still had his coat on. "Yes."

The man came over and untied his hands. Paddy stood
up and removed his coat. His hat, which had been stuffed inside
against his chest, fell to the floor. He felt a dizzy as he bent to
retrieve it and he placed one hand on the stool to brace himself.

The man pointed. "Hang on wall."

Paddy found a hook on the wall and hung up his hat and
coat. As he walked back, the man gestured to another chair at the
table, and Paddy sat down.

"You hungry?" the man asked.

To that moment, Paddy hadn't thought about it. "Yes."

"Food come."

They sat there, the man drumming his fingers, Paddy
continuing to check out the room. Two cots were placed about
five feet apart, against one wall, and by the far wall there were
two buckets with covers. Next to the buckets, stood a wash stand
with pitchers of water; towels hung from nails on the wall. Paddy
wondered how long the buckets and water would have to last.
The man got up and went to a small side table near one of the

cots. He came back with a deck of cards. "You play?" He plunked the deck in front of Paddy.

Paddy picked it up and began to shuffle. "Pinochle?"

The man nodded and, with his thumb, pointed to his chest. "Boris."

"Boris. Okay." He dealt the cards.

After twenty minutes of Boris winning handily, there was a soft knock at the door. Boris put his cards down, got up and opened the door just enough to accept a box. He placed it on the table, and went over to Paddy's coat where he reached into the sleeve, pulled out Paddy's hat and gave it to someone just outside the door. He closed the door, sat down, and picked up his cards. Paddy stared at him, wanting to ask what that was all about but he decided to wait until he had a better feel for what kind of guy Boris was.

Boris looked at him and tapped the box. "Food. Finish game first."

\*\*\*\*\*\*\*\*\*\*\*\*\*\*\*\*

After his conversation with Molly, Amos sat in the parlor, searching the paper for some distraction. He found himself reading an advertisement promoting a reliable home treatment for a beer or whiskey habit. It came in two forms: a pill for those wishing a voluntary cure; and a secret tasteless powder, which a mother, or wife, could mix with food or drink thereby effecting a cure without the son, or husband realizing the source.

It came with the promise of a refund to those not satisfied. The advertisement amused

him and he wondered if there might be such a product for love-sick young men.

There was a noise on the porch; Amos got up to investigate. There was no one at the door and no one outside. He opened the door to stick his head out and spotted Paddy's hat sitting on an envelope just in front of the door. He picked them up and closed the door. Molly was on her way from the kitchen; he flipped the hat onto the hall table.

"Was that someone at the door, Amos?"

"No. Someone left a note." He showed it to her and pointed to the hat.

"Oh, dear God. Open it."

The envelope was not sealed. He removed the note and held it under the hall light so they could read it together. In bold hand lettering, it said:

Do not tell anyone of this note

Do not inform anyone at the police department

Do not involve the newspapers

Tell no one

If you ever want to see your son again, Follow our instructions.

Drop the dynamite investigation.

Do not arrest Pitman

He folded the note and placed it in his pocket.

She clung to him. "Amos, you'll do what they say?"

He hugged her tightly, whispering, "We'll get him back." He reached for his coat, hanging near.

"Dear God. What are you doing?"

"I'm going to see Frank."

"But the note said…"

"I know. Frank would give his life for Paddy."

"Oh, Amos."

"I'll be home soon."

The windows were all dark at the Dunn house. He banged on the door; upstairs a light turned on, footsteps, and Terence, Frank's father, opened the door, still wrapping a robe around himself. "Amos!"

"Terry, I'm sorry for the hour, but it's urgent I talk with Frank."

"Is it Paddy? Is he all right?"

"Yes. But I need to see Frank."

"Yes, Amos. Step in. I'll get him."

A minute later, Frank came down the hall in a bathrobe. "Mister Flanagan, what's happened?"

"Nothing yet, Frank. I need your help."

Frank led him into a parlor, off the hall. "Tell me what to do."

"Frank, this is serious, Paddy's life may depend on you telling absolutely not a single soul what this is about."

Frank placed a hand over his heart. "I will tell no one."

Amos explained the situation and the note. Then he asked, "What do you know about these Sunday visits?"

"He goes to Haverhill, to a Mrs. Schultz, across the river in Bradford. She's the grandmother of Maria's friend. It's all very proper. Today was only his second visit."

"I need something else, some pictures of Paddy. You must have some good ones. I'd like to pick one and ask you to make some copies."

"When?"

"I need them early in the morning."

"Come downstairs. I'll show you what I have."

Amos returned home to comfort Molly and to try to get some sleep. Before turning out the light, they sat on the edge of the bed, his arm around her, her head against his neck. The only sound was her quiet snuffling. Finally, she pulled away and reached toward the light. "It's not fair," was all she said.

Up early the next morning, she got the children ready for school. He shaved and came into the kitchen for some oatmeal and tea. There was a rap at the door, Molly tried not to look frightened, and Amos went to the door. A cold-looking Frank Dunn handed him an envelope. "I'll be praying for Paddy."

"Thank you, Frank." He closed the door and went to the rack where he placed the envelope inside his coat.

He returned to the kitchen where the children were bolting down the last of their oatmeal. They ran into the back where Neal scrambled around, looking for his book bag while Kathleen brushed her teeth and hair. He told Molly he had the pictures from Frank. "I'll let you know as soon as I have any information."

"I'll be here waiting,"

Neal and Kathleen reemerged, putting on hats and coats.

Amos said, "I'll be walking to school with you."

They looked surprised.

"It seemed such a short weekend. I've hardly had a chance to talk with either of you."

As soon as they gained the street, Kathleen asked, "What time did Paddy get home?"

"It was late."

"Where was he?"

"At Frank's. Mother was right."

147

Neal said, "I didn't see him this morning."

"He went in early to beat the strikers."

They seemed satisfied and soon became more interested in the friends they encountered than in their father's unexpected company. He left them near the school where the nuns were organizing the children to enter in an orderly fashion. In warmer weather, they were obliged to get into a line—one for boys—one for girls, in each grade.

He hopped on a streetcar and went to the station house where Kerrigan was conducting morning roll-call. In the inspector's room, he tried to take an interest in his case reports while waiting for Kerrigan to be free. The Breen case was out of his hands for the time being, and there was nothing so far on the search for Carapatsi, the Anna Lopizzo shooting suspect. Amos wondered if he'd ever be caught, or if the bastard had already made it back to Sicily.

He came to the sheet on Wilcox. God damn it, he thought, why am I having to chase this son-of-a-bitch; why doesn't he just tell me who his lawyer is? He decided to put an end to it, he had no more time for Wilcox.

Finally, it appeared that Kerrigan was free; he went behind the desk to speak quietly. "Jimmy, I've got to trust you with my son's life."

"Amos, what in God's name?"

"He's been taken hostage."

Kerrigan bent his head close. "Do you know who did it?"

"No, but they left this last night." He slipped the note to Kerrigan below the desk. Kerrigan held it low and read it. "Ah, Jesus, Amos. Oh, Jesus. What do you want me to do?"

"Get Casey assigned so he can work with me and get somebody, who can keep his mouth shut, to follow my kids home from school."

"Consider it done. What else?"

"I don't know. I'm going to see my Italian friend. Keep your ears open."

"I will. Now, I hate to add to your troubles, but the son-in-law wants to see you. I have a sneaky feeling he knows about the Pitman arrest warrant."

"Yeah, and he's still mad at me for Breen, but John would never stoop to anything having to do with snatching my son."

Kerrigan nodded, without looking convinced.

Amos slipped into Sullivan's office and waited for him to get off the phone. Sullivan motioned him to a chair and wound up his conversation. "Amos, what do you think of this business of sending those children to New York?"

"John, you've said, from the beginning, that these Wobblies are crazy, and you're right."

"Can you see yourself sending a kid off to live with people you don't know from Adam?"

Amos felt a twinge in his chest. Was Sullivan in on it? Did he know about Paddy? Was he sending a message? "Maybe they think the kids will be better off. At least they'll have enough to eat."

"The Mayor's concerned. He's seen the papers from New York. They've got these kids plastered all over the front page. Makes us look bad, Amos. They got money for train tickets; why don't they just feed the kids here?"

He wanted to escape. The conversation felt ludicrous. "I can't do anything about the papers."

Sullivan smacked his desk. "No, but you can help us find out what the parents are thinking. Are these Wobblies twisting their arms? Do they really want to let their kids go? Get us some information."

"I'm going over there today, John. I'll make inquiries and report back."

"Good. And, Amos, remember what I said. We all want to be working here when this is over. Without the mills, there's nothing here for any of us."

When Amos emerged from Sullivan's office, Kerrigan motioned him over and handed him a letter-sized envelope. "That's Wilcox's store, isn't it?"

Amos looked at the return address in the upper left hand corner. "Yeah." He reached into his pocket, pulled out a pen-knife, and opened the envelope to find a cryptic note: Lawyer is Harris and Forbes, School Street, Boston.

Bill Wilcox

He sighed. "Ah, well." Shaking his head, he folded the note back into the envelope and stuffed it into his pocket. "I'm going upstairs to quash that warrant for Pitman."

From the hallway, Billy Conboy appeared to be a conscientious public servant, neatly dressed in a clean white shirt, tie and jacket. When he looked up as Amos entered, the image changed to that of an alcoholic suffering after a weekend bender. His eyes, which seemed to have difficulty focusing, were raw as though rubbed with sand, and his skin, although clean, was pasty white and scaly, especially around his eyebrows. His hands held a fluttering piece of paper. On seeing Amos, he placed the paper and his hands firmly on the desk. "Ah, Amos, good morning. The judge hasn't been in."

"That's fine, Billy. I want to hold off on that warrant."

"The one for Pitman?"

"Yes."

"Has he shown up? Is there some new development in the case?"

Amos hated to visit with Conboy, an old friend caught in a net made of steel wires that seemed to close ever tighter, squeezing every last vestige of dignity, every ounce of manhood from his person until all who knew him prayed for his merciful death. How low had he sunk? Did he trade confidences for booze? Amos promised himself to find a way to bypass Conboy in the future.

"There's something else I've got to do. I can't talk about it. Just quash the warrant. Okay?"

"I will, Amos. And best to the family."

He returned to the first floor where Kerrigan signaled with a small movement of his head. Amos passed close, and Kerrigan said, "He's in the boiler room." Amos kept moving to the basement stairs. He found Casey taking an interest in the dials on the boiler. He explained the situation and showed Casey the note.

"My God, Amos. My God! Why don't we find Pitman and hold him in a basement somewhere until we get Paddy back?"

"Pitman may not have anything to do with it. The whole thing could be from higher up. From somebody who doesn't give a damn about Pitman."

Casey looked surprised. "William Wood? Oh."

"It's too early to tell. Who knows?" Amos gave Casey a small envelope. "Here's a couple of pictures of Paddy. Don't use them yet. This had got to be kept secret."

Casey took the envelope. "What do you want me to do?"

"Go over to South Lawrence and, very discretely, check for any unusual activity around Pitman's place."

Casey left, and Amos stayed behind for a minute to examine the dials.

\*\*\*\*\*\*\*\*\*\*\*\*\*\*\*\*\*\*\*\*\*

Paddy lost hand after hand. "I think if we were playing at my house, I'd be winning."

Boris nodded his assent and motioned Paddy to keep playing. Finally, he seemed to tire of winning and set his cards aside to peek into the box. "You hungry?" He took out some sandwiches and gave a large one to Paddy along with a bottle of root beer.

Boris seemed to be getting more human. Maybe they could relax with each other. While they were eating, he asked Boris, "Where are you from—what country?"

Boris shook his head. They were not going to talk about him. They continued in silence for a while before Paddy asked, "Would you like to hear about me?"

This amused Boris. He shrugged as if to say, 'Why not?'

What could he tell Boris? Especially, what could he tell him that might prompt him to reveal something about what was going on and who was behind it.

"I work in the mills. I'm a supervisor with about fifty operatives working under me." Paddy noticed Boris's eyebrows lift slightly when he mentioned that he was a supervisor. "Of course, that means that I'm part of the management. I'm supposed to take the part of the mill owners. And I do, but I can't understand why the workers have to live in such poverty." He watched Boris's eyebrows—no reaction.

"How long your father a cop?"

The question caught Paddy off guard. "About twenty years."

"He is smart, yes?"

"Yes, very smart."

"That's good, less pain."

What kind of man was he dealing with? At one moment he seemed normal, in the next brutal and threatening. He tried again. "I live with my family, and…"

Boris raised his hand. "No more talk. Deal cards."

# CHAPTER FOURTEEN

Amos, his mind a blur of worry and guilt, went straight to Lamastro's store front and office. It was all about Paddy now. Entering from the street, he passed down an aisle lined with wooden crates on either side, some opened to display jugs of olive oil packed in straw. Connie looked up, obviously surprised to see him. There was no one else in the store or outer office, but he leaned over to whisper, "I need to see both of you. It's important."

She stood up. "He's got somebody with him. I'll slip him a note."

"It's got to be on the Q.T."

She took his arm and led him into a tiny, empty room, where she left him, closing the door on her way out. He took off his hat and coat before going to take a peek out a window overlooking an alleyway in the rear. A light snow was falling; a few people scurried along the alley with their heads down, scarves and collars pulled up against the snow.

The door opened and Connie slipped in. "He'll be a few more minutes, Amos. Would you like me to make you a cup of coffee?"

"No thanks, Connie. I won't keep you long. Something's come up. It can't wait."

"I'll be just outside."

Amos stood, blankly staring out the window while wondering what to say, and what kind of help Lamastro might be able to offer. He felt so helpless, and coming to Joe was a stab-in-the-dark, probably one of those useless, flailing-around, kind of actions that people take when they should be thinking about something more logical. But what?

The door opened; Connie and Joe came in—he with an extra chair so they could all crowd around the tiny desk.

"It's about Paddy. He didn't come home last night."

They waited.

Amos spread the note on the desk for them to read. Connie's hand went to her mouth. Joe said, "My God, Amos. What are you going to do?"

"I don't know. When he didn't come home for supper, I thought it might be the girl, and we'd have a little session when he got in. Then, the note came with his hat. Before that, when I still thought it might be the girl, I was thinking of coming to see you. And now, here I am anyway."

Connie said, "Molly must be crazy with worry."

Joe said, "Why don't you go after Pitman?"

"Might not be Pitman. Might be Wood, or someone else. And whoever it is, he probably hired outsiders to do it. I need to find Paddy before I can go after anybody. It's all I can think about."

"There are a lot of strange people in town. They can't all be working for the Wobblies. And some of them have money."

Connie added, "Some of them are having suits made."

Amos turned to her. "Suits?" What the hell was she talking about?

"Maria's father—the girl. He's a tailor."

He looked at her with a blank expression.

Joe said. "You should meet him, Amos. He's a real gentleman. If he can help Paddy, he'll do it, without question. You should meet him anyway."

He looked from one to the other. "This is about Paddy?"

Connie nodded. "Alessandro knows some people."

Joe said, "I'll go with you."

Connie said, "You should find some way to let Maria know about Paddy."

Amos shook his head out of disbelief; keeping Maria informed was the least of his worries. "Please, no one must know."

Joe said, "Let's go. I have to be back here soon."

Union Street was almost devoid of traffic and pedestrians; light snow continued to fall, and people in this part of town didn't have much money to spend even in the best of times. They didn't have far to walk before reaching the little shop with the manikin and bolts of cloth in the window.

The bell jangled to announce their arrival, and a startled-looking Maria turned to face them from under the dim bulb hanging by its wire in the middle of the room. She came forward to greet them. "Mister Lamastro, and Mister Flanagan, how delightful to see you. Especially you, Mister Flanagan. How is everyone in your family?"

Amos couldn't help a small smile. She, of course, knew the answer to her question—at least as of the previous afternoon. "We're all in good health, Maria. Thank you." He'd forgotten how beautiful and gracious she was. Poor Paddy, how could he be expected to resist? "Is your father about?"

Her expression changed to one of slight concern. "Yes, I just brought him some lunch. He's in the back."

Alessandro Petrella appeared at the curtain-entrance to the rear. He saw Lamastro and came forward with his hand extended. They shook hands, and he turned to Amos as Lamastro made the introductions. Petrella gave his hand to Amos. "Inspector Flanagan, I have looked forward to this moment. As a father, you must know what I feel in my heart for you and your family. I thank you for my daughter's life."

Years as a policeman imbedded in Amos a kind of calipers, which came forward instantly, even in social situations, to size up any new encounter. He sensed Petrella's intelligence, his smooth social grace (always a potential danger) and his genuine gratitude. The use of last names felt a little awkward, but Europeans seemed to be more relaxed using last names rather than first names. "I did next to nothing, Professor Petrella, my wife and daughter took care of Maria, and, of course, Paddy gets most of the credit."

"Ah, but the son comes from the father." He turned to his daughter. "Maria, did he not say that his father taught him to help those in need?"

"Yes, Papa." Her hand went to her mouth. A sign of concern?

Petrella said, "Gentlemen, I forget my manners. I have some coffee in the back. Please join me."

Lamastro said, "We're here on a matter of great confidentiality."

"Yes well, Maria was just leaving."

"Yes, Papa." She came forward to give him a kiss and then turned to take Amos's hand. "I'm so pleased to see you. Please give my love to your entire family."

She paused to give Lamastro a peck on the cheek and then left. Petrella gestured toward the rear.

The lighting there was better than that in front. Petrella cleared some garments from the worktable in the center of the room and set out three small cups. Lamastro spoke. "Alessandro, I believe Inspector Flanagan would prefer his coffee with hot water added and perhaps some sugar."

Amos nodded.

"But of course." Petrella got busy, and they all made polite conversation.

With the coffee served, and Amos attesting to it being very good, they got down to business. He produced the note and explained that he hoped to find Paddy without alerting the abductors. "I can't go back to working on the dynamite case, which might involve some highly placed people, until I get Paddy back."

Petrella sat quietly until Amos was clearly finished. "My friend, this is terrible, terrible news. I will do whatever you ask of me."

"I think that whoever did this is not from around here. I believe they were hired and brought from elsewhere to abduct and hold Paddy. Unfortunately, there are all kinds of strangers in town, Wobblies, reporters, soldiers, Pinkertons—you name it. On the other hand, the abductors probably don't fit in any of those categories. Joe and I are thinking that you have a lot of contacts and might be able to uncover some group that doesn't have a good reason to be here."

Petrella nodded. "I'm thinking of one already."

Lamastro said, "I told him that you had some strangers buying custom-made suits."

"Yes, there's a group of Serbians. The boss, who goes by the name Carlos, is having me make two suits for him. They come, three at a time, in a large black motor car. One stays with the car. They are all armed."

Amos asked, "Serbians, you say?"

"Yes, Carlos speaks some Italian, and they all speak English—poorly. I don't like the way they look at Maria. I make sure she's not here when they're coming."

"She's a beautiful young woman."

"Yes, but she's Italian."

Amos said nothing; he looked to Lamastro, who gave him a slight shake of his head.

Petrella continued. "You know, of course, about their liaisons?"

Amos searched for an appropriate response. "I, uh… I knew that Paddy was very attracted to her. And not much more than that, until yesterday."

"As Paddy's father, how do you feel about it?"

"I haven't given it much thought. These things have a way of taking care of themselves."

"But if it doesn't? If your daughter-in-law is going to be Italian? Your grandchildren Italian?"

Amos had thought about it. It would not be what he preferred, but a loving, united family was all important. He did not want his answers to Petrella's questions to become the basis for future problems and, given the circumstances, he certainly did not want to alienate him. "Tell me how *you* feel about it."

"I admire Paddy, and he has my undying gratitude, but I do not want this. I see nothing but problems. I intend to forbid Maria from seeing him again. But, of course, that's not important right now."

Amos was tempted to ask about the problems, but he felt the most significant ones would remain unmentionable. The daughter of an Italian professor marry an Irishman—the son of an Irish cop? He nodded to Petrella. "Paddy will get over it eventually. First I have to get him back."

"I will do all within my power to help you."

Lamastro said, "Alessandro, are there any other strangers that Inspector Flanagan should be aware of?"

"None that I know of, but I will make discrete inquiries."

Amos asked, "Do you know where the Serbians are staying?"

Petrella shook his head.

"Do you know the make of the automobile—the marque?"

Petrella thought for a moment. "Cadillac; they told me it was a Cadillac."

"Give me a description of them."

"Carlos is medium height, thin, has an aquiline nose, mustache and goatee, very black hair. The other two are taller, heavy, muscular men, one clean-shaven, the other with a mustache; both have black hair, bushy eyebrows. They all wear suits."

Amos penciled the information into his notebook and looked at Lamastro. "Am I forgetting anything?"

Lamastro got up. "You can always come back."

They got up, and Petrella extended his hand to Amos. "I will be most disappointed if you do not come back, especially when this matter is taken care of."

Amos held his hand. "I certainly hope that will be soon." He started to leave but turned back with an afterthought. "You didn't ask me, but I would welcome Maria into my family."

Petrella smiled and nodded his appreciation as they shook hands again.

As Lamastro came forward, Amos pushed through the curtain, nearly bumping into Lorenzo. Was he just coming in? Had he been standing there, listening? And for how long?

When they regained the street and were headed south along Union Street, he remembered Sullivan, he had to keep Sullivan off his back. He asked Lamastro, "Joe, what can you tell me about how the parents of those kids who got shipped to New York feel? Were they coerced by the Wobblies?"

"I don't know. I'll ask Connie."

161

Amos hopped a streetcar and headed for home; he was worried about Neal and Kathleen.

\*\*\*\*\*\*\*\*\*\*\*\*\*\*\*\*\*\*\*\*\*\*\*\*

By Monday evening, Paddy was tired of being scared; he hadn't slept and his mind was getting fuzzy. He was sick of playing cards, sick of trying to get information out of Boris, and sick of sandwiches. He had no toothbrush; his mouth felt dirty, and he was not looking forward to another night handcuffed to his cot. Boris gave him the Herald to read; he took refuge behind it and tried to think clearly. His whole world had become a ring of fear. He was helpless, just waiting to be squashed like an ant on a sidewalk. How could he help himself?

He sat on his cot with his back against the front wall of the building. He knew this because the main, outside, sliding door was in the same wall. From the sound of it opening and closing, he judged it to be about twenty-five feet away, on the other side of the interior wall separating the room he shared with Boris from the rest of the building. A second sliding door located at the center of that wall provided access to the room. There was no other exit.

Several times during the day and evening, visitors arrived to open and close the outside door and then knock at the interior one. Boris would go to the door, slide it open partway and slip through. Paddy heard a car door open and close when visitors arrived by motor car. These people brought the sandwiches and newspapers, and Boris sometimes had a lengthy conversation, in some strange foreign language, with one of them before coming back into the room.

Another visitor, Paddy assumed it to be a single person, came several times during the day to empty the slops, take out the ashes, bring scuttles of new coal, and lastly, to empty the

162

garbage. Boris carried all buckets outside of the interior door and back, so Paddy never saw this person either. He imagined some old guy who didn't give a damn what was going on inside, as long as he got paid. One look at Boris, with his big revolver, would make anybody think twice before mentioning his strange employer.

Paddy thought about running for it when Boris was in the corner with his pants down, but, in addition to the handcuffs at night, Boris used a padlock for the interior door whenever he was going to be busy. Paddy determined to steal a peek out one of the covered windows when Boris was out of the room having a conversation with one of the automobile people. Maybe that would lead to another idea.

His chance came the next morning. A car arrived, doors opened and slammed shut. The outside door opened, closed, the knock and Boris disappeared. He heard murmuring, only Boris's voice was distinguishable, but Paddy couldn't understand a word anyone was saying. He lost no time, going to the window near his cot and pulling on the canvas cover. He tore it off a nail at one corner and pulled it back just enough to peer outside. He could see the car out front—a black Cadillac. The drivers face remained hidden behind a newspaper, except when he flipped it to turn a page, revealing a prominent black mustache and eyebrows.

The buildings in the area were strangely familiar, low, warehouse-type buildings, some with railroad sidings. Yes. He was in Lawrence! He remembered playing with others around these buildings when he was a kid. They could get inside some of them, discover all kinds of things. He helped kids scavenge for coal around the rail yards and sometimes he felt guilty when some of them stole things to take home. One time, he hopped on a freight car with Frank; they were out for a joy-ride. When it started moving, they got scared, not having any idea of where it was going or how to get off. Lucky for them, it was only going to another part of the railroad yard. When his da found out he'd been playing there, that was the end of it. Neither he or Frank ever went back.

He pulled his head back and pressed the canvas back over the nail holding the corner down. Back at the table, he waited for Boris to come in with a breakfast sandwich to go with the undrinkable coffee simmering on the stove. As Boris opened the food package, Paddy had an idea, he reached for the paper and pencil Boris used for pinochle. Boris eyed him suspiciously.

"I like to draw pictures, okay?"

Boris shrugged.

# CHAPTER FIFTEEN

Amos arrived at Saint Patrick's School just before three. He noticed Patrolman John Dolan standing across the street and went over to talk with him.

"John, I appreciate your being here, but I'll see the kids home today."

"It's no sacrifice. I can tell you I'd rather be here, watching after some kids than across town getting into a fracas with some strikers."

Amos only thought of the strike now in terms of how it might effect Paddy; any increase in tensions might add to the threat on his life.

Ettor and Giovannitti would be up for a hearing in the Anna Lopizzo case that week. Surely, that would bring demonstrations—more trouble, and he heard that there would be another shipment of kids at the end of the week. Strikers, especially the women, goaded the police and troops, taunting them at every opportunity. Frustrations mounted—you could see it--something had to give. Molly would be sick with worry over possible added danger to Paddy and her family.

Dolan asked, "What's this all about, Amos—me watching the kids?"

"It's a family matter—very embarrassing."

"Oh. Is Molly giving you a bit of grief?"

"No, we're grand. But I can't talk about it. I appreciate your help, and I know you'll keep all this under your hat."

"You have my word."

Neal came out of the schoolyard, jostling with a classmate while attempting to button his coat over his uniform.

Amos crossed the street where they waited for Kathleen before heading home. Although his mind was elsewhere, he listened with pleasure to his children recounting their day. Once home, he and Molly retreated to the back bedroom where he told her what little he'd accomplished so far.

She asked, "Wouldn't it be better to involve the whole department and the State Police as well?"

He had been thinking the same thing, but he did not want to tell her why he hadn't done it. From long experience, he knew the chance of violence, the chance that strangers might kill their son and disappear was real. Once he opened it up, he would have no control, others would take over; someone could make a big mistake and spook the kidnappers. But if he waited *too* long to get help...

"If I don't do better tomorrow, I'll pull them in on it."

"What do we tell Neal and Kathleen tonight when Paddy doesn't show again?"

"We'll tell them that he's with Frank that they're working together on a very big job so Paddy's sleeping over there."

The tears started. "And tomorrow?"

He held her close. "I'll tell them the truth."


The next morning, he walked Neal and Kathleen to school. They didn't ask about Paddy, believing that he was with Frank, but they were very curious as to why their father was walking them to school again. Kathleen asked, "We noticed a patrolman behind us when we came home for lunch yesterday. Will he be there again today?"

"Yes."

"Why?"

"It has to do with the strike. I'm involved, and it never hurts to take extra precautions. Besides, I enjoy being with my children. And that patrolman has nothing better to do."

"Oh."

Hoping to divert their attention, he asked, "Are they making any plans for a Valentine's Day party at the school?"

Neal said, "Kathleen thinks she's going to get a card from Tommy Mahoney."

She tried to hit him on his shoulder, but he ducked.


Amos stood with his arms folded near the stairwell just inside the front door at the station house, waiting until Kerrigan noticed him and nodded, indicating that Casey was downstairs in the boiler room. He turned and descended.

"Good morning, Michael. Anything going on at Pitman's?"

"Except for getting in out of the cold now and then, I was there all day. Nothing seemed the least out of the ordinary. How was your day?"

"I've got one thing to follow up. But I'm thinking I should open it up and call in the State Police."

"That's probably best—get more people looking. What's the follow up?"

Amos told him of his visit with Petrella. When he spoke of the Serbians and the black Cadillac, Casey stopped him.

"Now, here's something. You know Ian McQuillan, he's only been in the department for a year and he rents a place somewhere on Franklin Street from a Jew named Gottlieb, who lives downstairs. Ian patrols the railroad yards in South Lawrence. Gottlieb owns a warehouse there. Ian keeps an eye on it for him and he kids Gottlieb about reducing his rent. Anyway, I bump into Ian yesterday in South Lawrence, and he tells me

167

about seeing this big Cadillac parked outside Gottlieb's warehouse. He slags Gottlieb about being so rich all of a sudden, and Gottlieb tells him he rented the warehouse to some guys from out of town for meetings."

Amos hung on every word as Casey spoke, pacing around the small space available in the boiler room. "Get a hold of McQuillan. Find out which warehouse and check it out without being seen. Tell McQuillan to stay away from there, and you meet me back here at two. I'll find Gottlieb and see what he can tell me about his warehouse renters."

After Casey left, Amos went upstairs to ask Kerrigan for McQuillan's address.

"Ah, Amos, any news?"

"I've got only one lead to follow. I need Ian McQuillan's address. His landlord lives downstairs. I need to talk to him."

Kerrigan reached under his desk to pull out a large ledger book. Before opening it, he leaned toward Amos. "I've got some news for you. Paul Martin asked me this morning why you weren't putting it out about Paddy. He knows he's been snatched."

"Shit. It will be all over. I don't have much time."

Kerrigan opened the book and scanned down a page. "He's on Franklin at Tremont—northwest corner."

Amos took a streetcar to Broadway and another up Broadway to Tremont where he walked over to Franklin Street. The two-story house on the corner was painted medium-gray with white trim. There was a small porch, and a single entrance indicated that the house had originally been built as a single family dwelling. Amos went to the door and turned the thumb piece attached to a rotary bell on the inside. He heard footsteps and then somebody struggling to undo the latch and open the door. A small, heavy-set woman looked up at him with a quizzical expression.

"Mrs. Gottlieb?"

She nodded. He identified himself and showed his badge. He noticed small shakes of her head. "I need to speak to Mister Gottlieb."

The head shaking became more pronounced. "Not here," she said, with a pronounced eastern-European accent.

He'd seen it before—an instinctive fear of police—an avoidance at almost any cost, even at times when he was trying his damnedest to help. This time, it was he who needed help; Gottlieb was the only prospect he had. He reached into his pocket and pulled out one of Frank's pictures of Paddy.

"This is my son. He's missing."

She looked at the picture but said nothing.

"My wife and I are going crazy with worry. He's a fine young man. He works hard and he's very good to his younger brother and sister. We're afraid that something has happened to him, and your husband may be able to help."

She nodded and stepped back, "He went to Post Office. You come in and wait."

She took his hat and coat. "It's so cold today. I give you some soup."

He started to protest.

"We have plenty. It will warm you. Come to kitchen."

He followed her as she passed through the living room. He paused in front of an array of framed photographs, including a few daguerreotypes. The topmost one contained a dark-haired, mustachioed man holding a violin in a classic pose. He peered close, and she came back. "My father," she said, "You should have heard him play. It was food for the spirit."

"The violin is such a beautiful, expressive instrument. I'd like our youngest son to take lessons, but I don't know how long he'd keep at it."

169

"You must love it. So many hours, practice, practice, practice. But in the end…"

He sat at a small, finely-finished table in the center of the room from where he observed a shelf loaded with knickknacks, including a gilded tea set.

She set a bowl of soup in front of him and noticed his interest in the shelf. "From my mother." She said. "It's all I have from her."

He looked down to see that, along with the soup, she had served him what looked like a shiny donut.

"That's a bagel. Eat it with the soup."

He picked up the spoon and tasted the soup. "It's delicious."

"I make it special. Since when is your son missing?"

"Since Sunday night. He's been abducted."

"Abducted?"

He took out the note and offered it to her. She took it and then went rummaging through a box near the stove, finally producing eyeglasses with one earpiece missing. She read the note. "This has to be kept a secret?"

He nodded. "Some people have found out. I don't have much time."

She handed the note back. "Ziggy will help you. Oh, your poor wife, she must be so afraid."

Ziggy turned out to be only about two inches taller than his wife and he surely weighed less. He came into the kitchen, wiping the steam from his glasses with a handkerchief. When he saw Amos, he pulled his head up and, putting the glasses back on, looked at Amos again and then at his wife.

"This is Inspector Flameagain. His son has been abducted. He needs your help. Here, Ziggy, sit down and tell the man what he wants."

Without a word, Ziggy sat down, gazing at Amos and waiting.

"It's true. He's been abducted; I think it has something to do with the strike." He handed the note to Gottlieb and waited while he read it. "The secret's out. I'm out of time and I don't have much to go on. I need your help, Mister Gottlieb."

Ziggy nodded, and Amos told him the story and how he learned about the Serbians and the Cadillac seen at his warehouse.

"Yes, the Serbians. They came to me, said they wanted the warehouse for meetings—paid me in advance. You think they have your son?"

"It's only a chance. I need to find out."

"They don't look like business people. They have guns; I could see that. You must be very careful, they don't harm your son."

"Yes, very careful."

Gottlieb reached into an inside pocket and pulled out a piece of paper. He unfolded it and examined both sides before spreading it out on the table. He reached into another pocket for a pencil. "Here is what it looks like inside." He drew a rectangle on the paper. Amos leaned forward to watch as Gottlieb continued to draw and explain.

"There is a room inside, like so. It has a coal stove in the middle and windows here and here, but they have been covered from inside. The sliding door to the room is here, and the outside sliding door is here. And here, around in the back, is a small door. I give you the key." He got up and went to a rack of keys hanging next to the door. Selecting one, he brought it over and

171

placed it on top of the paper. He sat down. "You bring it back, please."

Amos picked up the paper and studied the diagram. He folded it, put it in his pocket, and picked up the key. "I'll bring it back."

His wife came to stand next to Ziggy, and they held hands, looking at Amos. He said, "With your son. You bring it back with your son."

She insisted that Amos finish his soup. "You have a big job. You must be ready."

He gobbled it down, although there would be no difficulty getting back in time to meet Casey at two.

\*\*\*\*\*\*\*\*\*\*\*\*\*\*\*\*\*\*\*\*\*\*\*\*\*\*

Paddy went through the motions of drawing some pictures for Boris's benefit. They were terrible--under the best of circumstances, he did not draw well. Now, with Boris watching, he was nervous, scared, and his hands trembled. As he finished a drawing, he tore off the sheet and set it aside. Boris sat with his big, broad, hairy-backed hands folded on his belly. When he lost interest in Paddy's drawing, he pushed his hands out to his front and cracked the knuckles. Then he took out a knife, turned, picked up a piece of wood, and started to whittle.

Paddy had in mind to write a note and place it in the garbage. But what if the garbage guy couldn't read? And even if he could, he probably just took the garbage out and dumped it somewhere without looking at it. How to get his attention? He drew a picture of a man dumping out a garbage can and finding money. Maybe he'd see that and get curious.

172

During a restless night, Paddy thought of another way to get the attention of the garbage man. He still had his pocket watch, and fastened to it was a leather fob with a Saint Patrick's medal attached, a medal he won for a composition he wrote in the eighth grade. In the morning, after his cuffs were off, and Boris was occupied making coffee, he wrote on the back of the garbage man drawing, *$5,* and added his address. Using a pin, which held up his under draws, he attached the fob and medal to the paper and left it on his bunk, covered by two other drawings.

When to put it in the garbage was the question--too early and Boris might find it or cover it over with something else, and when the man came for the garbage, it would be too late. He had not paid close attention the day before but he thought the man did the slops first, then several trips for coal and ashes. His last trip was for the garbage.

The man came for the slops, and shortly after he finished, Paddy heard the car pull up to the front door. There was a knock at the inside door, and Boris opened it. Paddy expected him to go out, have a conversation and come back in with some food, but when he opened the door, a man stepped in. Compared to Boris, the man was small and thin, had a sharp nose, a goatee and mustache. He took off his gloves, hat and coat and then waved fingers at Paddy signaling him to come over to the table. Paddy complied, and the man set out a piece of paper and a pencil in front of him. "You will write a note to your father."

Paddy knew he should keep his mouth shut but he didn't. "Yes, I can ask him to send me some books to read."

The back of the man's hand whipped across Paddy's face, knocking him off the chair. "You will tell him that he must stop looking for you."

Paddy got up. His face felt hot with the sting of the blow and from the anger welling up inside. He judged the distance to the man's crotch, thinking of one swift kick, but the man stepped back and now held a revolver in his hand. Paddy snorted his contempt, and the man stepped forward and brought the barrel of his gun across Paddy's other cheek. This time, Paddy went down with a dull blur moving through his head and the syrupy taste of blood in his mouth.

The man ordered Boris. "Pick him up." And Paddy felt his arms pulled back as Boris raised him to his feet. "Hold him," the man said, as he stepped close and swung a sweeping punch into Paddy's middle. Suddenly, Paddy had no air. He couldn't pull in any air. The man grabbed his hair, pulled him over and kneed him in his face. Paddy heard a crunch, but all he could think about was air. Boris let him drop, and he curled up on the floor desperately pulling in tiny draughts of air.

The little man said, "I hate these Irish bastards. These goddamned smart Irish bastards. Pick him up."

He heard Boris ask, "You want the note, or you want to beat him?"

There was a pause before the man said, "Put him in the chair."

The air came more easily. He put his elbows on the table and took deep breaths as he became aware of the pain throbbing through his entire head. His mouth filled with blood, and his tongue found a molar coming out of its socket in the upper jaw on the left side. Blood dribbled from his nose, down his front and onto the table. A hand reached to slide the paper away from the blood. Another hand placed a pencil in his right hand and slid the paper back. A corner of it found a large drop of blood and began to soak it up.

The man said, "Blood is good. Makes the note more real. You ready?"

Paddy grunted and put his hand and pencil near the top of the paper, smearing a thin layer of blood over the middle of the sheet.

"You write, 'Papa,' 'Father,' whatever you call him."

174

He put his left hand up to hold the paper and wrote, "Father." It seemed so distorted; he didn't recognize his own writing.

"Do not look for me."

He struggled; it was as if he were moving heavy weights instead of a pencil. How could this be so difficult?

"They will kill me if you keep looking."

He wondered at the words appearing on the paper. They looked so strange and seemed to come from some far-off place.

"Sign your name."

He wrote, "Padd…" He ran off the page, and the 'y' wound up on the table.

The man picked up the note. "This is good. The blood gives it a nice touch."

Paddy slumped back in his chair, and his eyes began to focus. The man looked at him and smiled before turning to Boris. "We're moving out of here. I'll be back later." He leaned over Paddy and lifted his chin with his left hand, forcing him to look up at his leering grin. "I have more for you later."

Paddy registered the words without being able to consider the consequences. All he wanted to do was crawl over to his cot. The man left, and Boris watched as Paddy got up and staggered over to sit on the edge of the cot, wondering what to do about all the blood. Boris handed him a rag but said nothing. He dabbed the blood coming from his nose and reached in with a thumb to push the molar back into its socket. Then he pushed back to sit with his back against the wall. The drawings and fob were still there, next to him.

From the table, Boris continued to watch him. Was he smiling? Had he enjoyed the show? He held up a sandwich. How could any human being enjoy seeing another beaten like that? Paddy shook his head and pulled his knees up. He hugged his legs and stared across the room, trying to ignore the pain so he could think.

They were moving out. What did the fob and note matter now? It would be too late; he might as well hand the note to Boris. There was no way to tell where they were going. Probably Boris didn't know either. He looked down, noticing the patch of blood on his shirt. Be a shame to get blood all over the Cadillac. I must be going crazy, he thought. Cadillac. Cadillac. Not many around. William Wood might have one. He turned slowly, and with pain, to his coat, hanging next to his cot. Boris looked up but went back to eating and reading his paper. Paddy fished in a pocket to retrieve a pencil.

With Boris still occupied, he picked up the drawing with the fob attached and wrote on the back, *Going in black Cadillac.* He was surprised at how easy it was to write, and how legible the writing was.

Paddy closed his eyes and tried to doze off, but the pain still throbbed in his head. He did not lie down. Time passed until a knock at the door brought him to alertness. The man had brought a scuttle of coal. Boris gave him one full of ashes and went outside the door to talk to him. When he came back in, Paddy bowed his head, pretending not to notice anything.

He couldn't wait. If Boris found the note and fob, so what? Things couldn't get much worse. He moved to sit on the edge of his cot, waggling his head to see if he was still woozy. After a minute, he stood and walked tentatively to the table where he sat and reached for his sandwich. Breaking off small pieces, he chewed them on the right side of his mouth--even that hurt, and every bite tasted of blood. Boris opened a bottle of root beer and pushed it toward him. He drank half of it and went back to his cot but he did not sit down. He picked up the drawings, fob and all, walked to the table and picked up the remains of his sandwich. From there he went to the garbage where he deposited the sandwich and drawings, carefully placing the critical drawing on top with the fob and medal pinned to its underside. He went to his cot, putting on a bit of extra stagger for Boris's benefit. He had run the course, he sat down; there was nothing he could do but hope and pray and he had already done plenty of both. A strange calm came over him as he wondered what his face looked like. What would it look like the next time he saw Maria? He slid back, drew his knees up and tried to conjure up a vision of her, there was a glorious day coming when he would hold her again and kiss her incredible lips.

A knock at the door. Boris got up and went to the far wall for the garbage.

# CHAPTER SIXTEEN

When Amos left the Gottliebs, he was dying to go straight to the warehouse but he needed Casey and had no way to get word to him. He reached the police station a little before two, Kerrigan motioned him over. "The son-in-law wants to see you."

"Shit, shit! Tell Casey to wait for me."

Sullivan was on the phone when Amos walked in and he was in no hurry to get off. Amos sat with his arms folded, curling and uncurling his toes inside his shoes while he listened to a long-winded conversation about a congressional investigation into the strike. Sullivan finally hung up, pulled on his collar, and turned to him with an exasperated expression. "What have you got for us, Amos?"

"I've got several people talking to some Italian families."

Sullivan smacked his desk and then drummed his fingers. "We need something quick. There's more kids going on Saturday. The mayor, the mill owners, they want to stop them. It's all for the newspapers, they say, all to get money for the unions. The parents can't all be that stupid."

"John, I don't speak Italian. I can't just go busting into the tenements. Even with an interpreter, they wouldn't tell me. My friends understand the situation. They're getting real information"

"Get over there this afternoon. At least get us something to start."

"Uh, yeah, okay, John. I'll let you know."

He left the office and looked at the clock. It was almost two-thirty. Kerrigan signaled that Casey was downstairs. He found him sitting on a stool in the boiler room. "Sorry, Michael."

"How are things with the City Marshall?"

"They're all in a panic over these kids going to New York. They want to know if the parents approve."

"I can answer that."

"Paddy comes first. Did you find the warehouse?"

"I did, and a big black Cadillac came and went while I was there."

"Let's get over there. We need to know if Paddy's in there, or not."

"I'll leave first and wait for you on Essex Street."

"The hell with that. Let's go."

Constructed of heavy rough-finished wooden planks, the warehouse was one of several single-storied, flat roofed, buildings on Easton Street, a short service road running parallel to the tracks in the nearby railroad yard. A loading platform with steps on one side was located at the center of the front wall and it was covered by a sloping roof. The sliding door at the back of the platform was the only entrance on that side. Amos and Casey peered at it from behind the corner of a building across the street.

Casey said, "I went around, looking in all the windows. It looks like there are stacks of lumber in most of it, but the windows on that end are covered up from the inside."

Amos showed him Gottlieb's sketch. "That's where the room is."

"There's somebody in there. You can see the smoke from the stove."

"Yeah, but who?" Amos looked up and down the street. "C'mon." He headed across.

Just as they got to the corner of the warehouse and were about to go around to the back, the front door slid open, and a

180

small figure stepped out carrying a box. They waited as he came in their direction. Casey stepped into his path. "Come over here for a minute."

Amos watched as the man's eye's opened in a look of fear. He was about sixty years old, thin, unkempt, probably just scraping by doing errands and odd-jobs. He followed Casey, and all three of them grouped around the corner, out of sight.

Amos asked, "What's your name?"

"Scotty."

"What have you got there, Scotty?"

"It's the garbage. I'm taking out the garbage."

"How many are in there?"

"I don't know."

"You don't know?"

"I bring coal. I take away the garbage, the ashes, and the slops but I never get inside the room." Scotty was starting to shake.

"Take it easy, Scotty. This is not about you. You haven't done anything wrong, we just need information. You say you take out the slops—they must be living in there."

Scotty nodded. "Somebody else brings the food."

Casey asked, "You can't tell from the garbage, how many?"

Scotty shrugged. He was still holding the box.

Amos said, "Set it down. We'll have a look."

Amos looked at the drawing, still sitting on top. It meant nothing until he picked it up. The weight of it told him to turn it over. He read the note and handed it to Casey. He rummaged through the rest of the garbage. "Can't be more than three people in there."

Scotty said, "They're leaving today. This is my last trip."

"Thanks, Scotty. You can go. You've been very helpful."

Scotty picked up the box and ambled off. Amos and Casey stood, staring at the fob and medal in Casey's hand. Amos nodded. "It's Paddy's. You go for help. I'll stay here."

Casey stepped to the corner and peeked around to the front. "It's too late—they're here."

Amos peeked and saw a black Cadillac coming toward them. He turned and they headed around to the back door where Amos produced the key and removed the padlock. He opened the door a crack, and they listened as the front door slid open and closed. "How many did you see in the car?"

"Two. Just two," Casey said.

They heard a knock and the inside door opened and closed.

"Let's go." He led Casey inside and closed the door. "The driver may be still outside. You go by the front door."

It was that time on a winter's afternoon when the light fades quickly, but there was still enough coming through the dust and soot covered windows to see the stacks of lumber and to get around without bumping into things. To his left a beam of sunlight shone through, illuminating slow-moving dust motes, Amos cocked his revolver and positioned himself near the inside door on his right. He heard voices and scraping sounds as objects were moved around inside the room. One voice, Paddy's, said, "Ow. You son-of-a-bitch."

Another voice, "Move, you Irish shithead."

More movement and the door slid open. Light shone from inside, and a thin, well-dressed man stepped out. As he turned around, the room light on his face revealed a black goatee and mustache. He ordered someone inside, "If he doesn't move fast enough, kick the bastard." He turned to go and another figure appeared in the light--Paddy, bent and bloody, his hands manacled in front of him, peered into the dark.

Amos felt the juices boiling up inside; his son had been beaten; his son was injured. He raised his revolver and whispered. "Dear God, please help me." Bending his knees, both hands on the revolver, he took a deep breath and tried to steady his aim, a torrent of thoughts ringing through his head. When Paddy was about five years old, he became fascinated with Amos's revolver. Amos wanted to minimize his interest but also to teach him something about guns and the danger they represent. He taught Paddy to drop to the floor whenever he saw the gun. He made a game of it and sometimes made Paddy demonstrate for one of his colleagues. He yelled, "Paddy drop.", and Paddy did. One day, Paddy yelled, "Amos drop.", and Amos did. It became a running joke for both of them. Paddy would remember.

Paddy stepped forward behind the first man. The light went out and a third man, a huge man, carrying a bundle, stepped into the gloom. Amos steadied and yelled, "Paddy drop." The big man dropped his bundle and turned toward him, a revolver in his hand. Amos squeezed the trigger, felt the jolt against his palm as the roar blotted out all other senses. With both hands, he steadied the revolver for a second shot but held back as the big man collapsed. He looked for Paddy. A second roar came from the thin man's gun, and Amos froze as a bullet thwacked into some lumber near his head. He bent and moved ahead, squinting into the near-dark; he had to reach Paddy. Another roar, and Amos stiffened; he could almost feel the bullet coming his way. The next sound came from Casey. "I got him, Amos."

Amos moved forward to make sure that the Serbians were down for good. He found the big man with a stream of blood pouring out of his chest. He reached down to pick up the revolver. Paddy, who still was lying on the floor, spoke. "Get the key, Da. It's in his breast pocket." He ignored Paddy and stepped past him to check on the thin man, lying face down in a pool of blood. He couldn't find the man's gun. "I've got it, Da."

He returned to the big man and was reaching for the key when he heard the front door slide open. The engine of the car out front revved up, and another shot roared through the building. The engine went quiet. "Him too," Casey yelled.

Paddy stood up, and Amos removed his cuffs, getting a good look at his son for the first time. He looked away, not wanting to show the sick feeling that quickly pushed out the excitement of moments earlier.

Paddy said, "I'm grand, Da. You can clean me up before Mom sees me."

Amos looked down, fighting back the tears and the burn in his throat.

"Thanks for finding me."

Amos kissed his son, blood and all. He didn't think he was crying but he noticed the wet on his cheeks, he held Paddy back, patted him softly and let him go.

Casey conducted his own examination of the bodies on the floor. "I imagine that Sullivan will be disappointed with our afternoon's work." He looked at Paddy. "Mother of Jesus."

Amos asked, "Is there another body outside?"

"Yeah, in the car."

"Anybody around? Scotty?"

"I didn't see a soul."

The two men looked at each other. Paddy turned from one to the other, trying to understand the thrust of their words.

Casey said, "It would make nailing Pitman a lot easier. He'll be scared out of his wits from not knowing what happened, or where these guys are."

Amos said, "Only Kerrigan and Gottlieb know we're here. I think Gottlieb will be okay. I won't need to tell him much. Jimmy will understand, and we can clean up the blood in here."

Paddy understood. "Are you just going to dump them?"

Casey said, "I'm thinking the river."

Amos nodded. "I'll drive."

Paddy said, "I know a spot. Very secluded. There's an old dock; nobody ever uses it."

Amos turned to him. "I don't want you involved in any way."

"Da, I learned from you. We both know, I'm already involved."

Amos looked to Casey and back to Paddy. "Let's get it over with."


It was easy to move the thin man outside and onto the floor in the rear of the car, and the driver, while a little heavier, needed only to be moved to the rear from the front seat where Casey had shot him. They propped him up to one side of the seat with his hat tipped over his eyes so he'd look like a sleeping passenger. Boris was a problem. It took all three of them to drag his body out onto the loading platform. Amos had some difficulties but he managed to position the car so that they were able to slide Boris off the platform and flop him into the car in one continuous movement.

Casey got in the back where he removed his helmet and sat well back so that it would be difficult to see him. He managed to get one foot on the floor, but the other rested on Boris's chest. Amos, with his hat pulled down and collar up, drove the car while Paddy sat in the passenger's seat, holding his coat collar up around his face.

It was getting dark, very few people were out on the street, but tradesmen and workers were heading home, many of them driving horse-drawn wagons and carts. The Cadillac would stand out anywhere in Lawrence and especially in South Lawrence. But, in the dim light, few would notice, and it would take a sharp eye to spot the hole made by Casey's bullet in the passenger-side window. Even so, Paddy cringed every time he noticed someone looking in their direction. He prayed that Amos wouldn't stall the car or bang into something. He gave directions. "Go up South Union Street and turn right on Merrimack, toward North Andover."

They passed the, nearly two thousand foot long, Wood Mill, where the car seemed less conspicuous, and finally crossed the line into North Andover. Amos had not logged that many hours behind the wheel of an automobile, Paddy probably could have done a better job, but the big car tolerated his mistakes. He turned left off Sutton Street, toward the river. It was getting dark, and they did not know how to turn on the headlamps, but Amos got to the river without stalling or hitting anything. Once there, Amos and Casey got out to examine the dock; walking on it, they stomped their feet and bent to inspect the boards. Constructed of light timber, apparently intended for landing small boats and not to support heavy loads, it showed signs of age and weather damage.

Casey shook his head. "Oh, Amos, I don't think I'd be wanting to drive a car out onto this."

Amos looked to the sides where winter-browned grass and weeds grew to the river's edge. "I can't drive it on the bank; it will bog down in the mud before the wheels are covered."

"Maybe we should just leave it in the woods somewhere."

"It's got to disappear, or our story won't hold up. Too many people are involved."

Paddy slipped up behind them. "I know what to do. I saw a guy do it in the flickers."

The two men waited for the rest.

Paddy continued. "I get the car going and I leap out just before it goes out onto the dock."

Casey turned to Amos. "He's not having us on?"

Amos stared at his son. "You're in no condition to be attempting something like that."

"I'm bloodied up, Da, but I'm all right. And I'm much faster than you are."

Amos bent his head and put his hand up to his forehead. "I can't let you do this, Paddy. Why don't you show me what to do?"

"Da, I'm quick. I've been doing more driving than you have. I know I can get out on time."

Amos looked to Casey, who said, "If Paddy's sure he can do it. I believe he can."

Paddy turned and went back to the car. Casey said, "I'll be next to the dock, Lad, I'll catch you."

Paddy started the car and backed up to get it aligned to the dock. Amos looked out over the water where ice floes jammed the surface. How could Paddy get to the surface and swim through that if he went down with the car? He changed his mind and turned around to stop Paddy, but it was too late; the car roared out of the gloom, picking up speed as it headed for the dock. With one hand on the steering wheel, the other holding the door ajar, Paddy looked like a wild man. Amos's hands went to his head. "Please, dear God, just this one more time."

On the last dip down the hill before reaching the dock, the car picked up more speed, and Paddy came rolling and tumbling out. He crashed into Casey's legs and they both slid farther down the bank. Amos didn't even watch the car. He ran down the bank after Paddy and Casey. Paddy said, "Are you all right, Casey?"

"I'm a bit wet." He got up, moving his parts. "I think that's all."

187

Paddy, now up and feeling a little euphoric, said, "Nice catch. Thanks."

Amos, almost limp with relief, looked to see what happened to the car. They all turned to see it held afloat by ice and moving slowly downstream.

Casey muttered, "They're going to Haverhill."

Amos said, "This can't be."

They watched in silence as the car floated beyond reach. And then each of them caught his breath as the ice tipped slightly, and the car gently slipped, disappearing below the ice-strewn surface.

Casey said, "This has been a day."

Amos said, "I'll bring the lad home to his mother. Could you stop by the station and tell Kerrigan we've got him and I'll explain everything tomorrow?"

For a moment, they stood, a tight little band in the gathering twilight and looked at each other in silent recognition of the bond they felt, then turning they trudged up the bank and headed for home. No one spoke.

********************

There was a knock at the front door. Molly jumped to answer it. Heartsick with worry for Paddy, she had accomplished next to nothing all day. The children were due home from school. Could it be the policeman assigned to accompany them?

There was no one at the door, and she could see no one departing. Opening the door to take a better look, she found an envelope as it dropped to the floor. It was not mail; that came earlier. There was no address, no marking of any kind. She

188

closed the door and, now worried about Neal and Kathleen, she opened the envelope and, when she saw the blood, groped for a place to sit. She could barely breathe as she read the note from Paddy. She had to tell Amos, but where were the children? She put the note back into its envelope and got dressed to go out. She tried to stay away from the window as she prayed for the children to get home but she remained glued to it, staring out as if her eyes could pull Neal and Kathleen down the street.

Finally, she saw them, strolling along, not a care in the world. She wanted to yell to them—"Run.", but that might get them upset, especially went she raced out of the door as soon as they got in.

She told them that she had to meet Amos. It couldn't wait. She'd explain later.

"Is it about Paddy?" Kathleen asked.

"It might be. I'll explain later." She was out the door before they could react.

She boarded a streetcar on South Broadway and headed for the police station. It would take about twenty minutes—an eternity. They'd have to find Amos. But perhaps they wouldn't know where he was. Should she just go home? Hadn't he said that he'd turn matters over to the state police if he didn't get results today? Suppose he was already on his way home? She'd miss him, and he wouldn't know about the note.

At the station house, she practically ran up the steps, stormed in the door and made a bee-line for the desk. Kerrigan looked up, clearly surprised at the sight of her racing toward him. "Molly, how nice to see you."

"Jimmy, can you get a hold of Amos?" she said, almost gasping for air.

"I can, but he's due here shortly." He looked her over, quizzically. "He and Casey are working on something special."

"Well, I've got something special." She pulled the note from her bag and handed it to him.

He held it under his desk while he read it. "This is very upsetting."

"Upsetting?" She almost yelled it out.

He bent forward. "Molly, for Paddy's safety, we're trying to keep this thing close."

"Jimmy, I'm afraid we have no time for that. Amos said that he would involve the rest of the department and the state police if he didn't find Paddy today."

"Yes, well as soon as he comes in, I'll get things moving."

"Jimmy, this is my son. I want things moving now. A minute's delay could be critical."

"Of course, Molly, you've got every right. I'll do it."

She didn't move.

"And Neal and Kathleen, they're fine?"

She turned and ran out the door. Kerrigan sighed and slowly pulled out a fresh sheet of paper. He'd wait a bit longer for Amos—but not much longer.

# CHAPTER SEVENTEEN

On Merrimack Street, well away from the river, Casey flagged down a delivery wagon and they all got in the back for a ride over to Essex Street where Amos and Paddy boarded a streetcar for home, and Casey went on to see Kerrigan at the police station. Paddy drew a few stares on the streetcar, but he didn't recognize anyone. Amos toyed with the idea of stopping at Jack's Pub to get Paddy cleaned up, but the fewer who knew about his condition the less explaining later.

They paused at the front door. "Let your mother see me first. I'll explain a little before she sees you."

Paddy bent to hide behind his da as they went in and down the hall. Molly, a wild look in her eyes, roared toward them. "Amos, where in God's name have you been. I've been frantic."

He held up his hands. "Yes, Molly, it's been a terrible strain, but…"

"Do you see what I have?" She shoved the note onto him.

He looked past her to see Neal and Kathleen peeking out of the kitchen with frightened eyes. He didn't look at the note. "It's all right, Molly. It's over."

"Over?" She looked as though her knees might be buckling.

He reached to hold her. "He's here. He's right with me."

She held onto Amos for support and stared over his shoulder at Paddy. "Oh, my God. Oh, dear God."

"I'm all right, Mom. I need a bath, that's all."

191

She slipped from Amos to hold Paddy.

"Easy, Mom, it hurts a little."

"I'll get your clothes." She looked down the hall. "Kathleen, go draw a bath for your brother."

While Paddy was in the bathroom, Amos explained to the children. "Paddy was attacked by some bad men—some strikers, we think. I found him in an alley."

Neal said, "But you said he was with Frank."

Amos took a deep breath. "I know. I didn't know what to tell you. I lied."

Kathleen reached across the kitchen table to put her hand on his. "It's all right, Da. You must have been terribly worried." He looked to Molly, who said nothing as she went quietly about the business of feeding her family. Paddy reappeared, wearing a towel like a scarf to cover the lower part of his face. They all tried not to stare and to pretend that everything was normal, all except Molly, that is; her eyes went to him at every opportunity. She and Amos exchanged frequent looks, each sensing the other's pain. Paddy went to bed right after supper, and Amos read to the children; first a King Arthur story for Neal and then from a biography of Abraham Lincoln for Kathleen.

How would he explain the shootings and dumping of the bodies to Molly? Things were such a jumble in his head--had he botched the whole thing? Was it all a grotesque mistake, actions taken in the heat of the moment, taken in revenge at the sight of his son covered with blood?

All was quiet when they sat across the kitchen table, she, with her hands folded in her lap, saying, "Well?"

"The story we tell is what I told the kids. Here's what actually happened." When he finished, she asked, "Am I to understand that you did not involve the entire department and the state police because you wanted to catch the higher-ups?"

192

"No, I did that because I knew that these men cared nothing for Paddy's life. One clumsy cop stumbling onto them might have caused them to dump Paddy in the river and get out of town. I only wanted a few men, men I knew I could trust, to know. Dumping the bodies was to catch the higher-ups."

"They would have killed him wouldn't they?"

"Yes."

She sat without saying anything for a moment. "Amos, I was frantic when that bloody note came. I went to Jimmy Kerrigan…" She told him the rest.

"Casey went to see Jimmy. He'll know what to do."

She reached across the table, and for a moment, they held hands.

She pulled her hand back and said, "I've never experienced anything like this. I was so sick with worry for Paddy, it affected my thinking. I couldn't think."

He smiled. "You're not the only one with that problem. Dumping those bodies… It could turn out to be a big mistake."

"And do you know what he's worried about?"

"Paddy?"

"He's worried about how he's going to look when he sees Maria."

"Hmm. Her father told me he's going to forbid her seeing him again."

"Oh, Amos, you should tell him."

Amos put his knuckles up to his chin in a thoughtful pose. "I don't think so. For one thing, Petrella might not do it. Or he might tell her she can see him one more time. I don't want to interfere."

"Paddy's going to be devastated."

"Yeah."

They sat in silence, each thinking of their son, his pain, and that to come.

Amos left early the next morning with a bucket, a jug of water, rags, some bleach, a flashlight and a scrubbing brush all in a sack. It was still dark and quite cold; he encountered only a few people on his way to the warehouse where he let himself in and used his flashlight to get around. In the room where Paddy had been held, he found a kerosene lantern. He used it to look around the room for any signs of Paddy's presence. Finding none, he put some water and bleach into the bucket and went to where the big man fell the day before. He managed to reduce the blood stain to where it was barely noticeable. Then, using a broom he'd found in the first room, he swept some dirt over it and ground it in with his feet.

The second blood stain was much smaller. After working on it for fifteen minutes, Amos decided to hide the remainder by moving a stack of wood over it. That took longer, and he was feeling well warmed by the time he finished. He took his time, looking for any other evidence of what had transpired the previous day, he could find no sign of the bullet, that missed his head—lost in the stacks of wood. Back outside, he locked the door and searched for a convenient place to ditch his sack of supplies. A short walk to the railroad yards and a slow-moving freight train with empty coal cars solved his problem.

It was still too early to catch Kerrigan at the station so he stopped for breakfast at a tiny place frequented by railroad workers. In the steamy, smoky, interior, he felt anonymous. From there, he went to Lamastro's home; Joe and Connie were still wearing bathrobes but they assured him that he hadn't wakened them and offered him some coffee. Inside, he removed his coat and stood at his customary place at their kitchen table.

"We've got Paddy back," he said.

Joe shook his hand and patted his back, and Connie hugged him, wetting his shoulder with her tears.

"There's more," he said, sitting down. "And you've got to really keep this a secret."

They listened as he related most of what happened. He skipped over the part dealing with the kidnappers, and what he had done. "If you don't know about it, you won't have to lie." He then told them the story he was putting out about Paddy having been beaten by strikers.

"Do you want me to talk to Alessandro?" Joe asked.

"Will he keep it a secret?"

"We Italians have been keeping secrets for centuries. Besides, he'll be going back to Italy soon."

"I haven't told Paddy about that yet. He's worried about how he's going to look when he sees her."

Connie said, "Oh, Amos, I wish there was something we could do."

"Yeah. All part of growing up, I guess." He drained the last of his coffee. "Well, I've got to go give the key back to the guy who owns the warehouse."

Connie said, "Before you go I have some information. I've spoken to several Italian families, especially the mothers of children gone to New York. They're distraught. I don't think there is one of them who would do it again, and they want their children back as soon as possible. I saw some letters from children; they're heart rending."

He nodded as he listened. "Thanks, Connie. You know, I've almost completely forgotten the other things I'm supposed to be working on. Even Pitman doesn't seem important anymore, but I'm going to nail that bastard." He got up to go.

Connie gave him a hug. "Our love to Paddy."

Joe put a hand on his back and saw him to the door. "Perspective, Amos. You've always been good at that. It's one of your strengths. Don't focus too hard on Pitman."

At the door, Amos said, "Thanks for everything, Joe. And you're right; I've got to keep my wits about me."

From Lamastro's, he went to the Pacific Mill to tell the story of finding Paddy to Kevin O'Shay, Paddy's boss. "He'll be right as rain in a few days."

O'Shay thanked him and promised, "I'll see that he doesn't overdo the work here. Tell him not to rush things."

Next, Amos called on the Gottliebs. He returned the key and told them he'd found the place empty. He also told them that he'd found his son, badly beaten by strikers, and he promised to bring Paddy by when he was feeling better. As he left, a glance at his watch told him it was time to see Kerrigan.

Casey had already told Kerrigan the gist of what happened. He listened to Amos, adding frequent reassurances of secrecy and then asked, "And Paddy? Is he all right?"

"He's more worried about how he'll look to his lady friend than about himself."

"That's good, but this is not a good day, Amos. The son-in-law wants to see you."

"He doesn't know about the warehouse, does he?"

"No, it's another matter—Wilcox."

"Ah."

"He shot his son to death."

He stared at Kerrigan. It took time to sink in.

"You've had a lot on your plate, Amos. And I told Sullivan you've been working on Wilcox right along. But still, this will be embarrassing. Maybe there'll be some strike news to distract the newspapers. Charlie Vose has the case now."

Amos stood there feeling stunned and then slowly turned toward Sullivan's office. He entered, and Sullivan told him to shut the door and take a seat. When Amos was settled, Sullivan tapped his desk lightly and leaned forward.

"I don't know where to begin, Amos. You've been of little help on the strike. In fact, going after Pitman on this dynamite thing is just making matters worse. It's not a crime to give your undertaker friend a few sticks of dynamite and not ask any questions."

"It's a bit more serious than that, John."

"You're going after the wrong guys, Amos. It's like arresting the tellers after a bank robbery. But that's not what I want to talk about. Did Jimmy tell you about Wilcox?"

"He did."

"And you had this guy in here. How are we going to explain that? We had him and we let the lunatic go?"

"I've got his lawyer's name. There was supposed to be a formal arrangement, keeping him away from his wife and kid."

"I know all about that. But the kid is dead, and the wife is ready for a nut house."

"I know."

"Listen, Amos, I heard about Paddy. That had to be a distraction. I'll explain it to Con. Maybe we can squash this thing. Take some time. Try to stay out of trouble."

"I will. Do you want to hear about the mothers of those kids?"

Sullivan leaned back, pulled at his collar and took a deep breath. "Sure. Why not?"

Amos told him what he learned from Connie. "I think there's good reason to believe that the Wobblies don't give a damn about the kids, or their mothers. They're doing it to put on a show for the newspapers."

197

"Now you're talking. Maybe we can use this."

"It would be nice if somebody was looking out for the kids."

"Yeah, well, right now you've got your own problem. And it's a big one."

# CHAPTER EIGHTEEN

Paddy got up that morning feeling pain with even the simplest of movements. Molly was solicitous, offering to draw him a hot bath right after breakfast. She told him what Amos planned to do that day and how he planned to blame Paddy's disappearance and beating on a gang of striker hoodlums. "He said that if you're up to it, we can ask Frank to come over, so you can explain what we're doing. Frank knows the truth, of course, about the kidnapping but nothing about the rest of it. You should keep it that way."

When Neal came home from school, Molly sent him to Frank's with a note, asking him to come over, and when he arrived later that afternoon, Molly sent him up to Paddy's room.

Paddy sat next to the window overlooking the street. "I saw you coming up the street."

Frank stepped just inside the door. "My God, Paddy. My God."

"I look pretty bad, don't I?"

"What happened?" He sat on the edge of the bed.

"First, I'll tell you the official story and then I'll tell you the truth." Paddy proceeded to the story of hoodlum strikers beating him up and then told him about the kidnappers. He did not tell him about the shooting or its aftermath.

"How did you get away?"

"My da rescued me."

"And the kidnappers?"

Paddy said nothing, he gazed at his friend. "You're my best friend, Frank."

"Okay, I get it, there were no kidnappers. Right?"

"Right, there were no kidnappers. The story is what I told you about hoodlum strikers"

"When do you think you'll get back to work?"

"I wanted to talk to you about that."

Frank laughed.

Paddy said, "I'm thinking maybe I won't go back to the mill."

"Good. Maybe you can come into the photography business with me. We can be partners. There's not much money in it yet, but we can build it up."

"Would you close the door?"

Frank got up and quietly closed the door. He sat back down. "You're not thinking of joining the Navy, or anything?"

Paddy smiled and then put his hand up because it hurt. "I'm thinking of going to Boston to work for my grand da and I'm going to ask Maria to marry me."

"That's a big bite. A lot could go wrong—her family—your family. Does anybody know about this marriage but me?"

"Not even Maria knows yet."

Frank grinned and shook his head. "Wow. Are you going to wait until you look better, or are you going to ask her soon?"

"I'm going to ask her this Sunday."

"Well, I guess if she really loves you, it won't matter what you look like, or when you ask her."

There was a gentle knock on the door. Kathleen stuck her head in. "Mum wants to know if you two would like a cup of tea?"

Paddy nodded. "Stay for a bit, Frank. We can talk about something else."

Kathleen left, and Frank leaned forward, grinning. "We can talk about your wedding pictures."

\*\*\*\*\*\*\*\*\*\*\*\*\*\*\*\*\*\*\*\*\*\*\*\*

Amos was glad to get away from Sullivan. The enormity of the Wilcox murder weighed on every part of him, crowding against his need to concentrate on covering up the shooting and body dumping of the previous day. And what was all that for? To avenge Paddy? To take revenge for the kidnapping and beating, and somehow to get the higher-ups responsible— Pitman, and maybe William Wood? Was any of it that important any more? Sure, Paddy was important. But the rest of it? And Wilcox, that goddamned son-of-a-bitch, slipping between the cracks like a cockroach. He killed his kid. Paddy Flanagan was alive, but William Wilcox was dead, and Amos might just as well have pulled the trigger himself.

He entered Judge Waters's office with no sense of how he got there. Billy Conboy, looking as twitchy and scaly skinned as ever, greeted him. "Ah, Amos, what is it I can do for you today?"

"I need to see the Judge."

"Yes, of course. Is it something that I might be able to assist you with?"

"I'm afraid not, Billy. I need to deal with the Judge directly on this."

"He'll be asking me what it's about."

"This would be for the Judge's ears only, Billy. Please tell him that."

"He won't like it, but I'll tell him. Before you go, Amos, is Paddy all right?"

"He's a bit the worse for wear but he's young."

201

"I heard he was missing for a while?"

Amos felt an edginess building into anger. He did not want to be drawn out by Conboy. The man might be completely innocent of any kind of involvement in the flow of information about Pitman and not have any idea of Paddy's abduction, but the less he knew, the better. "Yeah, he was." He turned to leave before Conboy could ask any more questions and bumped into Judge Waters.

"Amos, good to see you. Did Billy take care of you?"

"I've just told him that I need to see you privately."

John Waters, a tall man, he held himself erect in spite of his advancing years. The narrowness of his face and features were accentuated by a full head of white hair. He neither drank nor smoked, and the sharp glitter of his blue eyes made lawyers think twice before answering his questions.

He pulled out his pocket watch and held it almost at arm's length. "Now's as good a time as any."

Amos followed Waters into his office and closed the door. The judge hung his hat and coat on a rack and turned, motioning Amos to a wooden arm-chair with a leather padded seat while he sat in a tall-backed, swivel-chair behind his desk and pulled out a pair of eye glasses, proceeding to hurr and clean them with his handkerchief. While doing this, he nodded for Amos to begin.

"It's about the dynamite plot, Your Honor."

Waters finished putting on his glasses and leaned forward. "Amos, we're not in a courtroom. I know you for a good and honest man. Call me John. Now, what about the dynamite plot?"

"You know about Breen. It was Ernest Pitman who delivered the dynamite to his funeral home, and I have a witness who overheard Pitman bragging about doing it at the behest of William Wood."

At the mention of William Wood, Waters straightened and sat back into his chair.

Amos continued. "Just as I was about to go after Pitman, the information seems to have leaked out. My son, Paddy, was badly beaten by hoodlums. I've been telling everyone that they were just striker hoodlums, but I suspect they were sent by Pitman, or maybe even Wood, as a warning to me."

"I needn't tell you, Amos, this is a very serious situation. What do you propose to do?"

"Arrest Pitman and lean on him for what it takes to get the higher-ups, whoever they may be."

Waters, arms folded, gazed out the window. "Nasty day, isn't it?"

Amos waited.

"You know, as a judge, I'm not supposed to have any opinion, or to intervene in any way, but there is the little matter of the strike that's going on. What are you sentiments on it, Amos?"

"Well, John, as a policeman, I'm not supposed to have any. But I do believe the workers need to have their lot improved."

Waters smiled at the 'policeman' comment and then said, "As do I. But we both know that Lawrence is only viable for as long as the mills are prosperous."

"Agreed, but right now we have too much prosperity at the expense of intolerable poverty."

"It's important that we not interfere in the give and take between the strikers and mill owners."

Amos thought about that. It made complete sense, but his heart said otherwise.

Waters added, "I wouldn't think it amiss if the owners felt a bit more urgency to get on with it. If you take my meaning?"

"You mean if they thought that this dynamite thing and Paddy's beating might be in the papers, they'd want to end the strike in a hurry?"

"Oh, Amos, for shame."

"We policemen have devious minds."

Waters grinned. "And some judges are such hypocrites. I'll give you a warrant." He opened a drawer and pulled out a form. "But you'll just be wanting to ask a few questions for now. Arrest him later."

"Do you want to know what's going on?"

"Go ahead on your own. But if you need me, you know where I live. Be discrete. I'll tell Eileen that you may come by."

Amos folded the warrant and put it in his pocket. They shook hands and he was out the door, waving to a concerned-looking Billy Conboy.

Given the way confidential information seemed to get into the wrong hands, he decided to go directly to Pitman's construction company in South Lawrence. He went alone and arrived just before noon. If the secretary tried to stall him, he intended to barge into Pitman's office, waving his warrant. He strode quickly across the open yard toward the office door. When he was about ten feet away, Pitman emerged, buttoning his coat, apparently on his way to an appointment. He took no particular notice of Amos until his path was blocked. He had to look up as Amos was a full head taller.

"Ah, Inspector Flanagan, I believe. Sorry I can't stay; I'm on my way to an important meeting."

"It will have to wait. I have a warrant for your arrest."

"Now?"

"Maybe now. Maybe later. It depends on the answers I get to some questions."

Pitman looked around. Several of his men had stopped work to observe the proceedings. "My office then." He turned and Amos followed him inside. Amos noticed the wide-eyed expression of the secretary and her nervous movements as they passed. Was she concerned for her boss? Or was the open magazine on her desk forbidden?

Pitman closed his office door behind them and stood behind his desk. He took off his hat but left his overcoat on. The message was that he was an important man with only moments to spare. Amos removed his own coat, took out his notebook and sat down. He looked up at Pitman but said nothing. Pitman heaved a sigh and sat down.

"Mister Pitman, I came here initially on the matter of the dynamite, which was discovered at the Syrian tailor shop, where it was apparently planted by John Breen. Now, I have a bigger concern."

"I know nothing about any dynamite."

"Ah, but you know everything about it. We have two eye witnesses to the delivery of that dynamite to John Breen."

"Even if you do, it's not a serious matter."

"But kidnapping is."

"What are you talking about?"

"Do you have any idea of where the Serbians are, or of what they've told me?"

"Serbians? I don't know any Serbians."

"They know you. Listen, it's clear that you were working for higher-ups on the dynamite business. You give me the connection to Mister 'W'. Then I'll see if I can disappear the Serbians."

"You're talking nonsense."

"It's up to you, Mister Pitman." Amos stood up and leaned across Pitman's desk, grabbing his coat collar and pulling him forward. "In the meantime, if there should be the slightest move against any member of my family—even if you have nothing to do with it—I'm going to kill you." His face was so close, he could smell Pitman's shaving lotion.

Pitman's mouth opened. He stared up at Amos without a word.

Amos kept his face close to Pitman's. "Mister Pitman, do we have complete understanding?"

Pitman nodded. Amos shoved him back into his chair, turned on his heel and left. Pitman's secretary and every worker in the yard stopped to watch him pass. From across the street, he observed as Pitman came chugging out the gate in his black Model T Ford and bounced over cobblestones and potholes as he sped west at a full throttle.

When Amos returned to the station, City Marshal Sullivan wanted to see him again, this time to give him a direct assignment.

"They're shipping off another bunch of kids on Saturday. We're going to have a lot of cops there to make sure that the parents are giving their full consent, and that it's not the Wobblies just snaring kids to go beg for money in New York. I want you to observe, to look for parents who might be doing this under pressure."

"What do I do if I see a mother looking like she'd rather keep her kid?"

"Pull her in—the kid too."

Amos was keenly aware of how the strikers and police were increasingly hostile to each other. The Wobblies called the tune, and the cops danced to it, they created a series of confrontations, using women where possible, provoking the police into actions on which the yellow journalists feasted. Police resentment of both strikers and journalists grew with each incident. More recently, the militia units, and not the police, performed most duties associated with the strike and they were even more inept than the police at avoiding provocation.

He had visions of cops rounding up children and manhandling mothers. He thought of telling Sullivan that he was doing the exact opposite of what would be best for the mill owners but he held back. His own situation was already precarious and he had a strong sense of fatalism regarding the course of the strike. The strikers, the mill owners, the politicians and the police were locked in a downward spiral, which would end only when the pain could no longer be endured. Why try to reason with Sullivan? It would only slow things up.

He got to the depot before 7:30 Saturday morning, the children were scheduled to arrive there around 9:00. The Wobblies had been processing them all night at the Belgian-Franco hall on the other side of town, each child would be tagged with a card displaying name, language, age, address and so on. According to Joe Lamastro every detail was being handled in a responsible manner. Maybe everything would go smoothly, and he would get home early.

It was bitter cold outside, and the air inside the depot seemed to be colder still; groups of cops stood around shuffling their feet and moving their arms to fight the cold. There was not much conversation. He spotted Casey on the other side of the hall and made his way in that direction, stopping frequently to exchange greetings with the men in his path. All comments seemed to be directed at the damn Wobblies, or the weather.

Casey held another view, he said, "They plan to march those kids all the way down Essex Street—in this weather. They'll do anything to wring every last bit of sympathy out of the reporters in Lawrence before the main event in New York."

"It's working. When they get the public on their side, the politicians will follow, and the mill owners won't know what hit them."

"Do we know what time they're coming?"

"Around nine, they're scheduled to depart from here at eleven."

Casey glanced up at the station clock, which had just passed eight. "And we're supposed to check all the permissions? It's going to be messy."

"I'm here looking for mothers that didn't exactly give their permission."

Casey turned giving him his best sardonic look. "That should be easy—you being so fluent in Italian, and all."

"I'll just have to look for one who's crying." They both smiled.

"Crying? They'll all be crying."

The children started to arrive shortly before nine, preceded by a group of reporters. Tattered clothes, blue hands and noses, they were herded into the middle of the hall. Mothers hovered about with grim faces and fierce looks for the police. Chaperons, mostly stern-looking women, Wobblies every one, were among the children, talking many languages and maintaining control. The small children remained docile and crowded together; the older ones moved along with wide eyes, some of them talking excitedly with each other. The police moved in demanding documents, and the chaperons, Wobbly functionaries, confronted them with voices loud enough for the reporters to hear. Like vultures with notepads, they gathered round.

Amos kept his eyes on the mothers, who seemed extremely tense, but there were few tears. Probably didn't want to upset the children. A loud altercation between a chaperon and a policeman drew his attention. The reporters gathered around as well. He watched with sadness as three cops pulled a chaperon and child outside to a police wagon. More confrontations followed with the same result. Another black-eye for the Lawrence Police Department. When will we learn?

Before eleven, things had calmed down and the bulk of the group boarded the train for Boston with a connection to New York. The train pulled away. That's when the tears came.

Casey stopped on his way out, jerking his head toward the women. "Wouldn't you think there'd be a better way?"

The Flanagans sat down to supper on Saturday night and followed their usual custom of sticking to small talk until the meal was nearly complete. On this evening, everyone gravitated to the exodus of the children, except for Paddy, whose mind was filled with anxiety over what Sunday would bring.

Neal looked at this father. "I heard that there are a lot of kids in jail."

"And they beat some mothers," Kathleen added.

Molly said, "Why don't you just tell us what you saw, Amos?"

He proceeded to describe the event as he witnessed it, and the questions flowed.

Neal asked, "Why don't the police just let them go?"

"There's a lot of confusion around that. Some feel that the entire city of Lawrence, the police, the strikers, the mill owners and politicians, are being manipulated by the Wobblies in order to build their own power. Others say that the working and living conditions for workers are so bad that it doesn't matter how it's done as long as there's improvement."

"But why do the police beat women?" Kathleen asked.

"I didn't see any women being beaten. They were pushed and shoved when they refused to go peaceably, and some of them fought back, scratching, kicking, swinging handbags and umbrellas, the whole lot."

Molly said, "It seems that the police are playing into the hands of the Wobblies."

Amos replied, "I agree with that. I think that the strikers are winning."

Paddy, who had said next to nothing so far, spoke up. "But Da, almost half the strikers are already back at work."

Everyone waited for Amos to answer. "That's true. It could still go either way. I'd certainly like to see the workers come out of this with a better life. They're not treated much better than animals. But the mills are already losing business to competitors in other states where wages are even lower."

Molly said, "If the workers win here, maybe the workers in other states will follow."

Paddy had the last word. "In the meantime, maybe Billy Wood can get by with fewer automobiles and chauffeurs." He exchanged glances with Amos, the others all nodded.

Kathleen got up to clear the table, and Paddy went back to agonizing over whether he'd see Maria the next day, and how she would react to his appearance—and proposal.

As Amos and Molly got ready for bed, he asked, "Do you think he's planning to go there tomorrow?"

"Oh definitely, it's written all over him."

Amos put on his heavy night shirt and got into bed, propped up against the pillows, while Molly fixed her hair.

He asked, "Do you think I should tell him what her father said?"

"He might think you've had a hand in it."

"He's probably going to think that anyway."

"I'd let it go. She might be as determined as he is and be there."

"Oh God, this is going to be painful."

# CHAPTER NINETEEN

Paddy spent a fitful night and got up early for Mass. Going to and from the church, he concentrated on walking erect, without limping. He dawdled over breakfast and tried to read the paper—anything to distract himself until it was time to go. On his visits to the bathroom, he couldn't help examining his face in the mirror; the bruises had spread out and taken on additional colors—yellows and greens alongside the original blues and reds.

He thought it strange that no one asked him about his plans for the day. When it was time, he didn't bother to offer an excuse; he just said he was going out. Before boarding the streetcar, he pulled his scarf and collar up high around his face and he sat in the back next to a window, staring blankly at the now-familiar passing scene while reviewing what he planned to say. A bundled up girl, about two years old, occupied the seat just in front of him. She spent most of the ride standing up and facing backwards, reaching out and otherwise trying to engage Paddy. Her mother seemed relieved to have her thus distracted. Paddy offered no encouragement but couldn't help taking her hand and wiggling it for a moment before he got off.

Crossing the bridge, he walked up South Main Street in Bradford, continuing to rehearse his proposal, all the while, struggling to contain his emotions which swung from glorious visions of his future life with Maria, to a panicky gloom. He was counting on some time alone with her, but if he had only a few minutes he still had to make her understand the complete meaning and significance of his plan. He would be asking her to take a very big step—leaving her family and moving to Boston. For all his concentration, he couldn't help but glance across the street as he passed 'Webster's Shoes and Ladies Slippers' factory--there were no Serbians waiting.

On Pleasant Street, he realized that he had not given much thought to what he would do if she put him off, or refused to go along with his grandiose scheme. He had been fully immersed in fantasizing about the wonders of a new life—with Maria, and working with automobiles and trucks—the wave of the future—while building a new family. He had no other plan. There couldn't be one.

He paused in front of the house, said a silent prayer and walked up the steps. Mrs. Schultz answered the door herself, surprising Paddy.

"I was wondering if I'd see you again. Please come in." She looked him over. "My, you've had a time of it."

"It looks much worse than it is."

She guided him into the living room. It was clear that neither Carla nor Maria were present. "Please sit down," she said, "I have something to tell you. But it would be best to talk over tea." She gestured to a chair and then turned to leave.

Paddy sat down as a gnawing, foreboding, feeling grew in his chest. She returned and prepared to serve tea. He wondered if this was a sign that things were not bad, or if the news was so terrible that she was stalling. She went about the business of serving tea, all the while maintaining a steady chatter about the cold winter weather.

"I do hope that those children, who were sent to New York, have enough clothing and are staying in warm houses."

Paddy was tempted to tell her what he thought about the children's exodus being nothing more than a fund raiser for the Wobblies but he didn't want to talk about that. He felt nervous, anxious for the preliminaries to be over so he could find out about Maria. He forced himself to make polite responses to her small talk and to take care with his tea; it wouldn't do to spill something, adding even more to his waiting time.

Finally, after what felt like a long time, she settled back and began. "I know that you are disappointed at not finding Maria here. I've been in touch with Carla, and she gave me a message in the event that you showed up today, there have been

214

some questions as to your whereabouts, I'm sure your bruises are part of that story. Anyway, it seems that Maria's father is very much against what he believes to be a serious relationship between you and his daughter. He has forbidden her to see you."

Paddy did not know how to react, how to respond; he sat, holding his tea cup, sensing the heaviness in every part of him. "I don't know what to say."

"It's not necessary to say anything. In the few times I saw you together, I could see that the two of you are hopelessly in love. This has got to be a heavy blow."

"I was going to ask her to marry me."

"Yes."

"Not right away. I've been working on a plan."

"I know that at a time like this it's difficult to believe that things have a way of turning out for the best in the end, but surely you understand the difficulties of such a marriage? Italians have a very strong sense of their culture and traditions."

"Maria is an American."

"Of course, she is, and, who knows, maybe a way can be found. I'm sure that Maria confided a great deal more to Carla than I know. You should see her."

"I will."

Mrs. Schultz set her cup onto the tea tray. "I have a feeling that you're anxious to get going. On a cold day like this, Carla will probably be at home. Should I call and tell her that you're coming?"

"Uh. Oh yes, but I do enjoy your company."

"I'll always be delighted to see you."

Paddy placed his cup on the tray. "You've been so kind. I don't know how to thank you."

215

"However things turn out, Paddy, remember you have a whole life ahead of you." She left him to call Carla and return. "She's expecting you." She gave him some brief directions to the house. He got up, and she saw him to the door. "Please come to visit me again."

"Thank you for everything."

He opened the gate and, as he turned to close it, glanced at the front door where she watched him through the curtain. He would not be back, not without Maria.

The cold and grayness of the day were appropriate to his mood; he almost enjoyed the emphasis added to the sympathy he felt for himself. Was he asking for too much? Other people fall in love all the time; they go on with joy to marriage and all its blessings, free from interference and obstacles placed in their path. He continued down the street toward the bridge and the place, on the other side, where he had been forced into the hack. It didn't matter. Nothing mattered. He needed a miracle.

In Lawrence, he got off the streetcar on East Haverhill Street in front of the German Lutheran church. He was not familiar with the neighborhood so he asked a passing woman for directions. She gestured to indicate that she did not speak English. He headed north and found Webster Street on his own.

Carla opened the door before he could knock. "Come into the living room. It's nice and warm." She took his hat and coat and hung them on a tall, curved, dark wooden rack and umbrella stand next to the door.

He wiped his feet on a thick door mat and then stepped onto an entryway floor covered with small, white tiles, similar to those found in some fancy saloons. The living room was just off the hallway, opposite an impressive stairway with a wide, well-polished banister.

She showed him to the couch and took a chair facing him. "Those bruises look like they must hurt a lot."

"The pain is going away, and it's not what I'm thinking about right now."

"My grand momma tells me that you've just had tea. Can I get you something?"

"No thanks." He rubbed his hands, wringing away the cold. "I guess I'm not feeling like much of anything right now."

"Maria's not feeling very good either."

That made him feel just a tad better—the idea that she was suffering for want of him. It was like some form of ethereal communication, a message from a far-off place.

"What did she say?"

"Well, she wanted me to tell you that she loves you very much, but she can not go directly against the wishes of her father."

"But I can. If there was only some place where I might find her?"

"She won't do it, Paddy. She has to find her own way."

"Did she say that she can do that?"

"Not yet."

She looked as though she was going to say more. Paddy waited.

"She's leaving."

"What?"

"They're going back to Italy, except for Lorenzo."

Paddy sunk back into the couch. "Italy?"

"Yes."

"It might as well be the moon."

"She plans to write; you can write back through me. She says she'll understand if you don't wait."

217

He stared at her. Wait? Wait for what? His life was being wiped away. "I was going to get a job in Boston. I wanted to get married."

"She wants that as much as you do, Paddy. Don't give up."

"When are they leaving?"

"This week."

"This week? Oh God. Oh my God."

"I'll see her before she goes. Is there anything you'd like me to say?"

Paddy leaned forward, holding his head. "Tell her I'm going to Boston to work in my grandfather's business. She could get a teaching job there—in Boston." He took his hands down and stared at her. "Tell her I'll wait."

"I will."

They sat in silence for a few minutes. Paddy shifted forward and stood up. She saw him to the door where he put on his hat and coat. "Thank you for everything, Carla." He gazed out through the lace curtains covering the window in the door. "I think I'll walk home."

It had started to snow, not heavy, just a dusting so far, and darkness was taking over the streets. With his hands jammed into his pockets and his head down, he moved along Union Street, feeling the cold creep in through his clothes to keep company with his mood. He passed within a block of Maria's house and glanced up to see if, by some miracle, like a vision of the Virgin, she would appear out of the snow.

By the time he reached Essex Street, he was so cold that a streetcar was irresistible. He rode all the way to South Lawrence and he was still cold when he got off. He thought about passing the house and going around to see if Frank was home but, at his own front door, he felt a lump in his throat and knew he needed to be in his own house. Entering quietly, he hung up his coat and listened to the sound of playing cards being shuffled on the kitchen table. He glanced into the living room and saw his da reading, slipping in, he picked up a copy of Colliers magazine and sat down.

Amos glanced up. "It's snowing, heh?"

"Yes, it's snowing."

Amos continued to look at him, and Paddy looked back, the magazine unopened on his lap.

Amos spoke. "Do you want to talk about it?"

Paddy said nothing; he stared at his da. Amos waited.

Almost a minute passed before Paddy said, "They're all going to Italy."

"The Petrellas?"

Paddy nodded. "I don't understand."

"Why they're going?"

"No, why she doesn't just walk out. She's an American citizen; she doesn't have to go."

"Hmm. They're a tight family. Her father has had a hard time here. Who knows what he'll be up against when they get back to Italy. She's a loyal daughter."

"He won't let her see me."

"Yeah, well..." Amos leaned forward. "You're going to be a father, yourself, someday. You'll see. You try never to hurt your children; you do the best you can. But sometimes..."

"I want to marry her."

"I know." Amos leaned back and folded his arms. "Were you thinking of bringing her here? It would be okay, you know."

Paddy shook his head. "I'm thinking of going to Boston, to work for grand da."

"Not a bad idea. Motor cars and trucks are going to take over."

"It's a good idea?"

"I think so. And it's only a short train ride—or perhaps you'll be driving out."

Paddy smiled, just a small smile. He knew his da was trying to cheer him up, but it only made him feel all the more sorry for himself. He left and walked down the hall to the kitchen. Molly was alone.

"I thought that was you coming in," she said. "Kathleen and Neal just went upstairs to wash for supper. Why don't you have a cup of tea and keep me company while I set out the dishes?"

"Yes. There's something I wanted to tell you."

She said nothing as she poured tea into a cup and set it at his place. He sat down, and she sat across the table and waited.

He stirred in some sugar. "You probably already know where I went today. Maybe you even knew what was going to happen?"

"I wanted to say something. I just didn't know; it might have made things worse."

"I'm not blaming you. There wasn't anything you could have done."

"She's going?"

"To Italy."

"I'm sorry, Paddy. It must be hard, and you've been through so much."

"I'm thinking of going to work for grand da." He picked up his cup and sipped, while watching her over the rim.

"Is this just because of Maria?"

"I was going to do it so we could get married. But I think I should do it anyway."

"It's a better future than you have in the mills. Does your grand da know?"

"I'm going to call him after supper."


Later that evening, Amos and Molly found themselves alone in the kitchen; Paddy had gone over to visit Frank Dunn, and the children were getting ready for school the next day. Amos sat at the table nursing a cup of tea until Molly put away the last dish and sat down with her own cup.

"What did he tell you?" Amos asked.

"He's going to Boston. You know that."

"Yes, he told me. He called your father. Did he say anything about that?"

"He did. He's to keep working at the mill until there's a place ready for him to live with my da. It will be a month, or two."

"That long?"

"It seems his housekeeper, Mrs. Burns, will be in charge of the arrangements."

"She must be a very capable woman."

"Indeed."

Amos detected more than Molly agreeing with him. "There's more?"

"I have a feeling that it may be Mrs. Burns, who will be needing a new arrangement."

Amos smiled and shook his head. "Well, that's your father's business, not mine, but we can't have Paddy moving into that kind of situation."

"He's old enough to handle it."

"Maybe, but that sort of thing can get ugly, and Paddy doesn't deserve to be caught in the middle."

"Yes." She paused. "I just realized it's been months since I last visited my father in Boston."

"And what about your sister? She must know what's going on."

"We'll see."

# CHAPTER TWENTY

Paddy finished the last of his breakfast as Amos strolled in wearing a heavy wool bathrobe, stretching one arm while he smothered a yawn with his other hand. Molly, who had just finished making breakfast and a big pot of tea, slipped past him to go and get dressed. Amos poured a cup of tea and sat across from Paddy.

"You're going in to work?"

"Yeah, I'll be needing the money."

"You still look a sight. How do you feel?"

"I'm a bit stiff, but the work's not hard."

"I guess we'll be able to rent your room out in a month or so, heh?"

Paddy smiled. That was his da's way, his way of showing affection, of boosting his son's spirits. He had to think of a good repost, downing the last of his tea, he wiped his mouth and got up. "By all means," he said. "I'll stay with Frank when I come home for a visit." He picked up his hat and coat from the adjacent chair, put them on and touched his cap to Amos.

Amos raised his cup. "A good day to you."

Fifteen minutes later, Paddy hung up his coat and greeted Kevin O'Shay.

O'Shay nodded and bent sideways to get a better look at Paddy's face. "Are you up for this, lad?"

"Yeah, I know I look like hell but I'm okay."

"Good. We've got sixty looms operating; you're going to be very busy—they're all scabs."

"Sixty? Wow."

223

"Looks like the strike is winding down. I hear the Italians are coming back."

"But not today?"

"Maybe next week. I don't know; it's just another rumor."

"Yeah." He scratched his neck and went out onto the production floor, thinking that he should have left his coat on—it was still cold. He went down the line, checking spools, belts, and setups. Loom fixers were still busy at scattered locations. Ernst Meyer was not among them. Too bad; what O'Shay said didn't make sense, everything he heard while convalescing led him to believe that the strike was still in full force. Women had come to the fore, confronting police and militia alike. Soup kitchens were well organized, and strikers held regular meetings and marches, each nationality singing in their native tongue to the others. And from what his da, and others, had said, sending kids to New York and elsewhere was helping to raise money from all over the country.

Workers showed up to stand in front of looms, and Paddy was soon up to his neck with teaching and helping. O'Shay was right; scabs were no prize when it came to getting the work done.

\*\*\*\*\*\*\*\*\*\*\*\*\*\*\*\*\*\*\*\*\*\*\*\*\*\*\*\*\*

Amos finished his breakfast and sat back to watch the usual Monday-morning frenetic activities of Neal and Kathleen as they wolfed down their food and got ready for school. Molly, unflappable as always, offered quiet reminders and a helping hand with coats and books. When they were ready, Amos put on his hat and coat and walked with them toward school.

"Is there some danger?" Kathleen wanted to know.

"No, everything's grand."

224

"Then why are you walking with us?"

"What's the point of having children if you can't be with them and enjoy them?"

They looked up at him, clearly not comprehending. Mickey, Tom Malone's kid, called to Neal from across the street.

"It's okay," Amos said. "You can walk with Mickey."

Neal left them to cross the street.

Kathleen said, "You can be with us lots of other times."

"Yes, but sometimes, we get so involved with other concerns we don't really see each other."

They walked quietly; she seeming to consider his words. "You're thinking of Paddy leaving, aren't you?"

"Yes," he said, "I suppose I am." He spotted a girl ahead, whom he knew to be Kathleen's friend. "You can go with Mary, if you like."

"I can walk home with her," she said, and they walked on together.


Kerrigan was busy, giving instructions to several patrolmen, when Amos entered the station. Before he could reach the hall, leading to the inspectors' office, Kerrigan signaled and pointed to Sullivan's office. Amos nodded, turned and headed in that direction.

He went in, sat down and waited for his boss to get off the telephone. When his conversation ended, Sullivan slipped the earpiece onto its hook, turned and smacked his desk. "Well now, Amos, please don't tell me that all you saw on Saturday was a bunch of grateful mothers eager to send their little tots off to the big city in order to keep them from starving here."

"You are correct. I did not see that. But I also did not see kids being ripped away from their mothers, or any evidence to indicate that the mothers were coerced. We let the Wobblies outsmart us on this one, John. Our cops are being maneuvered into confrontations, and the reporters are playing it up. We look bad."

Sullivan said nothing, he just stared at Amos, his face reddening. "They're Communists and Anarchists, Amos. They want to destroy Lawrence. They're the enemy." He sat back, looking angry. "Go back to work. I'll talk to you later."

He walked down the hall, thinking that Sullivan had been more contentious than usual. Was it the wrong side of the bed this morning? Or maybe pressures from the strike were getting to be too much?

Charlie Vose looked up when he entered the inspectors' room. "Amos, just the man I'm looking for."

Amos hung his coat on the rack and took a chair at the center table with Vose. "At your service, Charlie."

"I'm trying to put things together on the Wilcox case. I've got the basics, but what happened? Why didn't you nail him?"

"I don't have a good excuse. I was busy with other stuff. I let him buy me off with vague promises. His lawyer was supposed to work out something." Amos looked away. "The mother must be devastated."

"Yeah. She doesn't blame you though. She blames herself. Always a mistake isn't it, getting yourself into fixing things, instead of just being a cop?"

"I suppose."

"We all do it, Amos. The best cops always do it. I'm as guilty as you are. But I'm getting the impression that certain people are out to get you on this one. I think Sullivan wants your badge, and there's more to it than the Wilcox kid. What can you give me that I can use to help you out?"

Amos looked hard at Vose. "What I can give you is Billy Wood's head on a platter. He was behind the dynamite plot."

Vose leaned forward and spoke softly. "I didn't hear that. You should save it for latter." He grinned. "They might make you City Marshall just to keep you quiet."

\*\*\*\*\*\*\*\*\*\*\*\*\*\*\*\*\*\*\*\*\*\*\*\*\*\*\*\*

On Wednesday evening, Molly fed Neal and Kathleen at the usual time. Amos was home but he elected to wait and have his dinner with Paddy when he got home a little later.

Paddy quit work just after six o'clock. He passed through the gate and over the bridge without incident and walked home at a brisk pace in the dark, nose-biting air. After he turned the corner onto Crosby Street, he noticed a figure following him about twenty yards back. He reached the house and glanced over his shoulder as he mounted the stairs. Whoever it was darted behind a wagon parked at the curb. Inside, he waited behind the front door window to see if the person would pass. No one appeared. He hung up his hat and coat and passed into the kitchen where he washed his hands while wondering if he should mention having been followed. He decided that his recent experience was having an effect on his imagination and he dismissed the incident. Amos joined him at the table and they made small talk about Paddy's day at the mill.

Before Molly could dish out their food, the front doorbell rang. Paddy immediately sensed that there might be a connection to the person who had followed him. "Let me get it," he said.

Even through the curtain-covered window, the person had a familiar look about him. It wasn't Frank. It was Lorenzo. Paddy was so surprised he moved back and motioned Lorenzo inside. Stepping in, looking a bit sheepish and very cold, he held out a package to Paddy.

227

Paddy took it, saying, "Why don't you come in the kitchen for a minute and get warm?" He led Lorenzo down the hall into the kitchen and, putting the package aside, said, "You remember Lorenzo?"

Amos and Molly stared at Lorenzo and nodded.

Lorenzo said, "It's nice to see you again."

"Yes," Amos said.

Molly came over and placed a hand on his cheek. "You're half-frozen. Take off your coat and have some tea." She unbuttoned his coat and began to pull it off.

"I don't want to be a bother. I just came to bring…" He gestured at the package as he went along with getting his coat off.

She sat him next to Paddy and placed a cup in front of him. Back at the stove, she ladled out plates of stew. "There's plenty here," she said and she put a plate in front of Lorenzo.

Amos watched his eyes as the aroma reached his nostrils, and his hand moved to grasp the fork. He was hungry all right.

Not much was said, just a few polite questions from Amos and Molly: "Have you heard from your family?" "When do they expect to arrive in Italy?"

As Lorenzo filled his stomach, he became more communicative. "They should be there by now, but I have to wait for a letter. My father left that package" He gestured to where Paddy had left it on the sideboard and, reaching in his pocket, he pulled out an envelope. "This is for you, Paddy."

Paddy accepted the envelope. A glance at the handwriting, told him that it was not from Maria. He opened the envelope and scanned the letter before reading it aloud.

*"Dear Paddy,*

*I know that my actions regarding Maria have brought you great pain. I regret this because of what you did for us in saving her, and because I admire you as a good and worthy man.*

*In gratitude, I made a jacket for you. You can bring it to Antonio, the tailor who took over my shop, and he will do the finishing touches. Wear it in good health and try to forgive an old man, who cherishes his family and his heritage.*

*Respectfully,*

*Alessandro Petrella"*

Paddy folded the letter and held it on his lap.

They sat in silence until Lorenzo cleared his throat. "I'm grateful too."

Amos asked, "Why don't you try it on?"

Molly patted Amos's hand and said, "You can try it later, Paddy."

Lorenzo said, "A lot of people are grateful to *you*, Mister Flanagan. Your investigations are helping the strikers. And I think that Ettor and Giovannitti will probably go free. Don't you agree?"

Amos smiled at the irony implicit in Lorenzo's statement. If there was one thing he did not need it was a demonstration by the Wobblies on his behalf. "Thank you. But I don't take sides; I just try to see that justice is served." As the words spilled out, he felt like a pompous ass but let it go.

Molly asked, "Where are you staying?"

"I'm in a furnished room right now, but Mister Lamastro has invited me to stay at his home."

Amos leaned forward. "Joe Lamastro is one of the finest men I know. You listen to him and you won't go far wrong."

"I will."

229

It was time for Lorenzo to go, and Paddy saw him to the door. They shook hands. "Come again," Paddy said, "We're not as far apart as you think."

Lorenzo grinned and was out the door.

\*\*\*\*\*\*\*\*\*\*\*\*\*\*\*\*\*\*\*\*\*\*\*\*\*\*\*\*\*\*\*

Molly talked twice to her sister about their father's housekeeper, but Sarah had little to offer and she expressed surprise and mild shock at the suggestion of any impropriety between her father and Mrs. Burns. But Sarah had always been naïve and flighty; she married a teacher, who fancied himself a poet. Molly contacted her father and arranged to visit on Saturday morning.

Bundled up, she took the train to North Station in Boston where her father picked her up in his new motorcar, amazing her as he proudly drove it himself.

"These things are a gift from God," he said. "I can't wait to be rid of the horses."

The two-story house, in the Parker Hill section of Boston, was built on a slope. A retaining wall along the sidewalk contained a gateway at the center where stone steps led up the embankment to wooden stairs and the porch. The house seemed huge from the street, but there were not that many rooms inside—only ten. Molly recalled the small backyard where she played as a child; one never took a ball around to the front—it invariably went down the steps, into the street and down the hill.

Mrs. Burns opened the door as she and her father crossed the porch. She was a slender woman, tall with worried brown eyes. Molly judged her to be about the same age as herself, no more than forty-five. Her father had a series of housekeepers since her mother's death seven years earlier, but this one was probably the youngest and most attractive, although the sharp features of her face displayed the effects of a hard life. She made brief eye contact as she offered to take Molly's coat before helping Patrick with his.

Molly followed her father a short distance down the hall, noting the white-tiled floor with black-tile patterns and the same pictures of Irish landscapes on the walls she remembered from her childhood. The living room was different. New curtains and drapes let in more light; a new, rather expensive looking, Persian rug covered the floor, and there were new lamps with shades of light translucent cloth.

They sat in easy-chairs on either side of the fireplace, where a fire glowed red from under a grey layer of coal lumps. The heat on her face told her that she'd soon be over her chill and would have to move to another chair away from the fire.

Patrick said, "Even with central heating, there's nothing like a warm fire on a winter's day."

"Indeed. But central heating is one of the great blessings of our times, isn't it? Can you manage it all by yourself?"

"I hardly go near it. Mrs. Burns tends to it during the day, and I have a man come in early morning and at night to shake down the ashes, take them out and to bank the fire at bedtime."

"They say you'll be able to heat with gas before long."

"That will be the ultimate. Speaking of which, what did you think of the car?"

"I was amazed to see you driving it yourself."

"Ah. You'll be driving one yourself soon enough. Paddy will teach you."

"And when will that be?"

"Now, and I thought you came just to visit your da."

231

"You have noticed that I've been a wife and mother for some time now?"

He smiled and nodded his appreciation, as Mrs. Burns arrived with tea. She set the tray down between Molly and Patrick and, as she straightened, spoke to Molly. "I'm looking forward to meeting your son, Mrs. Flanagan, Mister Kelly speaks so highly of him."

"Thank you. He's a good boy. He'll not be any trouble to you."

Patrick said, "When we're finished here, Mrs. Burns, you can show Mrs. Flanagan our preparations for Paddy."

After Mrs. Burns left, and they served themselves tea, Molly said, "I was a bit surprised that it's taking some time before Paddy can start. You sounded so eager to have him?"

"I am eager to have him. He's too young to take over but he'll be a help. He's going to need a lot of teaching, and I want the other men prepared to welcome him. That's taking time. And I did not have the whole house done when we put in the central heating. We're having more rooms fitted up, and a bathroom for Paddy."

"You're going to spoil him."

"I am, but I'll be working him hard."

"He's looking forward to it. How long have you had Mrs. Burns?"

"You should visit more often, Molly. She's been here for almost a year."

"The house looks very clean."

He laughed and took a drink of tea. "She's a wonder. Best housekeeper I've had, and she's managing the carpenters, the plumbers, and the painters like a straw-boss. If I can't get Amos, I may bring her into the business."

"I'm working on Amos. Is she married?"

232

"Her husband was a fisherman, swept overboard, lost at sea three years ago. She has a son in a Franciscan seminary, a daughter and granddaughter living in New York. Her brother-in-law works for me; that's how I found her."

"And she's a good Catholic?"

He laughed again. "Indeed she is. You should see her room—all fitted up with a kneeler, holy pictures, candles. I feel like I'm living in a convent."

They sat quietly, sipping tea and munching on toast. He spoke. "I understand why you came, Molly. I'll see to Paddy as if he's my own son."

"You didn't do that well with William and Michael."

"I know. I know. A man can grow; I've changed; you'll see."

"They're doing very well in Australia."

"Yes, and they write more often now. I'm grateful for that, but I'll never see those grandchildren."

"I bet they come for a visit."

"If I live long enough."

"You could visit them."

He looked at her in an odd way, as if the idea were bizarre and had never occurred to him. "That would be something to think on, wouldn't it?"

Mrs. Burns came in to take the tea tray out and returned to escort Molly upstairs to view Paddy's new room. She asked, "Would you ask Paddy what colors he's like?"

"I will. Everything looks so nice. The house is better than I've seen it in years."

"Your father has been very kind to me. A generous man—I can even call my daughter once a week."

233

"My father is obviously pleased with you, Mrs. Burns."

"Thank you. Please call me Bridget."

Molly smiled but, unsure of a proper response, she said nothing.

\*\*\*\*\*\*\*\*\*\*\*\*\*\*\*\*\*\*\*\*\*\*\*\*\*\*\*\*\*\*

Molly arrived home late that afternoon, in time to fix supper. She told the family about her visit and that she liked Mrs. Burns. Paddy asked if she had any idea of how much longer he'd have to wait.

"It looked as though the house will be ready in a few weeks," she said, "but my father didn't indicate when things would be ready at his business."

Amos smiled. "And you liked Mrs. Burns?"

"She seems very nice."

"Nice?"

Molly gave him a look indicating that this was not appropriate humor for the children.

After supper, Amos stayed in the kitchen and went through the motions of helping Molly.

"You said your da is fixing up the whole house?"

"Yes. He said I wasn't to say anything to Mrs. Burns about anybody coming there besides Paddy. I wonder what the poor woman *is* thinking?"

"What are *you* thinking?"

She put down the dish she was cleaning and turned to him. "It's up to you, Amos. But if we do this, we should have our own place."

They went back to cleaning and drying. A moment later, he spoke. "I'm thinking I'm going to do it.

She kept on washing. "We'll work it out. I'm glad it's settled."

Settled? Is that what he said? It's what she heard, what she wanted, but it didn't feel right—too final. Yes, of course, it made sense. He should do it. He would do it. But so fast?

On Sunday afternoon Amos did something he had not done for years: he left the house for the sole purpose of being alone. All he said to Molly was that he was going out. He knew that she would assume that he meant that he was going down to Jack's for a pint. It was simpler that way; she wouldn't be concerned for him. A stop at Jack's on the way home might be a good idea; no need to make up a story.

He crossed South Broadway and, for the second time that day, ascended the steps of Saint Patrick's. The church had been jammed at the ten o'clock Mass that morning but it was virtually empty now. He crossed the vestibule, opened the inner door and stepped inside, waiting to ease the heavy door close with no sound. Quietly, he moved down the center aisle and selected a pew on the right side, about fifteen feet from the rear, he genuflected, made the sign-of-the-cross and slipped in to sit near the center. Placing his hat on the bench, he eased forward onto the kneeler for a short prayer while staring at the flickering red vigil candle and the white-spired altar behind it. He finished, crossed himself and remained kneeling for a moment before sitting back and looking around.

Why was he here? He knew the answer—he was scared. His whole life was swinging around—going off in an unfamiliar direction with unpredictable consequences. He was about to give up control. At age forty-five, he was going off on a new venture. What happens if it doesn't work? How do you pick up the pieces when you've got a wife and two kids still in school?

A sound distracted him: the clink of a coin dropping into the offering box in front of a bank of votive candles. There were

235

a half dozen women in the church—old women, poor souls with nothing better to do than come to the church and pray. One woman was lighting a candle at the side-altar dedicated to the Virgin Mary, others knelt, or sat in pews saying their beads, and one was making the Stations of the Cross. What would they go home to, a cold empty room and a crust of bread? Or a family, where no one gives them the time of day?

It was far too early for Amos to worry about such matters in his own life; he had more immediate concerns. He had made a break. He had not yet taken the actions but, in his heart, he had made the break. There was to be no onward and upward in Lawrence for him. This had been true for some time; the strike had simply brought matters to a head. He had to move on, or spend the rest of his life making excuses to himself.

He looked up at Christ on the Cross and whispered, "In for a penny, in for a pound." It wasn't a prayer exactly, but it felt like one. He moved forward to kneel and say a proper one.


Amos went to work that week with a strange sense of detachment. He felt as if he were marking time, just going through the motions. And yet, he had one clear objective—one item he had to bring to closure before he left: he had to connect William Wood to the dynamite plot.

He was surprised when the middle of the week arrived and he had heard nothing from Sullivan. Instead, Philip Fahey, the new Chief Inspector gave him a few routine assignments: a break-in at a store on Essex Street, a missing horse, and a shooting incident in which no one was hurt and for which there were no witnesses.

He stopped by the desk to see if Kerrigan had any sense of what was going on. "Charlie Vose thinks they're after my badge, Jimmy. What do you think?"

"Amos, if I were you. I'd just relax. They're not going to do anything until the strike is over—too many things to worry about as it is. And then, you've only got to wait until the next election, and a new crowd comes in."

"Yeah, you're right, but there are a couple of things I want to finish up before they bounce me out of here. The Anna Lopizzo shooter is one of them."

"There's no word on finding Carapatsi. My money says he's out of the country."

"You're probably right, but then what happens to those two Wobblies they've got locked up?"

"Who cares?"

Amos laughed. "Yeah. Still, there were a lot of guns going off in this town before those two showed up. Getting nailed because some crazy wop, a mile away, tries to shoot a cop and hits the girl by accident doesn't seem right."

"They won't get nailed. When the strike is over, everyone will want to kiss and make up. There'll be another parade when those two go to the train station." Kerrigan leaned forward. "Casey's by the door. I think he's looking to talk to you."

Amos nodded to Casey and walked downstairs to the men's toilet. Casey entered and made sure they were alone. "I found out today that an automobile—a black Cadillac town-car— was reported missing on the day after we rescued Paddy and put one exactly like it into the river. The owner is William Wood."

Amos took a moment to digest what he heard. "That car was one of a kind around here. This means the Serbians were using it with permission for some time *before* it was reported as missing."

"It does indeed."

237

"It could also mean that Wood didn't know about the Serbians and their use of his car. He has over thirty of them, you know. Whoever loaned them the car had to cover up by reporting it when Paddy showed up after we rescued him, and the Serbians along with the car went missing."

# CHAPTER TWENTY ONE

From what Lorenzo said during his visit, Paddy realized that he might not hear from Maria for some time. He telephoned Carla to commiserate.

"Yes," she said, "I thought she might write from New York but she didn't. That means they probably got a boat right away."

"How long does it take to get a letter from Italy?"

"I don't know; maybe a month." She tried to console him. "I'll contact you as soon as one comes."

Paddy struggled; every part of his world seemed to be coming apart. His most intimate relationships, those with his parents, his sister and brother, were changing. Outwardly, all was the same, they seemed not to notice any difference, but he felt a sense of parting, as if some kind of transparent barrier was growing between himself and the bedrock of his life.

He spent more time with Frank, discussing this and how life was changing for both of them. In his private thoughts, he wondered if their friendship would survive, or just change to something less satisfying.

For Paddy, the most clear-cut changes took place at work. He told no one of his plan to leave. This felt dishonest; he acted his way through each day while those around him remained unaware of his deception. As the days passed, his view of the mill and everyone in it changed. He had never thought of the operatives as human machines; he always tried to be polite and considerate but, in the past, he had mainly concentrated on achieving production quotas. Now he began to see each one of them as an individual human being, desperate to hold onto a job for the miserable life it provided.

Even Ernst Meyer took on a different identity. To Paddy, he was no longer a skilled German craftsman, taking pride in his work. He was an opportunist, who did his job in a perfunctory fashion while seeing himself as an industrial philosopher.

During a lunch break with Meyer, Paddy said. "When you look at the papers, it's hard to see how the mill owners can hold out. Those hearings in Congress are making them look like slave drivers."

"Congressmen and newspaper people don't own any mills."

"So what?"

"They don't have to worry about making cloth at a profit, only about getting elected or selling papers."

"You make it sound like the mill owners are victims."

Meyer grinned. "Think of it as divine retribution."

"But you don't believe in God."

"He comes in handy sometimes."

Until the day when Paddy returned to work after the kidnapping, and Kevin O'Shay expressed concern for his injuries, he had never spoken to Paddy about anything personal. All their dealings had to do with production, operatives, inventory and other work-related details. Paddy regarded him as a taciturn man, dissatisfied with his lot in life.

O'Shay now seemed more harried than ever. He looked sleep-deprived, and his skin more pasty and scaled than before. It occurred to Paddy that he was worried about his job. What would a man of his age do if for some reason the end of the strike resulted in his ouster? Perhaps he was worried that the strikers hated him personally for the way he had to treat them when they worked under him?

One evening at quitting time, Paddy went into the office for his hat and coat; O'Shay was busy, scribbling numbers into a ledger. He wore his jacket with the tattered cuffs and his bowler. Paddy passed close to his desk and paused. O'Shay looked up; something in his eyes told Paddy to talk to him. He sat in the chair next to his desk. "Is everything all right, Mister O'Shay?"

"Yes, everything seems in order." He patted the ledger.

"I mean it's a strange time—this strike and all."

"It is."

Paddy struggled to keep the conversation going. "Is your wife okay?"

"Yes. Yes, she's fine. And your family?"

"They're grand. Uh…" He almost gave up. "How do you think this strike will end?"

O'Shay sat up, took a deep breath, removed his glasses and started to clean them . "Different. Everything will be different. We'll have to learn everything all over again."

"You mean it will be different with the operatives—with their union, they'll have more to say?"

"I'm afraid so."

Paddy smiled and stood up. "Who knows? It might be better."

O'Shay did not look convinced.

Paddy left the mill and let his feet guide him home while his brain sizzled with an effort to make sense of the world coming into view around him—particularly that part defined by the mill and the strike. He'd try his ideas on Frank—always a good sounding board.

\*\*\*\*\*\*\*\*\*\*\*\*\*\*\*\*\*\*\*\*\*\*\*\*\*\*\*\*

241

Amos busied himself with the routine investigations assigned to him by Chief Inspector Fahey, while he waited to see if William Wood's missing car turned up, proving it to be *another* black Cadillac—not the one in the river. He had another "toilet room" conversation with Casey.

Amos said, "If it *was* the same car and only reported missing when we dumped it, we can assume that Wood, or someone very close to him, knew the Serbians had it. We also know that we are not the only ones who can connect the car and the Serbians."

"But we're the only ones, aside from Wood and his crowd, who know that the Serbians were up to no good."

Amos rubbed his chin. "True. Do you think Wood believes that the Serbians made off with his car?"

"Yeah. But then why would he report it? He wouldn't want the Serbians to be caught. They might squeal."

"Maybe Mister Wood is a little too aloof from his henchmen and doesn't understand some critical details."

Casey said, "Somebody had to be paying those Serbians."

"Yes. That would be a very interesting connection, wouldn't it?"

"A car like that would be noticed—possibly at some incriminating locations. I could make inquiries—after all, it's been reported missing."

Amos folded his arms and stared at the floor. "I suppose, but we already know of a few places where the car was spotted. Would their contact man be dumb enough to let them bring the car to his place? I think we're better off if we can trace where the Serbians went without the car."

"Yes, but the car is the thing that connects them to Wood."

They looked at each other; each man thinking his own thoughts until Amos said, "Are we thinking the same thing?"

"Arrange for the car to be found?"

"It's too dangerous."


Amos was overdue for a conversation with John Waters. His attempt to bluff Pitman had failed and he felt obliged to tell the judge. He thought constantly about the car and his conversation with Casey. If the car, with three, bullet-ridden, Serbian bodies, were discovered, the course of the strike and the dynamite case would be dramatically altered. But knowing that Waters would be duty and honor bound to act on the information, he decided to tell him nothing of the car and its contents.

Bill Conboy greeted him in his usual friendly way. If anything, he seemed more effusive in asking Amos about his family and in making small talk. Conboy's attempts at ingratiating himself had the opposite effect; Amos found the situation distasteful and was inwardly ashamed of the pity he felt for an inferior being. He responded politely but refused to give Conboy any inkling of why he wanted a meeting with Waters. Late that afternoon, Kerrigan told him that the judge wanted to see him.

In his office, with the door closed, Waters got right down to business. "I gather that our friend, Pitman, has not cooperated?"

"He was defiant, almost arrogant. And I think he went straight to his patron, William Wood, to tell him about my visit."

"I'd love to know how Wood reacted."

"He undoubtedly told Pitman to keep his mouth shut, and it's rumored that I won't have my badge much longer."

Waters sat back with his arms folded. "We can't let that happen, Amos."

"It's not something to worry about. It may be a blessing in disguise; I have other plans."

"I'll keep that to myself. But, when the time comes, the Attorney General will be interested in all this."

"I hope so. Meanwhile, I'll squeeze Pitman one more time, just to see if there are any cracks in the wall."

\*\*\*\*\*\*\*\*\*\*\*\*\*\*\*\*\*\*\*\*\*\*\*\*\*\*\*\*\*\*\*\*

"You can't believe in pre-destination, Paddy, you're a Catholic."

"Frank, I'm not talking about that kind of pre-destination. There's nothing religious about this. It has to do with circumstances and systems and organizations that are in place."

Frank sat on a stool in front of a workbench in the basement of the Flanagan home while Paddy tended the coal furnace, shaking down the ashes, shoveling them out into a barrel and stoking the coals. "So we don't get to make decisions, we just do what we have to do?"

Paddy closed the furnace door, set his poker aside and sat on another stool. "We don't get to decide as much as we think because we are already in situations which determine our choices."

"All right, but we were talking about the strike. Are you telling me that Wood can't settle the strike by giving in to the strikers?"

"Maybe he can *now*, but when this thing started, it looked like a huge threat to everything he thought he was supposed to be doing. He sees himself as the guardian of the mills, the investors, the banks—not the workers."

Frank laughed. "I can't believe this. Jesus, Paddy, anybody in this town—especially you—could have told him otherwise. The man is supposed to be good with numbers. All he had to do was walk through one of the tenements. How would he think people could live on what he was paying them?"

"You misunderstand. I'm not saying he should not have cared more for the workers. I'm saying that, in his situation, he would have had to be superhuman to even think that way."

"And everybody else in this town is also pre-destined that way?"

"Something like that."

"I'll have to digest this." Frank slipped off his stool. "Let's go down to Jack's."


\*\*\*\*\*\*\*\*\*\*\*\*\*\*\*\*\*\*\*\*\*\*\*\*


After his meeting with Judge Waters, Amos left the station. March 1$^{st}$ was only a few days away, but there had been no signs of spring so far, and the evening was cold and dark. At least, it wasn't snowing again, and there was no wind. At the bottom of the station house steps, he pulled up his collar and noticed the formidable figure of Casey standing across the street. Casey touched his night-stick to his helmet and turned to stroll toward the common. Amos glanced around to see if anyone was watching and then walked north on his side of the street before crossing to follow Casey.

There were enough lights on the common for Amos to see where he was going and to spot Casey waiting in front of the Civil War monument. There were times when he envied Casey's bulk; it seemed to make him almost impervious to the cold, although he suffered terribly on hot summer days. He approached. "It's warmer in the toilet."

"We won't be long—I'm late for my pint. It's about the car."

"I figured as much."

"It doesn't have to be found."

"Good."

"What I'm saying is: If Mister Wood knows it's there and what's in it…"

Amos forgot the cold. "He won't want it found either. But, of course, he'll realize that someone else knows it's there and what's in it."

"What do you think he'll do?"

Amos walked in a small circle, moving his shoulders to keep warm. "That will depend on what else he knows. It would not be good for him to know that we did it."

"So, he gets an anonymous tip."

"He'll want to find the car and get rid of it."

"We can tell him where it is."

"Sure." Amos laughed.

"He might settle the strike, just to calm everything down and get all the reporters out of town before he has to deal with the car."

"By rights, he should go to jail for the dynamite conspiracy and for kidnapping Paddy."

"That won't help the poor bastards in the tenements or bring the children back."

"You too? You're getting soft."

"I know you, Amos. Your heart's as big as my own."

The two looked at each other, and Amos said, "I can't do it on my own. Paddy and Molly are implicated."

# CHAPTER TWENTY TWO

Paddy came home a little later than usual. Everyone else had finished their suppers, and Molly was alone in the kitchen when he walked in. He sensed that something was different; he spotted a letter sitting on the table, at his place.

She turned to him. "Why don't you take that inside while I put your supper out?"

He nodded and picked it up, noting first Maria's handwriting and then the strange looking stamps and postmarks. In his room, he tossed his hat and coat on the bed and sat in his reading chair, arching his back and straightening his legs so as to get a hand into his pocket to fish out his penknife. Leaning toward the light, he slipped the blade into the envelope, mading sure he did not cut the letter inside.

He never thought to ask her for a picture of herself. It was difficult to conjure up her image as he unfolded the paper.

*Dear Paddy,*

*As is obvious, we have arrived in Rome. We are all well and getting settled in our new apartment near the University. My father's friends arranged everything. He can't wait to start teaching, and I have never seen him so happy.*

*I have been so busy helping my mother that I have only been out twice to do a little food shopping. It's amazing to me that things are not more different here. It seems that the Italians in Lawrence did a good job of making the neighborhood just like the real Italy.*

*Of course, I have not been too busy to miss you and I hope that you are thinking of me. Write to me right away and give the letter to Carla to mail. I will start to write a longer letter even before I get one from you. The mail takes so long; we must not wait before writing, or you might forget about me in between letters.*

*I'm putting my kisses for you on the paper right here.*

*With love for you,*

*Maria*

*P.S. Please check on Lorenzo.*

Paddy sunk back in his chair, held the letter to his lips and closed his eyes. He forgot his appetite and entered into a reverie, trying to imagine the paper as her lips. An inner voice reminded him that his mother was waiting. He put Maria's letter in his desk drawer and dream-walked his way toward the kitchen while clinging to his sense of Maria, his feeling that she was near even as his longing welled up, cruelly reminding him of the distance between them.

He sat down, and Molly put his supper in front of him. She sat across from him and studied his face. "I gather that all is well? God is in his heaven?"

Paddy broke into a broad grin.

"Be sure and tell me when she meets the Pope."

Still grinning, Paddy nodded. After supper, he returned to his desk where he reread her letter and took out a piece of paper.

*Dear Maria,*

*Your letter arrived today to make me the happiest man in Lawrence. I miss you and I am praying that we can be together again soon. In the meantime, letters will have to do. I will write often.*

*You mentioned your concern for Lorenzo. He was here a few nights ago to deliver the jacket your father made for me. My mother convinced him to stay for dinner, and before he left, we were getting to be friends. He still sees me as being on the side of the mill owners in the strike, but I have changed my mind.*

250

*Unfortunately, I still don't support the Wobblies and their methods.*

*Lorenzo said that he would be staying with the Lamastros. I will stop by and see how he's doing and I will write a letter, thanking your father for the wonderful jacket, and give it to Lorenzo to mail.*

*The strike is still going on, and I am back working at the mills. The owners believe that they will win, and all the strikers will return for the same pay. Many workers have already returned, and we are making cloth. I believe the strikers will win—they have such spirit and they deserve a better life. I don't know how this will happen and I have no experience with such matters, but it seems to me that it is not right for the owners to have so much and the workers so little.*

*I may not be here to see how it turns out; my grandfather is making arrangements for me to go to Boston and work for him. Don't worry; I'll still get your letters.*

*Writing to you makes me feel almost as if I'm with you. I love you. Keep sending kisses. Here are some for you. XXXXX*

*Paddy*

He folded the letter and then did something he had not done for years. He took out a stick of red sealing wax, melted the tip with a match and dabbed a spot onto the paper edge. When they were younger, he and Frank used to send each other secret messages this way. They even used some kind of seal to emboss the wax while it was still soft, but Paddy lost his years earlier. He addressed an envelope to Carla and placed his letter inside. She would mail it to Maria.

Just as he finished, Molly appeared in the doorway. "Do you need a stamp?"

"I have one, thanks."

"Your father wants to talk to us about something."

"Downstairs?"

251

She nodded, and he followed her down to the living room.

Amos set his paper aside and asked Molly, "Are the other two in bed?"

"Kathleen is still finishing some homework." She sat on the couch, next to Paddy.

Amos got up pulled over a small side chair and sat in front of them. "We'll keep our voices down, just in case. It's about the car."

"The one in the river?" Paddy asked.

"Yes, that one."

"Has it been found?"

"Not yet."

Molly asked, "Are you thinking of telling about what happened?"

Amos sat up straight and took a deep breath. "No. But I've been talking the situation over with Casey. We think the car belongs to William Wood. But even if it does, it still doesn't prove that he's behind the kidnapping or the dynamite plot. The man owns a number of automobiles, and chauffeurs take care of them. One of his subordinates could have been acting on his own. Whoever it is would not want the car and its contents found."

Molly turned to Paddy. "Do you have any idea of what all this means?"

Paddy stared at his da. "I think so."

"Well, I don't like the sound of it," she said.

"I'm thinking of sending an anonymous tip to Wood, telling him he'll be given the location of the car and Serbians after he gives the workers a raise and settles the strike."

Molly asked, "Won't he know that Paddy is involved?"

"Maybe. Whoever hired the Serbians will know, but he won't know how many other people are in on the secret."

"But you're Paddy's father; he'll know that you're one of them."

"He knows that already because we got Paddy back. What he does not know is where the car is or what happened to the Serbians. I don't think he'll make trouble."

Molly clasped her hands together. "I think it might be best to leave things well enough alone. Let nature take its course."

Amos turned to Paddy. "What do you think?"

"I don't want them to get away with it."

Molly stared hard at both of them. "Revenge is not a noble motive. And you have the rest of the family to think of."

Paddy answered. "Yes, you're speaking of revenge for the kidnapping and beating. But what about the way they treat the workers, like machines—worse, like animals? Somebody needs to stand up to them."

"It doesn't need to be you," she said.

Amos spoke. "We'll take precautions. I'll see that the kids are escorted back and forth to school. I'll meet Paddy at the mill gate. It should only be for a few days. If Wood settles the strike, it's a signal that he wants everything to quiet down—no more trouble."

"And if he doesn't?" she asked.

He reached over to take her hand. "You and Paddy take the kids and go to Boston."

"Oh, Amos."

"It's what your father wanted."

"I'll tell him that when we show up on his doorstep like a bunch of fugitives."

253

Paddy said, "I'll come back out and stay with Da."

Molly stood up. "I can see there's no sense in talking with either one of you."

The next morning, Amos placed a note in an envelope, marked it "Personal and Confidential" and mailed it to Wood's home in North Andover.

# CHAPTER TWENTY THREE

Tension began to build in the Flanagan home even before Amos mailed the letter. On the day after, they began the agreed precautions. Amos endeavored to make himself invisible at the station house, and Paddy tried, without success, to ignore the boredom and seemingly endless days in the mill. Neal and Kathleen busied themselves with school and play, even as Molly began to pack.

As the weekend passed, in place of the usual lively conversations, small talk filled in. No one went out except for brief trips to the stores and to Mass. As Amos watched Molly draw into herself and become increasingly quiet, he felt the poison of self-doubt creeping through his brain. He went to Paddy. "What are you thinking?"

Paddy, unsure at first of just what his da wanted from him, paused before answering. "I think Mom should take the kids and go to Boston."

He put his hand on Paddy's knee. "I think you're right."

They talked that night. She said, "I'll make the arrangements."

He put an arm around her and held her to him.

"This will be a first," she said.

"For what?"

"We've never been apart before."

"Yeah."

There was a bright spot for Paddy on Monday—another letter from Maria.

*Dear Paddy,*

*We are now almost settled. Rosa, Anna and Guido are in school. My mother has most of what she needs to cook and take care of the house, and I am able to get out on my own. I feel like such a foreigner, especially when I go sightseeing. There are so many things to see—so much history! You should see the Coliseum . The Wood Mill would fit inside.*

*My father has helped me to get work at the University. I am tutoring students in English. They waste a lot of our time together asking me questions about America instead of concentrating on learning English. I'm saving the money from this work so I can return to you. I don't know when that will be. I'm hoping that my father will be successful here and get so absorbed in his work that he won't mind so much.*

*I know that you have written a letter to me. I can't wait for the first one to arrive. We have not heard from Lorenzo yet. I hope that he is well and that you will look after him.*

*Rome is a very romantic city. I think I'm loving you even more since I arrived.*

*Love and kisses from me,*

*Maria*

Paddy had another letter almost ready to go. It was long, filled with expressions of love and yearning for her. He also related the news from Lawrence, mostly having to do with the strike, and he tried to explain his feelings of detachment from both the strike and the mill brought on by his coming move to Boston. He did not mention anything to do with the gamble he and his da were engaged in.

256

After reading her letter a second time, he added a note to the bottom of his own:

*Don't worry about the money. As soon as you can come, I will send as much as you need for the trip.*

*I love you,*

*Paddy*

Two days later, he was involved in teaching a new operative how to change the shuttle. She had been making the same mistakes for almost a week. At first, he thought it was mostly a language problem—she was Polish, but it was clear that she was not up to the job and would have to go. Maybe Kevin O'Shay could place her in a simpler job.

Ernst Meyer appeared near the stairwell. He motioned Paddy with his head; he wanted to talk. Paddy got the Syrian girl at the next workstation to look after the Polish girl and walked over to Meyer. He pulled out his earplugs.

"Did you hear the news?" Meyer asked.

Paddy looked back toward the Polish girl. "I've been pretty busy."

"The strike's over."

Paddy was sure he heard but he said, "What?"

"Wood's made an offer. It's what the strikers wanted. It'll be all over in a couple of days."

Paddy stood there, staring blankly at Meyer. He didn't feel anything and he thought he should.

Meyer leaned closer. "Are you all right? This is good news, isn't it?"

"Yeah. Yes, it's good news. I was just thinking."

"You were thinking? What were you thinking?"

Paddy smiled. "I was thinking that my da is a pretty smart man."

"Yeah well, that's nice. I gotta go."

Paddy walked back to the Polish girl. He was surprised to see that she was doing well. The Syrian girl smiled at him. He stood, pretending to watch the operatives while he digested Meyer's news. Was it the letter to Wood? His thoughts turned to Maria; if only she were still in Lawrence.

\*\*\*\*\*\*\*\*\*\*\*\*\*\*\*\*\*\*\*\*\*\*\*\*\*\*\*\*\*\*\*\*\*\*\*\*

Amos arrived at the station with an expectant feeling; Wood had made an offer and everyone seemed to believe that the end of the strike was a mere formality. As he walked in, he sensed a change in atmosphere; smiles seemed the order of the day. He waved to Kerrigan who motioned him over. "The son-in-law wants to see you."

Amos removed his hat and coat, leaving them on a bench behind Kerrigan's desk. He arrived at the office door, and Sullivan stood up to invite him in. "Amos, have a seat. Make yourself comfortable."

Amos sensed a marked change in Sullivan's demeanor. The end of the strike had to be a great relief, eliminating all kinds of pressure on the man. And now he wanted to make amends—butter up his old friend. He crossed the room and took his customary chair. Sullivan closed his office door and sat behind his desk.

"You've heard the news, of course?"

"I have, John, and good news it is."

"Indeed, assuming the mills can still compete."

"I'm sure Mister Wood has made careful calculations."

"One would hope so. But that's not what I wanted to see you about."

"I didn't think so."

"No, it's a more personal matter. You know, you were right when you said the police department was playing into the hands of the strikers. We made ourselves look foolish. It's going to take time to regain the public's respect."

"The public's memory is notoriously short."

"Maybe so, Amos. Maybe so. But the Wilcox case is now coming to the fore."

"Ah."

"Yes. Con and the Mayor both feel it would be best for the department if you were to resign."

Amos was stunned by his own reaction. He felt the blood drain from his face. But why was he reacting this way? He was leaving anyway. And yet, it felt as if his humanity—his manhood—was being ripped out of him. They had no right. No one had the right to cut a man down like this. He struggled for control. "Because of the Wilcox shooting?"

"Yes."

"No other influences involved?"

"I don't know what you're talking about."

"Sure you do." Amos noticed a reddening on Sullivan's neck as he pulled at his collar.

"Listen, Amos, make it easy on yourself. There will be a sweetener here, a going-away bonus. Maybe, when everything dies down, we can bring you back in."

Why argue? He wasn't going to show any weakness. "All right, John, I understand the spot you're in. I'll write my resignation and hand it in today." He got up to go.

Sullivan jumped to his feet and came out from behind his desk. "You're right, Amos, I'm in a spot. And I'm sorry. I'm deeply sorry." He held out his hand.

Amos shook his hand briefly, perfunctorily, and left the room. He returned to the main desk.

Kerrigan said, "That was quick. What happened?"

"Nothing that wasn't going to happen anyway, Jimmy. I'll be going into the trucking business in Boston."

"Ah, Amos."

"It's all right, Jimmy. I mean it; I was leaving anyway."

Kerrigan reached out to grab his forearm. "Don't go sudden like. Let's have a proper goodbye."

Amos knew that meant a drunken party—something he'd rather skip. But he could not. "Sure. Just let me know." He pointed to his coat. "Keep an eye on my coat; I'm going upstairs."

Bill Conboy made no effort to be his usual friendly and helpful self. Amos reflected on the fact that he rarely saw Conboy during the morning. Maybe he was still a bit hung-over? Conboy looked up, forcing a small, apparently painful, smile. "The Judge has to be in court in twenty minutes."

"I won't take long. Tell him I'm here."

Conboy got to his feet. "I doubt he'll see you." He turned to disappear into the Judge's office. In less than a minute, he came back out, jerking his head toward the door behind him. "He'll see you."

Amos went in, and Waters gestured to a chair. "Billy told you I haven't much time?"

"He did, John. I'll only take a few minutes. I've just been asked to hand in my resignation—ostensibly because of the Wilcox affair. I have the impression that Mister Wood's concern for the dynamite investigation is the real reason."

260

"Do you want to fight it?"

"No. I'm going to Boston. I was going anyway. But I'd like to leave a present for Wood."

Waters sat back, hooking his thumbs into his belt. "You're a brave man, Amos. Not many men would go off to make a new start at your age. And it's a shame; Lawrence needs men like you."

"I'm looking forward to the challenge. And I think it's best for my family. Paddy especially, but the younger two as well, they'll have better prospects in Boston."

"It's all about motorcars and trucks isn't it? I'll have to get one myself."

"They are here to stay. But I'm getting concerned about keeping you from court."

"They'll wait. What choice do they have? Anyway, back to business. I'll arrange for a confidential interview with the Attorney General. You can turn over what you have and give him a head start. And what about Pitman; he won't skip town will he?"

"I doubt it, but they should get him under surveillance soon."

"All right, Amos, I'll be in touch."

"Don't use Conboy."

"I understand."

Amos waved to Billy on his way past and returned to the front desk for his hat and coat. "I'll be back after lunch, Jimmy."

"Casey wants to know what's going on. What should I tell him?"

"Casey? Michael Casey? I barely know the man. Tell him nothing." Amos put on his coat and passed close to Kerrigan. "Tell him to keep his head down."

"I will, Amos. All the best."

Amos arrived at Saint Patrick's school before the noon recess. After Wood made his offer to end the strike, he and Molly decided to keep escorting the children and Paddy as well, until they were sure it was safe to stop. Since he was supposed to be working, she would be there. He watched as she came over the bridge, which spanned the railroad tracks, and waited for her to recognize him. When she spotted him, she approached with a look of concern.

"Has there been some kind of threat?" she asked.

"Not at all." He moved to her side, and they continued toward the school. "Actually, the threat is probably over. I've been fired. I think they believe that will end their problems."

"And does it?"

"No, but by the time they figure it out, we'll be in Boston."

"Are you going to tell the children?"

"Not right away. Let's go over things with Paddy and make the arrangements before we get them into it. It's better if we're ready to leave before they tell their friends."

After lunch, Amos walked Kathleen and Neal back to school and then returned home to write out his resignation and a note to William Wood, in which he included a diagram showing the car's location. As before, he addressed an envelope to Wood at his home. Before slipping the note in, he paused to check the diagram. He smiled; it looked, for all the world, like the pirate map in Neal's favorite book, *Treasure Island*. He went out to mail the letter, drop his resignation off in Sullivan's office, and loop back to escort the kids home after school.

Before she sent the children upstairs to change out of their school uniforms, Molly said, "I've made some cookies. You can have one after you change." They scampered off, and

262

she set out a cup for Amos. "Would you like a cookie with your tea?"

"I would," he said, taking his place.

"I called my father," she said, as she went about pouring his tea and placing a cookie on a saucer. "I never mentioned anything about you-know-what but I did tell him about the dynamite business. He wants us to come right away, to get the children out of any harm. He said the house is almost ready, and he'll get them to rush on the rest."

Amos folded his hands on the table and lowered his head, as if in prayer. Thoughts tumbled head-long through his brain. Why couldn't things stand still for at least a few hours? So many changes. There was no control; his whole life was being remade, and he felt like a bystander. "Is he ready to take Paddy into the business?"

"He is and yourself as well."

He picked up his cookie and idly examined it, seeing none of it, before taking a bite. "There will be some things to finish up here. The rest of you should go."

"I'll not leave you by yourself."

Neal ran in, ending the conversation. He jumped into his chair. "Timmy's coming over. Can he have a cookie too?"

"By all means," she said. "You may be wanting another one yourself."

He nodded, chomped on his cookie and drank his milk.

To Amos, it seemed that Molly's spirits had already picked up. At best, he was still confused. He needed time to think—for things to settle a bit. "We'll talk more later," he said.

It was dark when he put on his hat and coat and walked into the kitchen to tell Molly he was going to meet Paddy. "I'll tell him what's been going on. We can all work out a plan after the kids are in bed."

She put down her ladle, stepped away from the stove and put her arms around his neck. "I know you're worried, Amos. You feel so responsible for everything and everyone. But it will all be for the best—you'll see. And you've got a good woman." She squeezed him.

He kissed her forehead. "Yup. I guess I can always rent you out."

He turned to go and she paddled his fanny.

\*\*\*\*\*\*\*\*\*\*\*\*\*\*\*\*\*\*\*\*\*\*\*\*\*\*\*\*\*

It was almost quitting time. Paddy went into the office and found Kevin O'Shay in a talkative mood. "I guess it's all over but the shouting, Paddy. That's the word I get. I hope you're ready; they'll be wanting us to make up for lost time. Probably want us to cover the wage increase with extra production. I'm not looking forward to it, I can tell you."

Paddy folded his coat over his arm, held his cap and strolled over to sit next to O'Shay's desk. "Getting things up and going again will be a lot of work, but I doubt there's going to be much speeding up; the union is riding high right now."

"You're right; they are riding high. So who's going to get squeezed? You know who. I wish I was old enough to retire. As it is, I'll probably die at my desk."

Paddy smiled. "Nah. They need men like you. They'll be good to you." He got up. "I've got to meet someone."

"Young love, I suppose." O'Shay waved a hand, dismissing him.

He found Amos waiting at the gate and told him about the conversation with O'Shay.

Amos said, "We've had a few wrinkles ourselves today." As they walked briskly in the cold night air, he brought Paddy up

264

to date. When Amos told him how he'd been fired, Paddy said nothing at first. He turned to gauge his da's feelings. Then he said, "That kind of finalizes things, doesn't it?"

Amos said nothing,

"I mean, we're all going to Boston?"

"Yeah, we're all going to Boston."

They walked for another minute before Paddy said, "I think you're a lot better off than Kevin O'Shay."

Amos smiled and put a hand on his shoulder. "True."

They arrived on South Broadway, and Paddy offered to stand a round at Jack's.

"Your mother's worried as is; we don't want to keep her waiting. We can come down after supper."

They changed their minds and did not go to the pub after supper; there was too much to talk about at home. With Kathleen and Neal upstairs, doing homework and getting ready for bed, they convened in the living room. It was quickly agreed that Molly would leave as soon as possible with the children. She'd get them in a new school while Amos settled things in Lawrence, including putting the house up for sale.

Paddy said, "I want to stay for a few weeks. I can help O'Shay when the workers come back and keep Da company. And help with the packing, of course."

"I don't like that," she said. "There are surely others who can do the job. The mill won't fall down without you. I've got enough to worry about."

Paddy looked to his da.

"She's right. You go to Boston. I can manage here, and you can give me the lay of the land at the trucking company before I start."

It was settled. Paddy went upstairs to write another letter to Maria. He gave her his new address. The following weekend, he drove out from Boston in Patrick Kelly's Buick, stopping first at Frank's to show it off. He took Amos for a ride, but Amos drove most of the way—"just for the practice." Before leaving, Paddy loaded the car with boxes of dishes and clothing, lit the Prestolite gas headlights and headed back to Boston.

# CHAPTER TWENTY FOUR

Lawrence was finished with Amos Flanagan. The city where he was born, raised, schooled, worked and raised a family was spitting him out. He wanted it to be a good thing. He wanted to look forward to a new exciting future, but he couldn't escape his feelings of loss, of rejection. He knew every part of the city, where each neighborhood started and stopped. He had watched as new ethnic groups moved in vying for space within walking distance to the mills, sometimes dividing a street, the houses to one point being Polish the next one and beyond German.

He had friends everywhere, in the neighborhood, at church, on the job, and about town. Not a day passed without warm interactions with people he'd known since he was a boy. And now, he was to leave it all behind. He felt like an emigrant departing for a distant land. It would be different, he thought, if like his forebears, he had to leave the old country or starve to death. They had no choice, no doubts about whether they were doing the right thing.

He went through the motions of saying goodbye. The send-off shindig organized by Jimmy Kerrigan wasn't nearly as bad as he feared. It helped that neither Alderman Con Lynch nor Mayor Scanlon showed up to make hypocritical remarks. John Sullivan came by to shake his hand and say again how sorry he was. Amos knew he had no choice in the firing and said as much. It felt natural.

The party, held at Demsey's Saloon on Broadway, was tame in comparison to similar events, which Amos had attended. Only a few used the occasion to tie-one-on, Billy Conboy being one of the predictable offenders. So many came by to wish him well that Amos was touched in spite of his knowing it to be a

267

formality, a ritual for most of them. They almost all professed to believe that the parting was temporary, that he would be back. Amos never protested.

During one of the few quiet moments, Casey pulled him aside. "I'm just getting used to the excitement of working with you, and here you are, leaving me. With the strike over, I'll be back on the beat, a dumb copper cadging apples from fruit stands."

"Maybe you'd rather drive a truck in Boston?"

"A bit late for me, Amos, but you'll do well. I know you will. Just don't forget your friends."

"I'll not forget you, Michael."

There were a few surprises: Liam Turley, the undertaker, came by as did Willy McGreevy, who thanked him again for his help in getting Mary a place to go and have her baby. Fortunately, McGreevy's visit did not overlap that of the purported father, "Fast" Eddie Foyle.

When it was over, Casey walked with him as far as the bridge. Before they parted, he said, "I know there's a sadness in it for you, Amos."

"There is, Michael. There's so much of me here; so much I'm leaving behind."

"As losses go, it's not so bad, is it?"

"As losses go? No, you're right. There are lots worse."

"And there is a bright side in this."

Amos laughed and nodded. They shook hands. "God bless you, Michael."


He let himself into a dark and empty house. Like thousands of cobwebs, sadness draped itself over him as he went down the hall. He needed his wife. He needed Molly. But he had to settle for a telephone call. He let it ring ten times before recalling that Patrick Kelley never answered the telephone after nine at night, at which time he placed it inside a cabinet where it could barely be heard.

With the window shade up so he could see the moon, he lay in bed thinking of Molly's daffodils, which would soon burst out all over the yard for someone else to enjoy. He continued to gaze at the moon while extending an arm over to rub a strangely empty place.

He called her in the morning. "Some of your daffodils are blooming."

"We have some here," she said. "Mrs. Burns planted them last fall, and some tulips are on their way."

He told her about the shindig and about calling the night before.

"You sound lonely. I can come out."

"No need; I'm almost finished here—a few papers to sign. I'm going over to see Joe Lamastro this morning; he and Connie have been helping me with the paperwork on selling the house. How's Paddy, keeping busy?"

"He's up to his neck in it. I've never seen him so busy. Talks about all the problems, incessantly. And he has his long-distance romance to attend to. The letters are coming twice a week now."

"Does it look like she's actually coming back?"

"From the few details I get, it's hard for me to say. Paddy certainly thinks she is."

"There aren't any good-looking Irish girls in the neighborhood, are there?"

"If there are, it won't matter."

"I guess not. God, this could be awful."

"We'll just have to wait it out, Amos."

He took his time fixing breakfast, puttering around the kitchen that was to become part of his past life. Sun shown through the window, highlighting worn spots in the wood floor and chips in the white paint on the cabinets. He paused to gaze out at the small patch of yard between his house and the neighbors; bright green buds covered every branch and twig of the hedge along the fence. Why was he so sad? He'd be with his family soon enough. He moved away from the window just in time to catch his eggs before they turned into fried leather.

As soon as he hit the sidewalk, he knew something had happened. A neighbor approached, holding out a newspaper. "Have you seen this, Amos?"

The headline read, "TITANIC SINKS, 1200 LOST"

"My God, Mike, were there no survivors?"

"They say about eight hundred women and children. The ship hit an iceberg."

All along the street, they were talking of nothing else. Connie had coffee and some home-made pastry ready when he arrived twenty minutes later. Joe walked in nodding at Amos's paper on the table. "What a tragedy."

Connie said, "We need to pray for every soul that went down."

When they got down to business a few minutes later, Joe reminded Amos that he had to have everything out of the house by the end of April.

"It's going to be hard, walking out that door for the last time."

"You'll be into your new job and a whole new set of problems by then. You won't have time to think about it. How's Paddy doing?"

"Molly tells me she's never seen him so busy. He's also writing to Maria twice a week."

Joe shook his head, and Connie nodded. "It could work out, Amos. We're in the twentieth century; everything's changing."

"It seems that some things never change."

They laughed. Joe said, "Lorenzo's gone. He tried to get a job in the mills, but anyone associated with the Wobblies has been black listed."

"That's a shame. I thought he was turning into a nice young man."

"He is a nice young man. I think he was frustrated by his father's unrealistic demands."

"Where did he go?"

"Off with the Wobblies. They're organizing a strike in New Jersey somewhere."


Judge Waters arranged for Amos to have a private meeting with Suffolk County District Attorney White in Boston to tell him about the dynamite affair, Pitman and William Wood.

He had never been in such an impressive office; White was clearly a man of great importance. He greeted Amos in a cordial manner but seemed distracted, even a bit annoyed, with having to deal with a cop from Lawrence. He sat behind a huge oak desk and introduced two subordinates, Miss Roberta Forbes, a secretary, and Clarence Young, an Assistant District Attorney.

Amos thought that a "private" meeting meant just that. He felt compromised and unsure of how much he should say, how candid to be about his suspicions and the reasoning behind them. He envisioned everything he said appearing in The Boston Globe that afternoon. Feeling embarrassed, he clamped down,

271

telling only what he knew to be established fact and suggesting only what *might* be inferred.

The result was what he expected: A short, perfunctory meeting, followed by forced politeness and a quick trip out the door. He was angry, mostly at himself for being naïve enough to think that his efforts might result in bringing Pitman and Wood to justice.

An hour later, he sat in the living room in the house on Iroquois Street relating his experience to Molly. She told him the latest regarding Kathleen and Neal, who were still struggling to adjust to their new school and neighborhood. "It's hard to enter in the middle of a school year; the other children have all the friends they need, and the teaching is different."

"Maybe we can throw a couple of little parties, take the other kids for joy rides in Patrick's car."

"Just you being here will make a difference. I think they feel less secure without you around."

"I'll try to cheer them up. And how's my fellow conspirator?"

"Not happy. He got another letter yesterday; it obviously upset him, but I didn't want to pry."

"No hint?"

She shook her head. "He'll be home soon. I know he's dying to talk to you. Maybe you can get it out of him."

"I know your father wants to bend my ear. I'll put him off to tomorrow—I'll go to the office with him in the morning. Tonight is for Paddy and the kids."

Dinner that evening proved to be a lively affair with Amos the target of the children's stories while Paddy tried to interject some comments on the problems he saw in the business—ones he felt Amos would need to address. "Some of the older teamsters are worried they won't be able to handle motorized trucks and they'll lose their jobs."

Amos found it relaxing to just listen while he enjoyed Mrs. Burns' pot roast. He noted that Patrick remained uncharacteristically quiet, seemingly content to sit, enjoying the completeness of his family circle. After dinner, he excused himself; Paddy and Amos were to have time alone.

They went to the living room where Paddy occupied the chair Molly had sat in earlier. He leaned forward and began to tell his da of the things he'd learned. Amos caught a flatness in his voice when compared to earlier telephone conversations on the same subjects. He interrupted. "Is there something else?"

Paddy hesitated. "I got a letter—from Maria."

Amos waited.

"Her mother is real sick. She says her family needs her there."

"Maybe her mother will get better."

Pause. "That's not how it sounds."

"It's going to be tough for her. She's got two younger sisters and a little brother. Lorenzo won't be of any help; he couldn't get back into the mills so he's gone off with the Wobblies. They will need her."

"I know."

"It won't be forever."

"Guido, the youngest one, is only around ten years old."

Amos searched for a way to help. "You should plan a trip over there."

Paddy forced a grin. "Her father will love that."

"Well, don't give up. Keep writing."

"I will. I'm driving Carla nuts with all the mail I send. She thinks Alessandro is going to get suspicious."

With some instructions from its prideful owner, Amos drove the Buick when he and Patrick went to 'Kelly Trucking' the next morning. After making the rounds and introducing Amos to the men working in the shop, Patrick said, "We'll take another drive now. We're going to see the banker." He explained. "They're worried about advancing the money for new trucks to a business run by an old man like myself. They want to meet you."

"You're not planning to die very soon, are you?"

"Not if I can help it."

Amos felt that the meeting went well. Roger Hovey, the loan officer, expressed a willingness to finance more motor trucks as long as there were drivers and business for them. He wondered why Hovey wasn't worried about the business being run by someone with no experience if Patrick were to die unexpectedly. Hovey even suggested that it was time for Patrick to take a vacation—a trip somewhere. Amos kept his thoughts to himself.

\*\*\*\*\*\*\*\*\*\*\*\*\*\*\*\*\*\*\*\*

He returned to Lawrence the following day to arrange for the last furniture to be moved out and taken to Boston. He also had an appointment with Judge Waters to tell him about his meeting with the District Attorney. He described the meeting and his reaction to it.

Waters said, "They took you seriously, Amos. There was an assistant district attorney out here yesterday, questioning Pitman. He came by to see me and said that Pitman was obviously disturbed by his questioning and let on more than expected. They are planning to bring an indictment against William Wood. You're to keep that under your hat."

"I will, John. I just hope that my name doesn't come into it."

"The District Attorney promised me that you would remain anonymous. I believe he'll keep his word."

Amos clasped his hands together. "That's amazing. I'm really surprised—and pleased, I might add. After that meeting, I never thought anything would come of it."

Waters smiled. "You, of all people, Amos, should know that the system doesn't *always* fail."

They talked on other subjects for a short time before Amos took his leave, waving to Billy Conboy on his way past. Downstairs, he looked through the door and saw that Kerrigan was not busy. He walked over and extended his hand. "Did I thank you for that great shindig you put on?"

"You did, Amos, several times. But I'm glad you enjoyed it that much. And how are things in Boston?"

"Grand, but I'm just getting into it. Has it quieted down any here?"

"We're all taking a breather from the strike. But I heard this morning that they took a body out of the river in Haverhill. It's decomposed, but they said it's a well-dressed male with a bullet hole in him."

"Is that right? Was it a robbery, or didn't they say?"

"No robbery. He had a watch and two hundred dollars on him."

"Are they thinking he was dumped in Lawrence and washed down?"

"I don't think they know those kinds of details yet. Are you interested?"

"Just curious."

"Once a cop, always a cop, heh?

"Right. But this cop has got to get back over to South Lawrence and finish closing up the house. I want to catch the five o'clock train back to Boston."

# CHAPTER TWENTY FIVE

At four-thirty he left the house for the last time, trying not to look back. But he did, stopping to take a long look before clearing his throat and heading for the station. The train was not crowded; there was no difficulty finding a window seat. He checked his watch; the train would be in the station for another five minutes. Just as he opened his paper, he felt the hulk of a big man move into the seat next to him. He was annoyed when, glancing over his paper, he could see lots of empty seats just in front of his own. He flapped his paper and glanced at the man, only to laugh at himself—the hulk was Michael Casey, wearing the same suit he'd worn to the party.

"Have they promoted you to inspector, Michael?"

Casey stared straight forward. "No. Just less conspicuous this way."

Amos continued to pretend he was reading. "That will be the day—Michael Casey, inconspicuous."

"I'll ride with you as far as Andover. I wanted to tell you they found the car."

"Jesus. Who?"

"I'm sure they're working for Wood. I've been across the river at the Poor Farm, watching the river at night. They got some grappling hooks onto it and dragged it down toward Haverhill."

"You heard about the body?"

"Yeah. They must have ripped a door off, or something."

"Do you think the Haverhill cops or the state police will drag the river?"

"If they do, they'll find the car in Haverhill. Wood's done us all a big favor. Even if they find another body or identify this one, it won't matter. No one has been reported missing; they'll assume it's a gang murder, or maybe the Wobblies and something strike related."

"Any other good news?"

"No, and it looks like I can get off before the train pulls out."

"God bless you, Michael."

The train started to move. Amos turned to see Casey moving faster than he would have thought possible.

\*\*\*\*\*\*\*\*\*\*\*\*\*\*\*

It had been a good day. Paddy and his helper, Sean Anderson, performed the routine maintenance necessary to ready the truck for the next day. As they finished up, Paddy commented, "Isn't this great, Sean?"

"Yeah, if this was a horse, we'd be here another hour, washing and brushing and feeding and mucking out the shit."

Paddy went to the office to remind his grand da that it was time to go home. Once there, he found his mother in the dining room.

"We're home," he said.

She smiled. "So I see. Did you have a good day?"

"I did."

"Your father will be along shortly. There's a letter for you. I left it in your room."

"Already?"

The letter sat, propped against the ink stand on his desk. He picked it up to feel it and then put it down to remove his hat and coat before he opened it.

*Dearest Paddy*

*My heart is breaking. Our dear beloved mother has passed away. We are all devastated, and it has fallen on me to keep our family together. They all need me more than ever.*

*My father is drinking too much wine and saying it's all his fault for bringing us here. The doctor says that can't be true, her heart was weak, and it would have happened anyway. I think it doesn't matter and I must care for my father until he recovers his good sense and judgment. I know that reading this will make you unhappy. We were both hoping that the time would be short until we came together again. Now, I don't know how long it will be. Please try to understand.*

*I love you.*

*Maria*

Paddy returned the letter to its envelope, placed it on the desk and sat on his bed, staring at it. Sometime later, there was a soft knock and Neal stepped into the room.

"Da's home. They're putting supper out."

"Yeah, I'm not hungry, Neal. I'm just going to stay here. Okay?"

The family was still convening in the dining room when Neal reported back to Molly. Amos overheard and looked at her. "He got another letter," she said.

"I'll go up to him. Hold my dinner."

He knocked on Paddy's door and entered, taking note of the envelope on the desk. "I picked up some news in Lawrence today, but it can wait." He pulled out the chair from Paddy's desk and sat facing him.

279

"What's the news in Lawrence?" Paddy's voice betrayed his lack of interest.

"A body turned up in the river in Haverhill. Some well-dressed guy with a bullet hole in him."

Paddy sat up, showing some interest.

"It seems some guys got grappling hooks onto the car and dragged it toward Haverhill. Casey thinks they were working for Wood and maybe they tore a door off the car, and that's how the body came out."

"Wow. What's going to happen?"

"Most likely, nothing. Sounds like you got some news today?"

Paddy reached for the letter and gave it to Amos, who read it and placed it back on the desk. "That's a shame. The Petrellas are taking their knocks, aren't they?"

Paddy nodded.

Amos reached to put a hand on Paddy's knee. "And you too. I'm sorry—for the Petrellas—and for you."

"Do you think it will ever work?"

Amos leaned back and thought for a moment before answering. "I don't know. Give it a little time. Time can work wonders."

"I feel so helpless."

"Yes. I've been feeling a lot of that, myself, lately. Everything's changing."

"You've got mom."

"I'm blessed, but I need you too. I'm going to need your help."

"I'm not going anywhere, Da."

Amos smiled and looked at the envelope on the desk. "She's helping her father. Tell her you're helping me. You can give each other some advice—so to speak." He got up. "You can't help anybody on an empty stomach."

        "I'll be down in a bit."

        "We'll put something aside."

\*\*\*\*\*\*\*\*\*\*\*\*\*\*\*\*\*\*\*\*

        Letters continued to cross the Atlantic at the rate of one or two a week. They became a chronicle of the lives of two lovers, separated by what seemed to them an insurmountable barrier. Maria wrote of the details of her daily life as a housekeeper and surrogate mother in a world defined by the apartment and small neighborhood. Paddy wrote of the exciting and expanding world he'd found in Boston and the trucking business. The tone of their letters became more conversational, more like that of friends than lovers. Paddy worried about this. Was she becoming so immersed in her new life that he was fading from her heart? He wanted to write more intimately, to keep love's flame burning. But that felt awkward.

        He kept her up to date on events in Lawrence. In late August, Ernest Pitman committed suicide but not before confessing to his role in the dynamite plot. Days later, indictments were returned for William Wood and others. Ettor and Giovannitti, the Wobbly leaders, were tried for inciting the death of Anna Lopizzo but were found innocent in late November, engendering another round of celebrations. Caruso, who had been charged with the actual shooting, was also found innocent.

        Reporting strike related news to Maria made him despondent. As he mailed each letter off, he realized that the events in Lawrence, which had drawn them together, were coming to closure. But he and Maria were not. As the days shortened, and Boston gave its citizens a foretaste of winter, frustration led to days of despair. He began to believe that the waiting would never be over, that the letters and passion would taper off, and that they would come to realize, possibly without daring to say so, that they would never lie in each others arms.

He began to think of ways to force the issue. He could send her money for passage and insist that she join him. Better, he could go over and get her.


Frank Dunn came to town for photo supplies and to buy some Christmas presents. He stayed overnight with the Flanagans. He and Paddy stayed up, talking in Paddy's room.

Frank sat in the upright chair and fingered a stack of letters on the desk. "From Italy?"

"Yeah, we write often."

"About what?"

Paddy snorted and leaned back in his reading-chair. "About how we take care of our fathers."

"They're not love letters?"

"They're supposed to be, but I'm not sure where we're going—or when."

"So, she's still taking her mother's place. Is the father still drinking?"

"No. At least that's over with."

"But she doesn't say anything about getting away yet?"

"No. I'm going crazy. I've got to do something."

"Yeah. But what?"

"I'm thinking of going over there."

"Really?"

"The trouble is that it doesn't look like there's ever going to be a good time to go. We're really busy at work, and my da needs me."

"You can't wait forever."

"I know. I'm planning to talk to my grand da after Christmas. Maybe he can give my da some extra help while I'm gone."

\*\*\*\*\*\*\*\*\*\*\*\*\*\*\*\*\*\*\*\*

On Christmas morning, the family went to an early Mass before returning for breakfast and opening presents. Everyone loved their presents and watching the kids enjoy theirs. Paddy absorbed himself in helping Neal with his train set, all the while planning what he would say when he approached Patrick about a trip to Italy.

Mrs. Burns forbid everyone from the dining room until the dinner was ready. They entered to find the table decorated with sprigs of mistletoe, candles, oranges and nuts. There were new crystal water glasses, and, by each place, a tiny religious medal—a gift from Mrs. Burns. The dinner consisted of goose with every trimming, followed by mince pie with a topping of ice cream.

Patrick tapped on his water glass. "I too have an announcement." He leaned toward Neal. "Neal, would you ask Mrs. Burns to come back in. I want her to hear."

Amos and Molly exchanged glances. Paddy stared at the table cloth in front of him, and Kathleen fidgeted.

With Mrs. Burns standing at the sideboard, Patrick began. "I want to say, first, how pleased I am with the way in

283

which Amos and Paddy have taken over the business and done so well. And the same is true for everyone here; you have all managed the transition amazingly well. Which, of course is giving me some freedom that I haven't had before."

Like a shanachie, he paused for dramatic effect and to make sure that everyone was listening. He needn't have bothered; even Neal was leaning forward with his mouth open.

"I'm going to Australia. I want to see my other grandchildren. All the arrangements have been made; I'll be leaving in late January."

He turned to Amos. "I'm having everything prepared in the event that something happens to me. This house will belong to you and Molly when I leave on my trip. And should I not come back, the business goes to you, as well. You will have complete charge while I'm gone." He sat back and folded his hands, indicating that he was finished.

Only Kathleen and Neal reacted; they were excited and wanted to hear the details of his trip. Mrs. Burns exchanged glances with Molly before returning to the kitchen. Amos and Molly looked at each other, and Paddy stared into space, wondering if fate was bent on ruining every possibility of reuniting with Maria.


Amos and Molly stayed behind when the others left the table.

She said, "Paddy seemed upset."

"Yeah. Short of going over there and kidnapping Maria, I don't know how to help him."

"It would be better if it was just over."

"I agree. But how?"

She sighed. "And Mrs. Burns looked devastated. My father must have thought of her?"

"He probably thinks we'll just keep her on. What's wrong with that?"

"Everything. I want my own place, and she knows it."

Later on, Molly went into the kitchen. Without looking at her, Bridget said, "I'll be leaving soon. I'll not be any trouble."

"Please, do not do that. My father's announcement was a surprise and a shock to all of us. We need time to adjust. Things will work out—you'll see."

She looked at Molly. "Thank you. I'll stay at least until he's gone."


The next day, when Paddy finished working on the last truck, he strolled into the office to tell Amos he was going home. Amos motioned him to a chair and closed the door.

"Patrick's announcement didn't seem to sit well with you yesterday. I know you haven't been happy. How does this make it worse?"

Paddy studied his shoe tops for a moment. "I was planning a trip to Italy."

"Oh. And this puts a wrench in the works?"

Paddy nodded.

"When were you thinking of going?"

"Soon."

"Patrick might only be gone for a few months."

Paddy slowly shook his head.

Amos said, "That's a long time, I guess. But I think it's a good idea—a trip to Italy."

"I can't just keep waiting, Da."

285

Amos perched on the edge of the desk. He drummed his fingers on the wood. "I know. I know. I feel like I'm running some kind of three-ring-circus here. I need somebody to talk to, to help me look into things. I hardly know those men out there. Patrick knows them and he knows where everything is and where it's supposed to be."

He looked at his son for a moment. "I know you can't wait. It's not good. Let's work on it."


Connie and Joe Lamastro were invited to dinner on New Year's Day. Amos drove to North Station to pick them up. They arrived at the house, removed their coats and went into the living room where they warmed their hands by the fire and admired the tree. Patrick offered them whiskeys, but Joe had brought a bottle of Chianti, which Amos proceeded to open.


With the initial greetings and ceremonies over, Joe said, "We got some bad news yesterday. Lorenzo is in the hospital in Paterson, New Jersey. He was shot during some kind of labor disturbance. That's all we know at this point. Connie is going to go out there. I've sent a cablegram to Alessandro."

There were murmurs throughout the room. Amos summed it up. "We're all sorry to hear that. We want to help, if that's possible."

Paddy sat on a side chair with a glass of wine. He had just taken a sip when Lamastro gave them the news. He felt an immediate concern for Lorenzo, sympathy tinged with anger at his having been denied a job in the mills. His second thought was to wonder what this meant to him and Maria. Was there anything he could do, except wait to see how this latest disaster impacted his life?

Lamastro continued. "Of course, everything depends on Lorenzo's condition. If he can travel, Connie will bring him back to Lawrence, and we can keep Alessandro advised while he recovers. If he's in bad shape, Alessandro may want to come over and handle things himself."


Later, Molly took Connie for a tour of the house. They arrived in the sewing room where Molly felt free to talk without being overheard. "I used to make clothes for the children and do all the repairs. Now, I come here for different reasons." She proceeded to tell of her frustrations and her plan to move out. "Of course, that's all set aside now because of my father's trip. It affects everyone—even Paddy. He was planning to take a trip to Italy. I don't know what he thought to accomplish there, but he's miserable with waiting."

"Perhaps it's just as well; with what's happened to poor Lorenzo, he'd be there at a very bad time."

"That's true." Molly thought for a moment. "When are you planning to leave for Paterson?"

"The day after tomorrow."

"If you decide to bring him back, I'll come out and help you with the trip."

"That would be very generous. I'll see what's involved and contact you."


Amos and Paddy adjourned with Joe to the living room; they filled him in on the problems they associated with Patrick's departure. Paddy told him that he had planned on going to Italy.

Joe said, "Lucky you didn't leave yesterday. This Lorenzo business tops everything."

They all nodded in agreement.


When Paddy returned from work the next evening, he found a letter from Maria waiting. In it, she complained bitterly about her father's sister, her Aunt Cecilia, who had moved in and was taking over her life. He read it with an unfamiliar detachment, realizing that whatever she said would soon be overshadowed by the news of Lorenzo. He thought of himself, standing on a mountain, watching a worker in the valley—blissfully unaware of an avalanche that was about to bury him.

Days later, Joe Lamastro called Amos at work. . "A couple of things have happened, Amos. Connie says that Lorenzo is going to be okay. She thinks she can bring him home in a couple of days. She said that Molly agreed to go out and help her. Did you know about that?"

"I did. I'm all for it."

Lamastro proceeded with detailed instructions for Molly—how to get there and where to stay.

Amos took careful notes. "What's the other thing?" he asked.

"Ah. Alessandro is sending Maria over. She's supposed to go to the hospital in Paterson."

"When will she get there?"

"Her ship arrives in New York five days from now."

"Lorenzo will be in Lawrence well before she gets there."

Lamastro laughed. "No wonder they made you an inspector."

"Yeah, okay. I'm one of the thicks. You need to cut her off."

"Yes. Either Connie, or I, will meet her boat. If neither one of us can go, I'll have a message waiting for her, telling her to come straight to Lawrence."

"Will she be alone?"

"I don't know. This is a big expense for Alessandro, and I know that he thinks Maria is very capable. She's probably alone."

"I wonder if Paddy would be interested in going down to meet her?"

"That's the first thing I thought of, but Alessandro wouldn't like it."

"Who's going to tell him? Even Lorenzo doesn't have to know."

"Oh, Amos."

"Give me the particulars."


It was almost six before Paddy and Sean returned from their route and started the maintenance routine on their truck. Amos strolled out of the office to watch.

He spoke to Sean. "I understand you're able to drive this thing?"

"Paddy's been teaching me."

"Well then, you'll have your own route soon enough. What else has Paddy been teaching you?"

Sean straightened up, unsure of how to interpret the question. "Well, we talk about a lot of things."

"About girls?"

Sean stared straight back at Amos and then, loud enough for Paddy to hear, he said, "I'm not sure he knows much about that, Mister Flanagan."

Paddy, working on the other side of the truck, feigned a continued disinterest in the conversation while waiting to figure out what his father was up to.

Amos continued to address Sean. "Perhaps you can give him a bit of advice then? What would you do if a young woman, for whom you profess great affection, were about to arrive, all by herself, in New York City?"

Without skipping a beat, Sean replied. "Oh, Mister Flanagan, I would surely turn heaven and earth to be there for her protection."

Paddy picked up a rag and, slowly wiping his hands, rounded the front of the truck to stand in front of his father. Their eyes locked.

Amos nodded. "I've got all the information."

Paddy struggled to sort out the cross currents raging through his head.

Sean said, "I can finish up here, Paddy."

Paddy turned his head. "We'll do it together." He looked at Amos and, grinning softly, said, "Thanks, Da."

Amos cocked his head toward the office. "I'll wait and give you a ride home."

# CHAPTER TWENTY SIX

Paddy was not prepared for the chaos at Pier 67 on the west side of Manhattan. The Patria was not due to dock for another hour, and already there were people waiting, dozens of trucks, motorcars, horses and wagons lined up, and men were pushing handcarts and pulling wagons in every direction. More of all arrived by the minute.

As the crowding and activity grew, Paddy began to worry about being able to find Maria. Joe Lamastro had made it sound simple. He had sent a radiogram to Maria telling her that someone would meet her on the dock. "She'll be surprised to see that it's you," he said. Paddy worried that Lamastro didn't know what a sea of confusion would confront them.

There were New York policemen on the pier. He spotted one who looked distinctly Irish and went up to him. "I need some help," he said. The cop turned to look him over. Paddy felt uncomfortable. "My da's a cop. He said if I needed help, a New York policeman would help me."

The cop grinned, continuing to look him over. "Did he now?"

Paddy waited.

"What can I do for you, lad?"

Paddy explained his concern.

"You go in that office." He pointed. "Write a note to her telling her where you'll be." He looked around. "By column number ten. You have her paged. Give the kid a tip—twenty cents." He walked off, turning to say, "And give my regards to your da."

Paddy stood next to the column. The number could be seen from almost anywhere, high up, black numerals on a white background. Standing on his tip-toes, he saw the Patria in the river, three tug boats turning and nudging her toward the dock, passengers lining the rails. Maria was there, somewhere among those tiny heads and waving arms.

There were hundreds of people between him and the dock where the passengers would disembark. In spite of the cold, whole families, mostly Italian, had come to wait for a relative. And there were clergy, priests and nuns. Was some bishop or cardinal returning from Rome? First time emigrants would have landed at Ellis Island. And still, so many?

The crowd was held back while large hawsers were drawn taut and the gangplanks lowered into place. The men with wagons and handcarts made ready. Paddy squinted and scanned along each deck. Porters ran up the gangplanks before the first passengers descended. Then more passengers came down, following their baggage and melding into the crowd. But no Maria.

How many more were still on board? Had she gotten his note? Could he possibly have missed her? No, there she was, struggling with her suitcase. He waved frantically, but she wasn't even looking in his direction. She appeared a bit haggard. Not enough sleep, perhaps? But it was her; he was sure. He wanted to run to her, help her. But the crowding and milling around were worse than before. They might be kept apart, and she wouldn't find him where he said he'd be. He stayed put. She was expecting *someone* to meet her; she wouldn't leave the pier. He watched her disappear into the crowd.

At first, he waited quietly. Then he started jumping to see over the hats, hoping for a glimpse of her. He started to worry again. Where was she?

Someone tapped his shoulder. "You must be looking for someone."

She looked different. He didn't care. He wrapped his arms around her, pulling her to him, nearly knocking her hat off.

She pushed away, stepping back to straighten her hat. She smiled. "I'm very grateful that you've come to meet me."

'Grateful'? What did that mean? He hadn't come to do her a favor. He had come to claim his prize. His mother's last words came back to him. "Don't expect too much. Don't rush her." He smiled back and bent to pick up her suitcase and his own smaller one. She took his arm and they walked out to find a taxi.

Not much was said until they were on their way. Then, she wanted to know about Lorenzo.

"I understand he's doing very well. I haven't seen him, but my mom went to New Jersey to help Mrs. Lamastro bring him back. She said that he could almost have made the trip on his own."

She glanced at him, smiling. "I can't believe I'm going to see him tonight."

She wasn't going to see him that night, but he didn't want to upset her. There would be plenty of time to explain things on the train. He took out his schedule. "We shouldn't have to wait too long for a train."

She nodded, flicking her eyes over his face. She had been doing that a lot, as if checking to be sure that he was really Paddy Flanagan. He realized he'd been doing the same. She seemed a little older, thinner, and sad. He expected a more joyous reunion, she outgoing and affectionate—at least in small gestures. She hadn't yet so much as taken his hand.

It was a short ride to Penn Station, where the busyness started all over again. Tickets, track number, time, sandwiches to eat on route—he couldn't wait to be settled on the train, to be out of there. There was so much to say.

She sat next to the window, and he alongside. The train was almost full, and there was a lot of jostling and moving about, people finding seats and putting luggage overhead. They talked quietly, small details of her journey, and of his trip to meet her. Finally, the train pulled out and they were quiet until minutes later when they emerged from the tunnel into the half-light of early evening. He heaved a sigh, but she spoke first.

"Do you realize we've never been together in warm weather?"

He followed her lead. "That's something we can look forward to."

But she went off in another direction, asking about his work. "It sounds so exciting and important."

He answered her questions and talked enthusiastically about the future of trucks and automobiles. But he wanted to get past that. He wanted to tell her of his love, to talk about them.

She said, "We haven't seen each other for a long time. You're different, more mature, and you've been accomplishing so much. I've just been keeping house."

He almost told her she was different and was acting a bit strange but he didn't dare. "I thought your aunt was doing that, and you were going to teach English and attend some classes at the university?"

She looked down. "That was before my mother died. There have been problems." And then, "What time will I get to Lawrence?"

"We were all saddened by your mother's death." He could no longer put off telling her. "When we made plans for me to meet you, we couldn't be sure that the boat would be on time. If it was really late, we were going to stay with a cousin in New York City. Now, you're going to stay at our house in Boston. You'll be in Lawrence tomorrow morning."

"Oh." She turned away to look out the window.

He was scared. For days, he'd been dreaming of her arrival, how he would meet her and bring her home for this one night. How she would be impressed by the house. And how later, she would consent to live there for a while after they were married.

She turned back. "Will your mother be there?"

"Uh, yes. Yes, she will be."

She smiled—her old smile. It was the first thing he'd said that seemed to make her happy. But then, she turned serious again. "There are things I haven't told you."

His heart dropped. What would she say? And what could he say or do about it?

"My father made me promise not to see you."

"Oh, uh…" That didn't sound too awful; they were already together. He scrambled. "You haven't really broken your promise."

"When my mother died, we were all heartbroken, my father especially. We managed. My father stopped drinking. And then, my aunt, his sister, came to live with us. She never married, and she's horrible with my sisters and brother. They need me to protect them."

He felt like he's just been punched. Another obstacle, another reason to delay. Here she was, sitting next to him; he could touch her, and still there was no end. He wanted to jump up and scream, "NO." Instead, he held very still, staring at the seatback in front of him and saying nothing.

She bent around to look into his face and then sat back to talk of other things, inconsequential things. He listened, making polite responses, his mind elsewhere. He couldn't go on. If she went back to Italy without making a firm commitment to him, he had to end it. The pain of waiting, of continuing to love her through one delay after another was not a life—not for him—not for anyone.

She was saying something about him. "Carla told me what you looked like after those men beat you up. You look fine now."

He smiled and nodded.

She took his hand. "You've been very sweet."

He wanted to press her, to get her to say that she loved him but his confidence was shaken. He'd wait until he had a better feeling for what she might say.

They were almost in Boston when she teased him. "Have you met any nice girls while you've been traveling around Boston?"

That surprised him; he didn't know what to say. Racing through his mind was the idea that he should answer with a passionate kiss. But he only grinned and shook his head.


Amos met them; Paddy had sent a wire from Penn Station. Maria shyly extended her hand and then stepped forward to kiss his cheek. Amos couldn't believe it—he felt himself blushing.

Maria cried openly during the reception at the house. Molly was the first to greet her, continuing to fuss over her even after her hat and coat were off. Kathleen and Neal had been allowed to stay up. She hugged each of them. Mrs. Burns welcomed her, and Patrick, who had nodded off in his favorite chair, rousted himself to take both her hands and say, "Now, I understand. Now that I see you, I understand." And then he went to bed.

During all the greeting and fussing, Paddy stood by, wondering where all this was going. Then it occurred to him that he had to work in the morning, and Maria was about to go to bed. He stepped forward. "I may not see you before you go to Lawrence tomorrow. Give Lorenzo my best."

She studied his face. "It's not that far."

It felt like an invitation. "Yes, it's not that far. I'll see you soon."

She put a hand on his arm and then followed Molly to the room they had prepared for her. He watched her go and then turned.

Amos had been watching. "How did it go?"

Paddy shrugged.

Amos clasped his shoulder. "It seems okay. You'll never understand her completely, you know. I'm still working on your mother."

Paddy went up to bed. On his way back from the bathroom, he passed Maria's room very slowly. Muffled voices came from inside, and he thought he heard Maria sobbing. What, in God's name, did that mean?

With the light still on, he lay in his bed, staring at the ceiling. A gentle knock was followed by his mother's entrance. She stood over him. "Do you still love this girl? I mean, really love her?

He bolted to sit up and hold out his arms. "What? Yes, yes. What's happening?"

She sat next to him. "But you didn't tell her. She has to know, and I'm not the one to be doing it."

"It sounds like she's going back to Italy. I didn't know what to say."

"She doesn't want to go back. She's decided that her father will just have to manage the aunt." She got up. "I'm going to bed." She stood for a moment with her hand on his shoulder.

He gazed up at her while her words sunk in. He stood. "Me too," he said. "But not yet." He got his bathrobe from a hook behind the door and put it on.

She watched from the top of the stairs as he walked down the hall and knocked on Maria's door. When it opened a crack, she turned to go.

THE END

297

CPSIA information can be obtained at www.ICGtesting.com
Printed in the USA
BVOW030330080413

317541BV00001B/1/P